DIPLOMATIC INVESTIGATIONS

DIPLOMATIC INVESTIGATIONS

ESSAYS IN THE THEORY OF INTERNATIONAL POLITICS

EDITED BY

HERBERT BUTTERFIELD

AND

MARTIN WIGHT

HARVARD UNIVERSITY PRESS
Cambridge, Massachusetts
1966

FIRST PUBLISHED IN 1966

© *George Allen & Unwin Ltd, 1966*

Printed in Great Britain

THE CONTRIBUTORS

HEDLEY BULL	Reader in International Relations in the University of London
HERBERT BUTTERFIELD	Master of Peterhouse and Regius Professor of Modern History in the University of Cambridge
MICHAEL HOWARD	Professor of War Studies in the University of London
G. F. HUDSON	Fellow of St Antony's College, Oxford
DONALD MACKINNON	Norris-Hulse Professor of Divinity in the University of Cambridge
MARTIN WIGHT	Dean of the School of European Studies and a Professor of History in the University of Sussex

PREFACE

The papers composing this volume have been chosen from a number, written in recent years, by a group of scholars and others with an official or professional interest in the theoretical aspects of international politics.

The circle for which the papers were written had its origin in the enterprise and liberality of the Rockefeller Foundation. In 1954 two representatives of the Foundation, Mr Dean Rusk and Dr Kenneth W. Thompson, convened a committee of Americans who were interested in theoretical questions about international relations. They included publicists, university professors, and former members of the policy planning staff of the State Department. They met principally at Columbia University, and their discussions led to publication.[1] The success of the American group prompted Dr Thompson to suggest that there should be a similar committee in England. In 1958 the editors of the present volume acted upon the proposal, and invited colleagues who shared their interest in the theory of international politics to a preliminary talk. It was the beginning of regular weekend meetings, three times a year, in Peterhouse, Cambridge, under the chairmanship of the Master. Besides the contributors to this volume, Sir William Armstrong, Donald McLachlan, Adam Watson and Desmond Williams have been members. On one occasion, Kenneth Thompson was able to come to a meeting; on another occasion Sir Pierson Dixon was a guest.

The Rockefeller Foundation gave the group the name of the British Committee on the Theory of International Politics. 'The theory of international politics' is a phrase without wide currency or clear meaning in this country. The group took it to cover enquiry into the nature of the international states-system, the assumptions and ideas of diplomacy, the principles of foreign policy, the ethics of international relations and war. This is a region that still calls for new approaches and for academic treatment.[2] It marches with the domains of the political theorist, the international lawyer, the diplomatic historian, the student of international relations, and the strategic analyst. With each of these it blends, but it is something

---

[1] *Theoretical Aspects of International Relations*, ed. W. T. R. Fox (University of Notre Dame Press, 1959).
[2] 'What I do regret is that we have failed to establish, alongside international law, a parallel and articulate science of international ethics,' D. H. N. Johnson, *The English Tradition in International Law*, an inaugural lecture (Bell, for the London School of Economics, 1962), pp. 26–7.

different from all of them. The committee have not had the intention of undertaking the kind of discussions promoted by Chatham House or the Institute for Strategic Studies, and believe that no other body in England has made the theoretical aspects of international politics its central concern.

It soon became clear to the members of the British committee that within this ill-defined field they had different interests from their American colleagues. The connoisseur of national styles may notice the contrasts. The British have probably been more concerned with the historical than the contemporary, with the normative than the scientific, with the philosophical than the methodological, with principles than policy. But the discussions of the American committee were themselves in some respects traditional compared with the flourishing contemporary school of American and Australian international theory and systems analysis. Here the British committee have been conscious of the antithesis to their own approach. Some of their papers examining the differences between them may form the basis of a second volume which is in contemplation. Meanwhile, attention may be drawn to some of the characteristics of the present collection. These were not designed beforehand, but emerged by common consent as the discussions proceeded.

First, the frame of reference has been, not the limits and uses of international theory, nor the formulation of foreign policy, but the diplomatic community itself, international society, the states-system. The committee found themselves investigating the nature and distinguishing marks of the diplomatic community, the way it functions, the obligations of its members, its tested and established principles of political intercourse. The longest essay in the book examines whether there is a distinct Western tradition in international relations. The last three essays discuss aspects of conflict and change within international society, and look to what might be the problems of a future disarmed world.

Secondly, the committee have not been concerned with an all-embracing theoretical framework, a general theory, for international politics. Their procedure has been, rather, empirical and inductive. Their point of view has on the whole been historical. They have tended to suppose that the continuities in international relations are more important than the innovations; that statecraft is an historical deposit of practical wisdom growing very slowly; that the political, diplomatic, legal and military writers who might loosely be termed 'classical' have not been superseded as a result of recent developments in sociology and psychology, and that it is a useful enterprise to explore the corpus of diplomatic and military experience in order to reformulate its lessons in relation to contemporary needs.

Thirdly, it might be claimed that these papers have a pervading moral concern. In their discussions the committee have not been able to forget that foreign affairs and international relations, however they may be studied or analysed, are in themselves not a closed theoretical system. They are the political region pre-eminently of the contingent and the unforeseen, in which the survival of nations may be at stake, and agonizing decisions have to be made. The underlying aim of the present collection is to clarify the principles of prudence and moral obligation which have held together the international society of states throughout its history, and still hold it together.

To begin with, the committee's discussions were discursive rather than systematic. The first paper printed here was also the first paper offered to the group; its title was intended to be provocative. At the same first full meeting, in January 1959, Donald MacKinnon read a paper entitled 'What is the attraction of Communism today?' Thus launched, the discussions took their own course, following the wind of the argument. A record of the discussions was made and circulated afterwards. Subsequent papers arose out of the discussions. Sometimes two independent papers on the same topic were offered for discussion at the same meeting; sometimes one treatment of a theme evoked an alternative treatment later—thus the two essays on 'The Balance of Power'.

After some time it was seen that the papers, though not systematically planned, had a community of assumptions and treatment that might make them of interest to a wider circle of readers, and one of the editors made a selection for publication. Each contributor has had the opportunity to revise his paper to whatever extent the discussions upon it and further reflection have seemed to him to require. The editors have tried to respect the varied length and nature of the papers, but to give them some uniformity by bringing them up to date and supplying references so far as possible. Only one essay, that on 'Threats of Force in International Relations', has been left entirely as it was written in April 1961.

The paper entitled 'Why is there no International Theory?' has already been published in *International Relations*, vol. ii, no. 1, April 1960. We thank the editor of that journal for permission to reprint it, with some changes and additions. It remains for the editors, on behalf of all the members of the committee, to express their gratitude to the Rockefeller Foundation for the grant that made possible their meetings and discussions.

H. BUTTERFIELD
M. WIGHT

CONTENTS

CONTENTS

CHAPTER 1

WHY IS THERE NO INTERNATIONAL THEORY?

MARTIN WIGHT

'Political theory' is a phrase that in general requires no explanation. It is used here to denote speculation about the state, which is its traditional meaning from Plato onwards. On the other hand, the phrase 'international theory' does require explanation. At first hearing, it is likely to be taken as meaning either the methodology of the study of international relations, or some conceptual system which offers a unified explanation of international phenomena—'the theory of international relations'. In this paper neither of these is intended. By 'international theory' is meant a tradition of speculation about relations between states, a tradition imagined as the twin of speculation about the state to which the name 'political theory' is appropriated. And international theory in this sense does not, at first sight, exist.

Some qualification, of course, is needed. There are many theoretical writings about international relations; some of them bear names as eminent as Machiavelli or Kant; and in the twentieth century they have become a flood.[1] Yet it is difficult to say that any of them has the status of a political classic. This is a problem that besets the teacher of International Relations if he conceives of International Relations as a twin subject, distinct from but parallel with, the subject commonly known as Political Science or Government. Political Science has its tensions and internecine conflicts, to be sure, but it is in some sense held together by Political Theory, or as it is sometimes called the History of Political Ideas. The student of Government, however else he may be misled, is given an introduction to the tradition of speculation and the body of writings about the state from Plato to Laski. But the student of International Relations cannot, it seems, be similarly directed to classics in his branch of politics, of the stature of Aristotle or Hobbes or Locke or Rousseau. Is it because they do not exist?

The question may be put in a different way. The teacher of International Relations is often given the impression that his subject

[1] For recent writings there is a valuable critical study in Stanley H. Hoffman, *Contemporary Theory in International Relations* (Englewood Cliffs, N.J., Prentice-Hall, 1960).

B

sprang fully-armed from the head of David Davies or of Sir Montague Burton. But if he seeks to trace it further back, behind the memorable Endowment whereby Andrew Carnegie left ten million dollars for 'the speedy abolition of war between the so-called civilized nations' (to be applied when this end was achieved to other social and educational purposes), he finds himself involved in obscurity. In the nineteenth century and earlier, there is no succession of first-rank books about the states-system and diplomacy like the succession of political classics from Bodin to Mill. What international theory, then, was there before 1914? And if there was any, is it worth rediscovering?

One answer to the question is plain. If political theory is the tradition of speculation about the state, then international theory may be supposed to be a tradition of speculation about the society of states, or the family of nations, or the international community. And speculation of this kind was formerly comprehended under International Law. The public law of Europe in the eighteenth century has been described as 'an amalgam of formulae, jurisprudence, political speculation and recorded practice'.[1] (Indeed, the very speculative breadth of international lawyers did something to create their reputation as futile metaphysicians among practical men, even after the influence of positivism disciplined them to neglect metalegal questions.) When Tocqueville gave his presidential address to the Académie des Sciences Morales et Politiques in 1852, he made one of the earliest attempts to place the study of international relations among the political and social sciences. He distinguished on the one side the study of the rights of society and of the individual, what laws are appropriate to particular societies, what forms of government to particular circumstances, citing as examples the names of Plato, Aristotle, Machiavelli, Montesquieu, Rousseau. He continued:

'D'autres essayent le même travail à l'égard de cette société des nations où chaque peuple est un citoyen, société toujours un peu barbare, même dans les siècles les plus civilisés, quelque effort que l'on fasse pour adoucit et régler les rapports de ceux qui la composent. Ils ont découvert et indiqué quel était, en dehors des traités particuliers, le droit international. C'est l'oeuvre de Grotius et de Puffendorf.'[2]

It is, he says, to the classical international lawyers that we must look

---

[1] Sir Geoffrey Butler and Simon Maccoby, *The Development of International Law* (Longmans, 1928), p. 7.
[2] *Oeuvres*, vol. ix, pp. 120–1. Cf. below, p. 96.

in the first place for any body of international theory before the twentieth century.[1]

It is worth asking where else international theory is found. We might answer in four kinds of writing: (a) Those whom Nys called the irenists—Erasmus, Sully, Campanella, Crucé, Penn, the Abbé de St Pierre, and Pierre-André Gargaz. When Melian Stawell wrote a book on *The Growth of International Thought* for the Home University Library, writers of this kind provided her central line of progress from the Truce of God to the Kellogg Pact. But it is hard to consider them as other than the curiosities of political literature. They are not rich in ideas; the best of them grope with the problem of how to secure common action between sovereign states, and thus gain a mention in the prehistory of the League of Nations.[2]

(b) Those whom it is convenient to call the Machiavellians: the succession of writers on *raison d'état* of whom Meinecke is the great interpreter. In a footnote about the followers of Botero, Meinecke says, 'There are real catacombs of forgotten literature here by mediocrities'.[3] He does not so mean it, but one suspects that the phrase will cover all the writers in his own book apart from those who are notable in another sphere, whether as statesmen, like Frederick, or as philosophers, like Hegel, or as historians, like Ranke and Treitschke. Botero and Boccalini, Henri de Rohan and Gabriel Naudé, Courtilz de Sandras and Rousset: can we see in them forgotten or potential classics? One difficulty in answering is that they are inaccessible except to the scholar, and this perhaps itself conveys the answer.

(c) The *parerga* of political philosophers, philosophers and historians. As examples of this kind might be named Hume's Essay on 'The Balance of Power', Rousseau's *Project of Perpetual Peace*, Bentham's *Plan for an Universal Peace*, Burke's *Thoughts on French Affairs* and *Letters on a Regicide Peace*, Ranke's essay on the Great Powers, and J. S. Mill's essay on the law of nations. Apart from the classical international lawyers, these are the most rewarding source in the quest for international theory. Is it more interesting that so many great minds have been drawn, at the margin of their activities,

---

[1] It may be worth adding that international law gained academic recognition in Britain well before political theory. The Chichele Chair of International Law and Diplomacy at Oxford and the Whewell Chair of International Law at Cambridge were founded in 1859 and 1866 respectively, and the Gladstone Chair of Political Theory and Institutions and the Cambridge Chair of Political Science only in 1912 and 1928.

[2] They have now been admirably surveyed by F. H. Hinsley, *Power and the Pursuit of Peace* (Cambridge University Press, 1963), part i.

[3] F. Meinecke, *Machiavellism* (English translation, Routledge, 1957), p. 67, n. 1.

to consider basic problems of international politics, or that so few great minds have been drawn to make these problems their central interest? The only political philosopher who has turned wholly from political theory to international theory is Burke. The only political philosopher of whom it is possible to argue whether his principal interest was not in the relations between states rather than—or even more than—the state itself, is Machiavelli. With him, the foreign and domestic conditions for the establishment and maintenance of state power are not distinguished systematically; and this alone— without other reasons—would have justified his being annexed, by detractors and admirers alike, as the tutelary hero of International Relations. In this class, again, it would be necessary to place such miscellaneous political writers as Bolingbroke, whose *Letters on the Study and Use of History* contain a primitive philosophy of inter- national politics, or Mably, whose *Principes des Négociations* is one of the more enduring pieces of his large output, or the Gentz of *Fragments upon the Balance of Power*.

(d) The speeches, despatches, memoirs and essays of statesmen and diplomatists. To illustrate speeches and despatches as a source of international theory, one might cite the authority of Canning over a generation of British foreign policy—for instance, the classic despatch of 1823 containing his doctrine of guarantees. To illustrate memoirs, Bismarck's *Gedanken und Erinnerungen*, perhaps the supreme example. To illustrate essays, Lord Salisbury's early essays on foreign affairs in the *Quarterly Review*.

It is clear, therefore, that international theory, or what there is of it, is scattered, unsystematic, and mostly inaccessible to the layman. Moreover, it is largely repellent and intractable in form. Grotius has to be read at large to be understood; the only possible extract is the Prolegomena, which gives a pallid notion of whether or why he deserves his reputation. Students cannot be expected to tackle Pufendorf's *De jure naturae et gentium libri octo*, nor even his *De officio hominis et civis juxta legem naturalem libri duo*. There is little intellectual nourishment in the Abbé de St Pierre, or Hume on the balance of power; and Bismarck's international theory has to be dis- tilled with care from the historical falsehoods in which it is seductively enclosed.

Yet these are external matters. I believe it can be argued that inter- national theory is marked, not only by paucity but also by intellectual and moral poverty. For this we must look to internal reasons. The most obvious are, first, the intellectual prejudice imposed by the sovereign state, and secondly, the belief in progress.

Since the sixteenth century, international society has been so organized that no individuals except sovereign princes can be members of it, and these only in their representative capacity. All other individuals have had to be subjects or citizens of sovereign states. By a famous paradox of international law, the only persons emancipated from this necessity are pirates, by virtue of being *hostes humani generis*. Erasmus could still wander about Europe without bothering himself where his ultimate temporal allegiance was due. Scaliger and Casaubon already learned, two and three generation later, that the only safe way to be citizens of the intellectual world was to exchange a disagreeable allegiance for one less disagreeable. The main difference in the age of Einstein and Thomas Mann has been that change of allegiance has become impossible for an increasingly large proportion of the human race. Even Mr Hammarskjöld, we must suppose, will retire to write his memoirs as a Swedish citizen under the shelter of the world's fourth air force.[1] Even the Pope, to take the supreme instance, believed his position in international society anomalous and insecure until he had re-established himself as sovereign of a territorial state.

The principle that every individual requires the protection of a state, which represents him in the international community, is a juristic expression of the belief in the sovereign state as the consummation of political experience and activity which has marked Western political thought since the Renaissance. That belief has absorbed almost all the intellectual energy devoted to political study. It has become natural to think of international politics as the untidy fringe of domestic politics (as Baldwin thought of them in Cabinet), and to see international theory in the manner of the political theory textbooks, as an additional chapter which can be omitted by all save the interested student. The masterpiece of international politics is the system of the balance of power, as it operated from the time of Elizabeth down to that of Bismarck; but if we ask why the balance of power has inspired no great political writer to analysis and reflection, the answer surely is that it has flourished with the flourishing of the modern state, and has been seen as a means to that end. Even today, when circumstances have made the study of international relations fashionable, they are often still thought of and even taught as 'foreign affairs' or 'problems of foreign policy' (meaning our foreign policy, not Nasser's or Khrushchev's), and the world's present predicament will be described in some such parochial phrase as 'the crisis of the modern state'. Professor Morgenthau, who has had a great influence among international relationists in the United States since 1945, has consistently maintained that 'a theory of international politics must be

[1] The sentence was written in 1958.

focused on the concept of the national interest'.[1] Practical problems of international politics are often described in terms of building a bigger and better state—a European Union or an Atlantic Community or an Arab Union, without seeing that such an achievement would leave the problems of inter-state politics precisely where they were. Few political thinkers have made it their business to study the states-system, the diplomatic community *itself*.

It might be a good argument for subordinating international theory to political theory, to maintain that the division of international society into separate states is a temporary historical phase, emerging out of the medieval unity (however this be characterized) and destined to be replaced by a world state. In his inaugural lecture at Oxford, Zimmern remarked on the historical conditions that make International Relations a topical subject in place of International Government.[2] And it may seem one of the weaknesses of the concluding volumes of Toynbee's *Study of History*, that he resists the logic of his own analysis and supposes that Western civilization will defy all his precedents by achieving a stable international anarchy instead of a universal empire. But this is how international theorists have usually talked. They have seen the maintenance of the states-system as the condition for the continuance of the existing state—a small-scale field of political theory. They have not been attracted by the possibility of maximizing the field of political theory through establishing a world state. None of the successive attempts by a single Great Power to achieve international hegemony has produced any notable international (or political) theory. 'The monarchy of the World' was apparently a phrase used by Spanish diplomats under Philip II, but the idea was never embodied in a serious treatise.[3] Still less was any such thing inspired by Louis XIV or Napoleon.

Formal international theory has traditionally resisted the case for a world state. At the very outset, Vitoria unconsciously took over Dante's conception of *universalis civilitas humani generis*, and strengthened it into an affirmation that mankind constitutes a legal community, but he repudiated the Dantean corollary of a universal empire.[4] Grotius and Pufendorf did the same, with the argument that

---

[1] H. J. Morgenthau, *Dilemmas of Politics* (University of Chicago Press, 1958), p. 54. Cf. *In Defense of the National Interest* (Knopf, 1951).
[2] A. E. Zimmern, *The Study of International Relations* (Clarendon Press, 1931), pp. 13–14.
[3] Bohdan Chudoba, *Spain and the Empire 1519-1643* (University Chicago Press, 1952), p. 190.
[4] Dante, *De Monarchia*, book i, ch. 2. Vitoria, *De Potestate Civili*, section xxi, para. 4; and *De Indis recenter inventis Relectio prior*, section III, first title. Vitoria nowhere mentions Dante.

a world empire would be too large to be efficient.[1] For seventeenth-century writers this was a reasonable assumption: they saw the Spanish monarchy manifestly incapable of maintaining its inter-continental responsibilities, the Empire disintegrating, the French and English monarchies having to undergo fundamental reconstruction. In the eighteenth century, when the necessity of the balance of power has become a commonplace of pamphlet literature, a different and perhaps a contrary argument appears—that a world state might be so efficient as to be intolerable. For Kant as for Gibbon the division of mankind into many states is the guarantee of freedom; not only for states themselves, through the balance of power, but for individuals also, for whom it means the possibility of foreign asylum.[2] After the middle of the nineteenth century American experience provides a new argument against a super-state; that it would simply transform the admitted evil of international war into civil war, so that the advantage would be nil. 'Even if it were possible to leap over so many intermediate stages, and to set up a world government,' said Sir Llewellyn Woodward recently, 'the political result might be to substitute civil war for international war or, on the other hand, to surrender our existing safeguards of public and private liberty to a centralized executive authority of unparalleled and irresistible strength.'[3] Hence an almost uniform assumption among international theorists up to 1914 that the structure of international society is unalterable, and the division of the world into sovereign states is necessary and natural. Nor is it unfair to see the League and the United Nations as the expression of a belief that it may be possible to secure the benefits of a world state without the inconveniences of instituting and maintaining it. If in the twentieth century crude doctrines of world imperialism have become influential is it not partly because they have found a vacuum in international theory to fill? One of the very few reasoned arguments for a world state was put forward by Middleton Murry, when America had the atomic monopoly. He drew a different moral from the American Civil War.

'There is a manifest analogy between the situation which forced Lincoln's reluctant but unshakable decision to compel the Southern states to remain in the Union, and the situation today. A modern

[1] Grotius, *De jure belli ac pacis*, book II, ch. xxii, section 13; Pufendorf, *Elementa jurisprudentiae universalis*, book II, obs. v. 1.
[2] Gibbon, *Decline and Fall of the Roman Empire*, ch. iii, last paragraph; Kant *Eternal Peace*, first addendum, 2.
[3] *The Listener*, August 5, 1954, p. 207.

Lincoln would apply himself to making the issue crystal-clear to his fellow-countrymen, and if he could find means, to the Russian people also. The issue is world-union or world-anarchy; world-union or world-slavery. The rulers of Russia, he would say, cannot be permitted to refuse world-union, and thereby to condemn the world to anarchy and slavery. If they will not consent, they must be compelled to come in.'[1]

This is interesting, not only as an example of the union between pacifist convictions and what might be called a realist attitude to international politics; but also because the argument never had the slightest chance of being listened to by those to whom it was addressed.

The ascendancy of political theory over international theory can be illustrated in another way. Since the society of states came into recognizable existence in the sixteenth century, the three most powerful influences on its development have been the Reformation and Counter-Reformation, the French Revolution, and the totalitarian revolutions of the twentieth century. But none of these upheavals has produced any notable body of international theory; each has written only a chapter of political theory. To put it crudely, the Reformation and Counter-Reformation were concerned with Church and state, the French Revolution with the state simply, Communism and Fascism with the state and society. In the end, all these revolutionaries found themselves operating in international politics in a big way, but it requires wide reading and considerable discrimination to elicit the principles or theories of international politics by which they believed they were guided. The Jesuits are the exception: for they had the old equipment of the supreme temporal power to refashion. But what was Calvin's international theory? In some of his sermons it is possible to discern a conception of a *civitas maxima* whose absolute monarch is God, with the princes of the earth as His lieutenants; but it is a pale thing beside the vigorous intervention and subversion undertaken by his foreign policy in practice, whose principles get a kind of formulation in the last part of the *Vindiciae contra Tyrannos*. It is only when it begins to slide into the casuistry of *raison d'état* that Calvinist international theory acquires richness or subtlety, and then it ceases to be distinctively Calvinist. It is even more difficult to find any Jacobin international theory. The Rights of Man were transformed into universal conquest without, it seems, any theorizing more sophisticated or less negative than the statement by Genêt which Fox quoted in the House of

[1] J. M. Murry, *The Free Society* (Dakers, 1948), p. 63.

Commons: 'I would throw Vattel and Grotius into the sea whenever their principles interfere with my notions of the rights of nations.'[1]

The same may be said of Communism. It is a theory of domestic society, a political theory, which since Russia after Lenin's death came to acquiesce for the time being in remaining the only Socialist state in international society, has been tugged and cut about to cover a much wider range of political circumstances than it was designed for. Marx and Lenin saw the three principal contradictions of capitalism as, first, the struggle between proletariat and bourgeoisie in the advanced industrial states; secondly, the struggle between these imperialist states themselves, as exemplified by the First World War; thirdly, the struggle between the colonial masses and their alien exploiters. This was the hierarchy of importance that they gave to these three struggles, and it is a commonplace that the course of events has reversed the order, so that the struggle between proletariat and bourgeoisie in the Western world has almost ceased, and the struggle between the colonial peoples and their imperialist masters and former masters has become the main theme of international politics. According to Mr Deutscher, it was Trotsky who first saw that this was happening, and who coined the phrase about the path to London and Paris lying through Calcutta and Peking.[2] Neither Marx, Lenin nor Stalin made any systematic contribution to international theory; Lenin's *Imperialism* comes nearest to such a thing, and this has little to say about international politics. The absence of Marxist international theory has a wider importance than making it difficult to recommend reading to an undergraduate who wants to study the principles of Communist foreign policy in the original sources. It creates the obscurity, so fruitful to the Communists themselves, about what these principles actually are: so that only an expert sovietologist can usefully discuss what Lenin really said (and where) about the inevitability of conflict between the socialist and capitalist camps, and how this doctrine has been revised by Malenkov and Khrushchev. Perhaps it is a misconception, however, to say that all these revolutionary political theories are primarily concerned with the state. It may be truer to see them as attempts to reconstitute that older political phenomenon, a universal church of true believers; and in the light of such an undertaking the realm of the diplomatic system and sovereign states and international law is necessarily irrelevant, transitory, trivial, and doomed to pass away. At the heart of Calvinism and Jacobinism there was something like the exaltation

[1] House of Commons, January 21, 1794 (*Speeches during the French Revolutionary War Period*, Everyman's Library, p. 124). Cf. below, p. 95.
[2] Isaac Deutscher, *The Prophet Armed* (Oxford University Press, 1954), pp. 457–8.

and impatience with international politics which Trotsky showed, when he defined his task on becoming the Soviet Republic's first Foreign Commissar: 'I shall publish a few revolutionary proclamations and then close shop.'[1]

And secondly, international politics differ from domestic politics in being less susceptible of a progressivist interpretation. In Western Europe, at least, national histories considered in isolation do show evidence of progress—even when, as in the case of Germany, they are marked by recurrent catastrophe. There has been growing social cohesion, growing interdependence among the people, growth of state power, increasing flexibility in its operation, increasing wealth and its better distribution, diffusion of culture among the masses, the softening of manners, perhaps the lessening of violence—everything that the Victorians believed was inevitable. If Sir Thomas More or Henry IV, let us say, were to return to England and France in 1960, it is not beyond plausibility that they would admit that their countries had moved domestically towards goals and along paths which they could approve. But if they contemplated the international scene, it is more likely that they would be struck by resemblances to what they remembered: a state-system apportioned between two Great Powers each with its associates and satellites, smaller Powers improving their position by playing off one side against the other, universal doctrines contending against local patriotism, the duty of intervention overriding the right of independence, the empty professions of peaceful purpose and common interest, the general preference for going down to defeat fighting rather than consenting to unresisted subjugation. The stage would have become much wider, the actors fewer, their weapons more alarming, but the play would be the same old melodrama. International politics is the realm of recurrence and repetition; it is the field in which political action is most regularly necessitous. This, I take it, is what Burke means when he says that because commonwealths are not physical but moral essences, the internal causes which affect their fortunes 'are infinitely uncertain and much more obscure, and much more difficult to trace, than the foreign causes that tend to raise, to depress, and sometimes to overwhelm a community.'[2]

If this is indeed the character of international politics, it is incompatible with progressivist theory. Therefore international theory that remains true to diplomatic experience will be at a discount in an age when the belief in progress is prevalent. This may

---

[1] *Ibid.*, p. 327.

[2] *Letters on a Regicide Peace*, No. 1, third paragraph (*Works*, ed. H. Rogers Holdsworth, 1842, vol. ii, p. 275).

be illustrated by the penetrating observations upon international politics that are to be found scattered about in earlier political writers. Here is an eighteenth-century description of the competition in armaments:

'Une maladie nouvelle s'est répandue en Europe; elle a saisi nos princes, et leur fait entretenir un nombre désordonné de troupes. Elle a ses redoublements, et elle devient nécessairement contagieuse; car, sitôt qu'un Etat augmente ce qu'il appelle ses troupes, les autres soudain augmentent les leurs: de façon qu'on ne gagne rien par là que la ruine commune. Chaque monarque tient sur pied toutes les armées qu'il pourroit avoir si ses peuples étoient en danger d'être exterminés; et on nomme paix cet état d'effort de tous contre tous. (Il est vrai que c'est cet état d'effort qui maintient principalement l'équilibre, parce qu'il éreinte les grandes puissances.) Aussi l'Europe est-elle si ruinée, que les particuliers qui seroient dans la situation où sont les trois puissances de cette partie du monde les plus opulentes, n'auroient pas de quoi vivre. Nous sommes pauvres avec les richesses et le commerce de tout l'univers; et bientôt, à force d'avoir des soldats, nour n'aurons plus que des soldats, et nous serons comme les Tartares.'[1]

In its exaggeration as well as its perception, this passage written during the War of the Austrian Succession has a timeless quality when read during the Cold War. One seeks to separate the truth from the changing circumstances, asking how far industrialism may have altered the economic burden of armaments, and so on. But no sooner is one in the posture of recognizing a perennial truth in Montesquieu's words, than all one's progressivist instincts revolt. By now, we say, we have seen the arms race run its full cycle sufficiently often to know what it means; our protest is born of knowledge and experience and not, like his, of intuition alone; because our knowledge is greater our strength to break the circle is greater; and to accept Montesquieu's words as a description of our own predicament would be treason to mankind, because it implies the fatalistic doctrine that what has been will be.

In progressivist international theories, the conviction usually precedes the evidence. And when the conviction is analysed or disintegrates, one is apt to find at the centre of it what might be called the argument from desperation. This is already used by Kant, who first channelled the doctrine of progress into international theory through his *Eternal Peace*. Having established the three definite articles of an eternal peace, he argues that such a peace is guaranteed

[1] *De l'Esprit des Lois*, book xiii, ch. 17.

by Nature herself, who wills that we should do what reason presents to us as a duty; *volentem ducit, nolentem trahit*. And she effects this by means of the commercial spirit, which cannot coexist with war, and sooner or later controls every nation.[1] 'In this way Nature guarantees the conditions of perpetual peace by the mechanism involved in our human inclinations themselves.'[2] But a little later, in discussing the disagreement between morals and politics in relation to eternal peace, he seems to reach the ultimate point of his argument, and to take a flying leap beyond it:

'The process of creation, by which such a brood of corrupt beings has been put upon the earth, can apparently be justified by no theodicy or theory of Providence, if we assume that it never will be better, nor can be better, with the human race. But such a standpoint of judgment is really much too high for us to assume, as if we could be entitled theoretically to apply our notions of wisdom to the supreme and unfathomable Power. We shall thus be inevitably driven to a position of despair in consequence of such reasonings [zu solchen verzweifelten Folgerungen werden wir unvermeidlich hingetrieben], if we do not admit that the pure principles of right and justice have objective reality and that they can be realized in fact.'[3]

It is surely not a good argument for a theory of international politics that we shall be driven to despair if we do not accept it. But it is an argument that comes naturally to the children of Hegel (and Kant) when they are faced with defeat. Communists, as the Germans neared Moscow, and Nazis, as the Russians returned upon Germany, alike cried that defeat was unthinkable because if they were defeated history would be meaningless. 'To imagine for a moment the possibility of Hitler's victory meant to forego all reason; if it were to happen then there could be no truth, logic, nor light in the development of human society, only chaos, darkness and lunacy;

[1] The best English translation is still that by W. Hastie, in *Kant's Principles of Politics* (Clark, 1891). See pp. 105, 111.
[2] *Ibid.*, p. 115.
[3] *Ibid.*, p. 136; *Werke* (Academy edition), vol. viii, p. 380. Cf. *Idee zu einer allgemeinen Geschichte*, ninth principle: 'Denn was hilfts, die Herrlichkeit und Weisheit der Schöpfung im vernunftlosen Naturreiche zu preisen und der Betrachtung zu empfehlen, wenn der Theil des grossen Schauplatzes der obersten Weisheit, der von allem diesem den Zweck enthält,—die Geschichte des menschlichen Geschlechts—ein unaufhörlicher Einwurf dagegen bleiben soll, dessen Anblick uns nöthigt unsere Augen von ihm mit Unwillen wegzuwenden und, **indem** wir verzweifeln jemals darin eine vollendete vernünftige Absicht anzutreffen, uns dahin bringt, sie nur in einer andern Welt zu hoffen?' (*Werke*, vol. viii, p. 30; Hastie, p. 28).

and it would be better not to live.'[1] 'We shall conquer, because it lies in the logic of history, because a higher destiny wills it, . . . because without our victory history would have lost its meaning; and history is not meaningless.'[2]

Perhaps the prevalent belief that nuclear weapons have transformed international politics, giving the Great Powers something to fear more than they fear one another, and so making war impossible, has a similar root. It is clear, at least, that it is the latest in a series of optimistic constructions going back more than a hundred years. In the nineteenth century, public opinion was given the first place as transformer of international politics; in the twentieth century it has usually been the fear of war. The argument that the hydrogen bomb has made war impossible usually contains two propositions: first, that war waged with the new weapons will destroy civilization; secondly, that it is therefore too horrible to happen. Joad used it in 1939 in respect of the bombing aeroplane.[3] Bloch used it in 1900 in respect of mass armies, quick-firing artillery, small-bore rifles, and smokeless powder.[4]

It may be an illusion produced by treating the material selectively; but it sometimes seems that whereas political theory generally is in unison with political activity, international theory (at least in its chief embodiment as international law) sings a kind of descant over against the movement of diplomacy. Political theory is in a direct relation with political activity—whether justifying recent developments as Hooker did the Anglican settlement and Locke the Glorious Revolution, or providing a programme of action that the next generation carries out, as Bentham did for administrative reform in England or Marx and the other socialist writers for the working-class movement. But international law seems to follow an inverse movement to that of international politics. When diplomacy is violent and unscrupulous, international law soars into the regions of natural law; when diplomacy acquires a certain habit of co-operation, international law crawls in the mud of legal positivism. It was in 1612, in the armistice between the Western European wars of religion and the Thirty Years' War, that Suarez enunciated his belief that mankind 'constitutes a political and moral unity bound up by charity and compassion.'[5] The old view that Grotius had a human-

---

[1] Evgeny Krieger, *From Moscow to the Prussian Frontier* (Hutchinson, 1945), p. 8: of November 1941.
[2] Goebbels, speech in the Berliner Sportpalast, October 3, 1943 (*Völkischer Beobachter*, October 4, 1943).
[3] C. E. M. Joad, *Why War?* (Penguin, 1939), pp. 50, 52.
[4] Ivan Bloch, *Modern Weapons and Modern War* (Grant Richards, 1900).
[5] *De Legibus*, book II, ch. xix, section 9. Cf. below, p. 95–6.

izing influence on the later stages of the Thirty Years' War no longer has any credit. 'Undoubtedly, the general picture of international relations in the two centuries which followed the publication of *De Jure Belli ac Pacis*', Lauterpacht has written, 'was not one pointing to any direct influence, in the sphere of practice, of the essential features of the Grotian teaching.'[1] International theory did not approximate to international practice until the doctrine of natural law had become completely subjectivized in Wolff and Vattel, and transformed into a doctrine of autonomy of the national will, a counterpart of the theory of the rights of man. Frederick the Great's reign might be taken as the point of intersection of theory and practice. It saw the last stage of naturalism pass over into positivism, and the first great work of positivist jurisprudence, J. J. Moser's *Versuch des neuesten europäischen Volkerrechts*, which came as near to codifying *Realpolitik* as any work of international law can do, was published in 1777–80. Moser set the prevailing tone of nineteenth-century theory. Yet it is curious that a theory which starts from the axiom of legal self-sufficiency, separating the law both from the other normative spheres and from its social context— which sees the will of sovereign states as the exclusive source of international law, and defines international law as nothing but such rules as states have consented to—should have flourished in an age when the conception of Europe as a cultural and moral community acquired a new vigour, and the diplomatic system of the Concert maintained standards of good faith, mutual consideration and restraint higher probably than at any other time in international history. 'Chaque Nation a ses droits particuliers; mais l'Europe aussi a son droit; c'est l'ordre social qui le lui a donné', ran a protocol of the London Conference on Belgium of 1831.[2] It is surely a deeper theory of international law than the consensual principle could offer. With the signing of the League Covenant (if not indeed with the Hague Conferences) the relation of theory and practice was once more reversed, and positivist jurisprudence itself by an agreeable irony followed its naturalist predecessor into altitudes of fiction through the multiplication of worthless agreements in the age of Mussolini and Hitler.

The tension between international theory and diplomatic practice can be traced to the heart of international theory itself. It may be seen in the identification of international politics with the pre-

---

[1] 'The Grotian Tradition in International Law', *British Year Book of International Law*, 1946, p. 16.
[2] See C. K. Webster, *Foreign Policy of Palmerston* (Bell, 1951), vol. i, pp. 109, 132.

contractual state of nature by the classical international lawyers. This identification was apparently first made by Hobbes, and was carried from him into the law of nations by Pufendorf. But already in Hobbes one can detect an inconsistency. He describes the state of nature, when men live without a common power to keep them all in awe, as a condition of war of every man against every man; and forestalling the argument that such a condition never existed, he points to the relations of sovereign states as exemplifying it. But he adds this sentence: 'But because they uphold thereby (viz., by their 'posture of war'), the industry of their subjects; there does not follow from it, that misery, which accompanies the liberty of particular men.'[1] This is empirically true. Competition in armaments secures full employment as well as bringing war; tariff barriers protect as well as obstruct. Or at least it has been empirically true until the present day, when for the first time we may be beginning to ask whether there may not follow from international anarchy as much misery as follows from civil anarchy. But it is theoretically odd. It introduces an ambiguity into the conception of the state of nature which becomes a persistent feature of international theory. For individuals, the state of nature, whether it is imagined in Hobbesian or Lockean terms, leads to the social contract. For sovereign states, it does no such thing. International anarchy is the one manifestation of the state of nature that is not intolerable. The coexistence of states, said Pufendorf, 'lacks those inconveniences which are attendant upon a pure state of nature.'[2] Wolff conceived of international society as a *civitas maxima*, of which states were citizens, but this was a deliberate fiction constructed to support the theory of an international legal order. Vattel gives the fullest account of the ambiguity.

'It is clear that there is by no means the same necessity for a civil society among Nations as among individuals. It cannot be said, therefore, that nature recommends it to an equal degree, far less that it prescribes it. Individuals are so constituted that they could accomplish but little by themselves and could scarcely get on without the assistance of civil society and its law. But as soon as a sufficient number have united under a government, they are able to provide for most of their needs, and they find the help of other political societies not so necessary to them as the state itself is to individuals.'[3]

It was left to nineteenth century writers such as Laurent and Oppen-

[1] *Leviathan*, ch. xiii (cf. below, p. 45.)
[2] *De jure naturae et gentium*, book II, ch. ii, section 4.
[3] *Le Droit des Gens*, preface.

heim to crown the argument by pointing out that sovereign states are more moral than individuals.

'There is a profound difference between individuals and nations; the former have their vices and their passions which are continually leading them to do wrong; the others are fictitious beings whose agents are generally the most intelligent and most ethical of their time. And even where intelligence and morality are lacking, public opinion contains them and will increasingly contain them within the limits of duty.'[1]

It may seem puzzling that, while the acknowledged classics of political study are the political philosophers, the only acknowledged counterpart in the study of international relations is Thucydides, a work of history. And that the quality of international politics, the preoccupations of diplomacy, are embodied and communicated less in works of political or international theory than in historical writings. It would be possible to argue that the highest form of statecraft, both in the end pursued and in the moral and intellectual qualities required, is the regulation of the balance of power, as seen in Lorenzo the Magnificent or Queen Elizabeth, Richelieu or William III, Palmerston or Bismarck. But to understand this statecraft one can turn to no work of international theory; in the way, for example, that to understand the Founding Fathers one reads *The Federalist*. One turns rather to historical writing; to Ranke or Sorel. Works of international history, whether of wide chronological range (for example, Seeley's *Growth of British Policy*, Mattingly's *Renaissance Diplomacy*, or Hudson's *The Far East in World Politics*), or detailed studies (for example, Sumner's *Russia and the Balkans*, Wheeler-Bennett's *Brest-Litovsk*, or even Sorensen's account of Kennedy's handling of the Cuba crisis), convey the nature of foreign policy and the working of the states-system better than much recent theoretical writing based on the new methodologies. It is not simply that historical literature is doing a different job from systems analysis. Historical literature at the same time does the same job— the job of offering a coherent structure of hypotheses that will provide a common explanation of phenomena; but it does the job with more judiciousness and modesty, and with closer attention to the record of international experience. So one might venture tentatively to put forward the equation:

[1] Francois Laurent, *Etudes sur l'histoire de humanite*, vol. i (2nd ed., 1879), p. 42. I owe this quotation to Walter Schiffer, *The Legal Community of Mankind* (Columbia University Press, 1954), p. 160.

Politics: International Politics=Political Theory: Historical
                                                  Interpretation.
By another intellectual route, Henry Adams came to a similar
conclusion. 'For history, international relations are the only sure
standards of movement; the only foundation for a map. For this
reason, Adams had always insisted that international relations was
the only sure base for a chart of history.'[1]

What I have been trying to express is the sense of a kind of
disharmony between international theory and diplomatic practice,
a kind of recalcitrance of international politics to being theorized
about. The reason is that the theorizing has to be done in the
language of political theory and law. But this is the language appropriate to man's control of his social life. Political theory and law are
maps of experience or systems of action within the realm of normal
relationships and calculable results. They are the theory of the good
life. International theory is the theory of survival. What for political
theory is the extreme case (as revolution, or civil war) is for international theory the regular case. The traditional effort of international
lawyers to define the right of devastation and pillage in war; the long
diplomatic debate in the nineteenth century about the right of
intervention in aid of oppressed nationalities; the Anglo-French
argument in the nineteen-twenties about which precedes the other,
security or disarmament; the controversy over appeasement; the
present debate about the nuclear deterrent—all this is the stuff
of international theory, and it is constantly bursting the bounds of
the language in which we try to handle it. For it all involves the
ultimate experience of life and death, national existence and national
extinction.

It is tempting to answer the question with which this paper begins
by saying that there is no international theory except the kind of
rumination about human destiny to which we give the unsatisfactory
name of philosophy of history. The passage from Kant quoted above
illustrates the slide-over into theodicy that seems to occur after a
certain point with all international theory. At all events, it is
necessary to see the domain of international theory stretching all the
way from the noble attempt of Grotius and his successors to establish
the laws of war, at one extreme, to de Maistre's 'occult and terrible
law' of the violent destruction of the human species at the other.[2]
'La terre entière, continuellement imbibée de sang, n'est qu'un autel
immense ou tout ce qui vit doit être immolé sans fin, sans mesure,

---

[1] *The Education of Henry Adams* (New York, Modern Library, 1931), p. 422.
[2] *Soirées de St. Pétersbourg*, 7me entretien (Paris, Emmanuel Vitte, 1924, vol. ii,
p. 14); cf. *Considérations sur la France*, ch. iii.

C

sans relâche, jusqu'à la consommation des choses, jusqu'à l'extinction du mal, jusqu'à la mort de la mort'[1]—which de Maistre, at least, supposed to be political theology. An extra-galactic examiner in tellurian international theory might well hold that the writer of this answer, however curious the language in which it was couched, deserved a mark over some other candidates for not misrepresenting the historical record.

---

[1] *Soirées de St. Pétersbourg*, 7me entretien (vol. ii, p. 25).

CHAPTER 2

SOCIETY AND ANARCHY IN INTERNATIONAL RELATIONS[1]

HEDLEY BULL

I

Whereas men within each state are subject to a common government, sovereign states in their mutual relations are not. This anarchy it is possible to regard as the central fact of international life and the starting-point of theorizing about it.[2] A great deal of the most fruitful reflection about international life has been concerned with tracing the consequences in it of this absence of government. We can, indeed, give some account in these terms of what it is that distinguishes the international from the domestic field of politics, morals and law.

One persistent theme in the modern discussion of international relations has been that as a consequence of this anarchy states do not form together any kind of society; and that if they were to do so it could only be by subordinating themselves to a common authority. One of the chief intellectual supports of this doctrine is what may be called the domestic analogy, the argument from the experience of individual men in domestic society to the experience of states, according to which the need of individual men to stand in awe of a common power in order to live in peace is a ground for holding that states must do the same. The conditions of an orderly social life, on this view, are the same among states as they are within them: they require that the institutions of domestic society be reproduced on a universal scale.

The present essay has two purposes. First, to examine the opinion that anarchy in international relations is incompatible with society, or that the progress of the latter has been, or necessarily will be, a matter of the degree to which government comes to prevail. And secondly, to determine the limits of the domestic analogy and thus

[1] A number of the leading ideas in this essay derive, in a process in which they may have lost their original shape, from Martin Wight; and a number of others from C. A. W. Manning.

[2] Anarchy: 'Absence of rule; disorder; confusion' (*O.E.D.*). The term here is used exclusively in the first of these senses. The question with which the essay is concerned is whether in the international context it is to be identified also with the second and the third.

establish the autonomy of international relations.

It might be thought that the opinions I propose to consider are to be found at the present time only among the small group of people who advocate the establishment of a world government. This is far from being the case. The feeling of unease about the system of sovereign states is a deep-rooted one in Western thinking about international relations. It exists not only among those who explicitly espouse the elimination of this system, but also where we might least expect to find it, in the pronouncements of the servants of sovereign states themselves, by whose daily acts the system is preserved. These pronouncements often betray a sense of the inadequacy of the anarchical system, a lack of confidence in its institutions, a tendency guiltily to disguise their operation of the system or to apologize for doing so. The League of Nations and the United Nations we are invited to see not as diplomatic machinery in the tradition of the Concert of Europe, but as first steps towards a world state. Military alliances, in this manner of speaking, become regional security systems; exclusive political groupings, like Little Europe or the British Commonwealth, experiments in world order; war, police action. Men of affairs, even while in their actions they are seeking them, in their words are sometimes suggesting that solutions cannot in the long run be found within the framework of the existing system. Whether by a social contract among the nations or by conquest, whether gradually or at once, whether by a frontal assault on national sovereignty or a silent undermining of its foundations, the problem of international relations, if it is soluble at all, is taken to be in the last analysis the problem of bringing international relations to an end.

The view that anarchy is incompatible with society among nations has been especially prominent in the years since the First World War. It was the First World War that gave currency to the doctrine of a 'fresh start' in international relations and set the habit of disparaging the past. Nineteenth century thought had regarded both the existence of international society and its further consolidation as entirely consistent with the continuation of international anarchy. The ideas of 1919 were in part a mere extension of the liberal, progressive strand of this nineteenth century anarchist view: the strengthening of international law, the creation of new procedures for arbitration, the establishment of permanent institutions for co-operation among sovereign states, a reduction and limitation of armaments, the pressure of public opinion, the aspiration that states should be popularly based and that their boundaries should coincide with the boundaries of nations. But there was now voiced also a view that is not to be found in Cobden or Gladstone or Mazzini: a rejection of international anarchy itself, expressed on the one hand in the view that the true value of the League and the United Nations lay not in themselves, but in their presumed final cause, a world government; and on the other hand in the endorsement of world government as an immediately valid objective, and a depreciation of the League and its successor as destined to 'failure' on account of their preservation of state sovereignty.

The twentieth century view of international anarchy is not, however, something new. Such a doctrine was stated at the outset of modern international history and has since found a succession of embodiments. The European system of sovereign states did not, of course, arise as a result of the outward growth and collision of hitherto isolated communities. Its origin lay in the disintegration of a single community: the waning on the one hand of central authorities, and on the other hand of local authorities, within Western Christendom, and the exclusion of both from particular territories by the princely power. Throughout its history modern European international society has been conscious of the memory of the theoretical imperium of Pope and Emperor and the actual imperium of Rome. When in the sixteenth and early seventeenth centuries the question was raised of the nature of relationships between sovereign princes and states, order and justice on a universal scale were readily associated with the idea of a universal state: not merely because the supremacy of the prince was observed to be a condition of order within the confines of the state, but also because order throughout Western Christendom as a whole was associated with the vanished authority of the Papacy and the Holy Roman Empire. The idea that international anarchy has as its consequence the absence of society among states, and the associated but opposite idea of the domestic analogy, became and have remained persistent doctrines about the international predicament.

The first of these doctrines describes international relations in terms of a Hobbesian state of nature, which is a state of war. Sovereign states, on this view, find themselves in a situation in which their behaviour in relation to one another, although it may be circumscribed by considerations of prudence, is not limited by rules or law or morality. Either, as in the Machiavellian version of this doctrine, moral and legal rules are taken not to impinge on the sphere of action of the state: the political life and the moral life being presented as alternatives, as in the theory of quietism. Or, as in the Hegelian version, moral imperatives are thought to exist in international relations, but are believed to endorse the self-assertion of states in relation to one another, and to be incapable of imposing limits upon it. In this first doctrine the conditions of social life are asserted to be the same for states as they are for individuals. In the case of Hobbes, whose views we shall examine more closely, government is stated to be a necessary condition of social life among men, and the same is said to hold of sovereign princes. But the domestic analogy stops short at this point; it is not the view of Hobbes, or of other thinkers of this school, that a social contract of states that would bring the international anarchy to an end either should or can take place.

The second doctrine accepts the description of international relations embodied in the first, but combines with it the demand that the international anarchy be brought to an end. Where the domestic analogy is employed to buttress this doctrine, it is taken further, to embrace the concept of the social contract as well as that of the state of nature. This search for an alternative to international anarchy may be sustained by the memory of an alternative actually experienced, as in the backward-looking tradition of a return to Roman or to Western Christian unity. The other variety, the forward-looking tradition of which we may take Kant to be representative, finds its sustenance in the belief in human progress, in the possibility of achieving in the future what has not been achieved in the past.

Even as these two doctrines were taking shape there was asserted against them both the third possibility of a society of sovereign states; and along with it the beginnings of the idea that the conditions of order among states were different from what they were among individual men. Like the two doctrines against which it has been directed, this third doctrine consists in part of a description of what is taken to be the actual character of relations between states, and in part of a set of prescriptions. The description is one which sees sovereign states in intercourse with one another as consciously united together for certain purposes, which modify their conduct in relation to one another. The salient fact of international relations is taken to be not that of conflict among states within the international anarchy, as on the Hobbesian view; nor that of the transience of the international anarchy and the availability of materials with which to replace it, as on the Kantian view; but co-operation among sovereign states in a society without government. The prescriptions which accompany this account of the nature of international relations enjoin respect for the legal and moral rules upon which the working of the international society depends. In place of the Hobbesian view that states are not limited by legal or moral rules in their relations with one another, and the Kantian view that the rules to which appeal may be had derive from the higher morality of a cosmopolitan society and enjoin the overthrow of international society, there are asserted the duties and rights attaching to states as members of international society. ⌐

⌐ Two traditions, in particular, have advanced this third conception of an international society. One is the body of theory to which modern international law is the heir, which depicts states as constituting a society in the course of showing them to be bound by a system of legal rules: whether these rules are thought to derive from natural law or positive law, whether the subjects of the rules are taken to be states or the men who rule them, and whether the rules are regarded as universally valid, or as binding only upon the states of Christendom or Europe. In the systems of sixteenth century writers like Vitoria and Suarez, and of seventeenth century thinkers like Grotius and Pufendorf, the idea of the domestic analogy was still strong; the alternative notion of the uniqueness of international society was fully worked out only by the positivist international lawyers of the nineteenth century.[1] The other tradition is that of the analysis of the political relations of states in terms of the system of balance of power. According to such analyses states throughout modern history have been engaged in the operation of a 'political system' or 'states-system', which makes its own demands upon their freedom of action and requires them in particular to act so as to maintain a balance of power. In so far as such theories have presented the balance of power as a product of policies consciously directed towards it, and in so far as they have asserted that states are obliged to act so as to maintain it, they must be taken also to embody the idea of international society and of rules binding upon its members. In the sixteenth and seventeenth centuries the predominant theories of the law of nations and of the balance of power were held by different groups of persons and in their respective content were largely antithetical. But in the eighteenth century the two streams converged, as in the writings of Vattel international law came to take account of the balance of power, and in the writings of Burke and later Gentz the political maxim enjoining the preservation of a balance of power came to be defined in a more legalistic way. In the nineteenth century the predominant doctrines moved close together: although it may still be doubted whether either theory can be reconciled to the other without sacrifice of an essential part of its content.

[1] I have explored the domestic analogy in the theory of Grotius and of the twentieth-century neo-Grotians in chapter 3, below, 'The Grotian Conception of International Society'.

It is the validity of this third conception of an international society, either as a description of the past or as a guide for the present and the future, that is called in question by the doctrine that the international anarchy is, or has become, intolerable. It is not my purpose to vindicate the idea of an international society, nor to argue against the desirability or feasibility of a universal state. In my view the questions with which this essay deals do not lend themselves to clear-cut answers, one way or the other: the future course of history is liable to be richer in its possibilities than our categories for theorizing about it can comprehend. But it would seem important to examine carefully an idea that has stood for so long at the centre of the theory and practice of modern international relations before concluding that it should be cast aside. It is proposed to consider the idea of international society first in relation to the doctrine that states find themselves in a Hobbesian state of nature; and then in relation to the doctrine that they should attempt to emerge from it by constructing a universal state.

II

The identification of international relations as a variety of the Hobbesian state of nature derives from Hobbes himself. Hobbes' account of relations between sovereign princes is a subordinate part of his explanation and justification of government among individual men. As evidence for his speculations as to how men would live were they to find themselves in a situation of anarchy, Hobbes mentions the experience of civil war, the life of certain American tribes and the facts of international relations:

'But though there had never been any time wherein particular men were in a condition of warre one against another; yet in all times Kings, and Persons of Soveraigne authority, because of their Independency, are in continual jealousies, and in the state and posture of Gladiators; having their weapons pointing, and their eyes fixed on one another; that is, their Forts, Garrisons and Guns, upon the Frontiers of their Kingdomes; and continual Spyes upon their neighbours; which is a posture of war.'[1]

The situation in which men live without a common power to keep them in awe has three principal characteristics, in Hobbes' account. In it there can be no industry, agriculture, navigation, trade or other refinements of living, because the strength and invention of men is

[1] Hobbes, *Leviathan*, ch. xiii (Everyman ed., p. 65).

absorbed in providing security against one another. There are no legal or moral rules: 'The notions of Right and Wrong, Justice and Injustice have there no place . . . It is consequent also to the same condition, that there can be no Propriety, no Dominion, no *Mine* and *Thine* distinct; but only that to be every mans, that he can get; and for so long, as he can keep it.'[1] Finally, the state of nature is a state of war: war understood to consist 'not in actual fighting; but in the known disposition thereto, during all the time there is no assurance to the contrary'; and to be 'such a warre, as is of every man, against every man.'[2]

It may be claimed for the Hobbesian view of international relations as conflict among sovereign states that it distils certain qualities that are present in the situation of international anarchy at all times and in all places and that in certain areas and at certain moments seem to drive all other qualities away. It may be claimed also for that other description of international relations as a potential community of mankind that it draws attention to qualities similarly permanent and universal: those arising from the bonds which men have in common as men, and in relation to which the division of mankind into sovereign states must be regarded as something accidental and transient, whether the relations of these states are taken to consist chiefly in conflict or in collaboration. But there is a great area of international experience which is not taken into account by either theory; and which can be accommodated only by the doctrine that there exists in the international anarchy a society of sovereign states.

The theorists of international society have been able to question the applicability to relations between states of each of the three elements in Hobbes' account of the state of nature. In the first place they have often remarked that sovereign states do not so exhaust their strength and invention in providing security against one another that industry and other refinements of living do not flourish. States do not as a rule invest resources in war and military preparations to such an extent that their economic fabric is ruined; even if it may be argued that the allocation of resources to war and armaments is not the best allocation from the point of view of economic development. On the contrary the armed forces of the state by providing security against external attack and internal disorder, establish the conditions under which economic improvement may take place within its borders. The absence of universal government and the fragmentation among sovereign states of responsibility for military security is not incompatible, moreover, with economic interdependence. The

[1] *Ibid.*, p. 66.
[2] *Ibid.*, p. 64.

relative economic self-sufficiency of states as compared with individuals, has often been taken to explain why states are able to tolerate a looser form of social organization than that enjoyed by individuals within the modern state. At the same time, these theorists may point to the mutual advantages which states derive from economic relationships; and argue that trade, symbolic as it is of the existence of overlapping through different interests, is the activity most characteristic of international relationships as a whole.

[As regards the second feature of the Hobbesian state of nature, the absence in it of notions of right and wrong, it is a matter of observation that this is not true of modern international relations.] The theorist of international society has often begun his inquiries, as Grotius did, by remarking the extent to which states depart from rules of law and morality, and by uttering a protest against this situation in asserting the binding character of the rules. However, he has also been able to draw attention to the recognition of legal and moral rules by statesmen themselves, and to traditions of positive law and morality which have been a continuous feature of international life. International action which, although it is contrary to recognized principles of international law and morality, is accompanied by pretexts stated in terms of those principles, attests the force in international relations of notions of right and wrong, just as does action which conforms to them. By contrast, action which in addition to involving a violation of the legal and moral rules of international society is accompanied by no legal and moral pretext, action which, to use Grotius' terms, is 'not persuasive' as well as 'not justifiable', is widely taken by legal theorists to be quite uncharacteristic of the behaviour of member states of modern international society (as well as to be hostile to its working in a way in which illegal behaviour accompanied by a pretext is not).

The element in the Hobbesian state of nature which appears most clearly to apply to international relations is the third. It is the fact of war which appears to provide the chief evidence for the view that states do not form a society. On the one hand, if we take the modern state to illustrate the idea of a society, one of its salient features is that in it, apart from certain residual rights of self-defence, the private use of force is proscribed. But on the other hand, it cannot be denied that sovereign states in relation to one another are in a state of war, in Hobbes' sense that they are disposed to it over a period of time. It must be conceded also that this war is one of all against all. At any single moment in the history of the modern states-system, it is true, certain states will not be disposed to war against certain other states. That is to say, certain pairs of states will be pursuing common purposes and will be allied to one another; certain other pairs of states will be pursuing purposes which are different but do not cross, and will therefore treat one another with indifference; and certain pairs of states, although they have purposes which are conflicting, nevertheless share such a sense of community that (as now among the English-speaking states) war is not contemplated as a possible outcome of the conflict. But if we consider the states-system not at a single moment but in motion throughout the whole of its life (say, from 1648) then we shall find that every state that has survived the period has at some point or other been disposed to war with every other one.

The theorist of international society has sought to deal with this difficulty not by denying the ubiquity of war, but by questioning the relevance of the model of the modern state. If sovereign states are understood to form a society of a different sort from that constituted by the modern state—one, in particular, whose operation not merely tolerates certain private uses of force but actually requires them— then the fact of a disposition to war can no longer be regarded as evidence that international society does not exist. Theorists of the law of nations and of the system of balance of power have thus sought to show that war does not indicate the absence of international society, or its break-down, but can occur as a part of its functioning. Thus some international legal writers have seen in war a means by which the law of international society is enforced by individual members; others have seen in it a means of settling political conflicts. Theorists of the balance of power have seen war as the ultimate means by which threats to the international equilibrium are redressed. It may even be argued, in line with these theories, that the element in international relations of a 'war of all against all' so far from being detrimental to the working of international society, is in a certain sense positively favourable to it. For if the enforcement of law depends upon the willingness of particular law-abiding states to undertake war against particular law-breaking ones, then the prospects of law enforcement will be best if every state is willing to take up arms against any state that breaks the law. The fact that at any one time certain states are unwilling to contemplate war with certain other states, either because they are allied to them, or because they are indifferent to one another's policies, or because they are bound by a particular sense of community, is an obstacle to the enforcement of international law. In the same way the balance of power is best preserved if states are willing to take up arms against any state that threatens the balance, to focus their attention upon its recalcitrance in this respect and to disregard all special claims it may have on them.

⌊ If, then, we were tempted to compare international relations with a pre-contractual state of nature among individual men, it might be argued that we should choose not Hobbes' description of that condition, but Locke's. ⌉In the conception of a society without government, whose members must themselves judge and enforce the law, which is therefore crude and uncertain, we can recognize the international society of many thinkers in the tradition of international law⌉ And although Locke's speculations about life of men in anarchy will leave us dissatisfied, we may turn to modern anthropological studies of actual societies of this kind, which have been 'forced to consider what, in the absence of explicit forms of government, could be held to constitute the political structure of a people'.[1] Such studies widen our view of the devices for cohesion in a society, and suggest a number of parallels in the international field.

There are a number of these which are worth exploring. One, which has received some attention from international lawyers is the principle of the 'hue and cry'. Another is the place of ritual. Another is the principle of loyalty—among kinsmen in primitive society, among allies in international society. International society and certain sorts of primitive society would seem also to be alike in respect of the function performed within them by the principle that might is right. This we are inclined to dismiss as the contrary of a moral principle, a mere way of saying that the question of right does not arise. This, indeed, is what, according to Thucydides, the Athenians said to the Melians: they did not appeal to the principle that might is right, but said that the question of right arose only when the parties were equal, which in this case they were not⌉ Yet in international relations the parties are frequently not equal, and the society of states has had to evolve principles which will take account of this fact and lead to settlements⌉ The rule that the will of the stronger party should be accepted provides a means of going directly to what the outcome of a violent struggle would be, without actually going through that struggle. To say that the principle that might is right fulfils a function in international society is not to provide a justification of it or to regard it as a necessary element in international life; but it is to argue that the working of a social order may be recognized even in a feature of relations between states sometimes taken to demonstrate the absence of any kind of order.[2]

[1] M. Fortes and E. E. Evans-Pritchard, *African Political Systems* (Oxford University Press, 1940), p. 6.
[2] On the functioning of the principle that might is right in primitive and in international society, see Ernest Gellner, 'How to Live in Anarchy', *The Listener*, April 3, 1958, pp. 579–83.

We must, however, at some point abandon the domestic analogy altogether. Not only is this because the attempt to understand something by means of analogies with something else is a sign of infancy in a subject, an indication of lack of familiarity with our own subject-matter. But also because international society is unique, and owes its character to qualities that are peculiar to the situation of sovereign states, as well as to those it has in common with the lives of individuals in domestic society. One of the themes that has accompanied the statement of the idea of international society has been that anarchy among states is tolerable to a degree to which among individuals it is not. This has been recognized in some measure even by those who originated the description of international relations in terms of the Hobbesian state of nature.

In the first place, as we have noted, it is not consequent upon the international anarchy that in it there can be no industry or other refinements of living; unlike the individual in Hobbes' state of nature, the state does not find its energies so absorbed in the pursuit of security that the life of its activities is that of mere brutes. Hobbes himself recognizes this when having observed that persons of sovereign authority are in 'a posture of war', he goes on to say: 'But because they uphold thereby the industry of their subjects, there does not follow from it that misery which accompanies the liberty of particular men.'[1] The same sovereigns that find themselves in the state of nature in relation to one another have provided with particular territories, the conditions in which the refinements of life can flourish.

In the second place states have not been vulnerable to violent attack to the same degree that individuals are. Spinoza, echoing Hobbes in his assertion that 'two states are in the same relation to one another as two men in the condition of nature,' goes on to add 'with this exception, that a commonwealth can guard itself against being subjugated by another, as a man in the state of nature cannot do. For, of course, a man is overcome by sleep every day, is often afflicted by disease of body or mind, and is finally prostrated by old age; in addition, he is subject to other troubles against which a commonwealth can make itself secure.'[2] One human being in the state of nature cannot make himself secure against violent attack; and this attack carries with it the prospect of sudden death. Groups of human beings organized as states, however, may provide themselves with a means of defence that exists independently of the frailties

[1] Hobbes, *op. cit.*, p. 65.
[2] Spinoza, *Tractatus Politicus*, ch. iii, para. 11 (*The Political Works*, ed. A. G. Wernham (Clarendon Press, 1958), p. 295).

of any one of them. And armed attack by one state upon another has not brought with it a prospect comparable to the killing of one individual by another. For one man's death may be brought about suddenly, in a single act; and once it has occurred, it cannot be undone. But war has only occasionally resulted in the physical extinction of the vanquished people. In modern history it has been possible to take Clausewitz's view that 'war is never absolute in its results' and that defeat in it may be merely 'a passing evil which can be remedied'. Moreover, war in the past, even if it could in principle lead to the physical extermination of one or both of the belligerent peoples, could not be thought capable of doing so at once in the course of a single act. Clausewitz, in holding that war does not consist of a single instantaneous blow, but always of a succession of separate actions, was drawing attention to something that in the past has always held true and has rendered public violence distinct from private. It is only in the context of recent military technology that it has become pertinent to ask whether war could not now both be 'absolute in its results' and 'take the form of a single, instantaneous blow,' in Clausewitz's understanding of these terms; and whether therefore violence does not now confront the state with the same sort of prospect it has always held for the individual.[1]

This second difference, that states have been less vulnerable to violent attack by one another than individual men, is reinforced by a third contingency of great importance; that in so far as states have been vulnerable in this sense they have not been equally so. Hobbes builds his account of the state of nature upon the proposition that 'Nature hath made men so equal, in the faculties of body and mind . . . (that) the weakest has strength enough to kill the strongest'.[2] It is this equal vulnerability of every man to every other that, in Hobbes' view, renders the condition of anarchy intolerable. In modern international society, however, there has been a persistent distinction between Great Powers and small. Great Powers have been secure against the attacks of small Powers; and have had to fear only other Great Powers, and hostile combinations of Powers. We have only to think of the security enjoyed by Great Britain in the nineteenth century to appreciate that the insecurity which is a feature of the Hobbesian state of nature, in so far as it exists in international society, is not distributed equally among all its members. It is interesting to find Gentz writing of 'the European Commonwealth' that

---

[1] I have deliberately excluded from this essay any consideration of how far recent military technology should lead us to alter the answers that have been given to these questions in the past.

[2] Hobbes, *op. cit.*, p. 63.

'The original inequality of the parties in such a union as is here described is not an accidental circumstance, much less a casual evil; but is in a certain degree to be considered as the previous condition and foundation of the whole system'.[1] A footnote follows: 'Had the surface of the globe been divided into equal parts, no such union would ever have taken place; and an eternal war of each against the whole is probably the only event we should have heard of.' If Great Powers are relatively safe from attack and do not stand in need of the protection of a central authority, then by the same token they are themselves in a position to attack others and to withstand the pressures which other states may seek to bring to bear upon them. If an even distribution of strength among states would seem unfavourable to the development of international society, it is also true that great discrepancies in strength may obstruct its working or even prove irreconcilable with it. One of the central contentions of theorists of the balance of power has been that if international society is to be maintained, no one state may be in a position to dominate the rest. Other writers have gone beyond this, to assert with Gentz himself, in a doctrine in which the principle of the balance of power becomes difficult to disentangle from that of collective security, 'That if that system is not merely to exist, but to be maintained without constant perils and violent concussions, each member which infringes it must be in a condition to be coerced, not only by the collective strength of the other members, but by any majority of them, if not by one individual'.[2] Ancillon, writing sixteen years later, saw the same principle at work in the early development in Italy of the principle of equilibrium: 'Le voisinage d'un grand nombre d'états, trop inégaux pour résister l'un à l'autre, y avait fait saisir, suivre et appliquer de bonne heure ces maximes de prudence qui servent de sauvegarde au droit, et qui allaient passer de ce petit théâtre sur un théâtre plus vaste.'[3]

A fourth point of contrast that has often been remarked is that states in their economic lives enjoy a degree of self-sufficiency beyond comparison with that of individual men. Thus while it has been one of the themes of theorists of international society to stress the mutual dependence of states in trade, at the same time their relative economic independence of one another, by contrast with

---

[1] Friedrich von Gentz, *Fragments upon the Balance of Power in Europe* (London, Peltier, 1806), p. 63.
[2] *Ibid.*, p. 62.
    J. P. F. Ancillon, *Tableau des Révolutions du Système Politique de l'Europe, depuis la Fin du Quinzième Siècle* (Paris, Anselin et Pochard, 1823), vol. i, pp. 262–3.

individuals, has provided support for the argument that states are able to tolerate a form of society looser than that which is crowned by a government.

As against the Hobbesian view that states find themselves in a state of nature which is a state of war, it may be argued, therefore, that they constitute a society without a government. This society may be compared with the anarchical society among individual men of Locke's imagining, and also with primitive anarchical societies that have been studied by anthropologists. But although we may employ such analogies, we must in the end abandon them, for the fact that states form a society without a government reflects also the features of their situation that are unique. The working of international society must be understood in terms of its own, distinctive institutions. These include international law, diplomacy and the system of balance of power. There may be others which should be ranked alongside these; it is arguable, for example, that collaboration among the Great Powers to manage the affairs of international society as a whole and impart to them a degree of central direction— seen in operation in the series of conferences from Westphalia to Potsdam, and finding its most perfect embodiment in the Concert of Europe—also represents such an institution, even though it has functioned only intermittently.

III

The idea that sovereign states find themselves in a Hobbesian state of nature, as well as standing on its own as a description of what international politics is like, is also to be found linked to demands for the establishment of a universal state. In doctrines like that of Kant in *Perpetual Peace*, the Hobbesian domestic analogy is applied to international relations, but in this case taken further to embrace not only the idea of the state of nature but also that of the social contract.

The Kantian view of international relations involves a dilemma. If states are indeed in a Hobbesian state of nature, the contract by means of which they are to emerge from it cannot take place. For if covenants without the sword are but words, this will be true of covenants directed towards the establishment of universal government, just as it will hold true of agreements on other subjects. The difficulty with the Kantian position is that the description it contains of the actual condition of international relations, and the prescription it provides for its improvement, are inconsistent with one another. Action within the context of continuing international anarchy is held to be of no avail; but at the same time it is in the international anarchy that the grand solution of the international social contract is held to take place.

The advocate of a universal state can show his scheme to be feasible as well as desirable only by admitting that international relations do not resemble a Hobbesian state of nature; that in it covenants without the sword are more than words and the materials may be found with which to bring about collaboration between sovereign governments. But to make this admission is to weaken the case for bringing the international anarchy to an end. For the establishment of a universal government cannot then be regarded as a *sine qua non* of the world order. If a Hobbesian description of the international state of nature is abandoned for a Lockean one, then the case for a fundamental change is simply that which Locke presents for a contract of government: that to crown the anarchical society with a government would be to render it more efficient.

However, such a case might still be a quite formidable one. It may rest essentially on something which the Lockean description of international society itself admits: that in it the private use of force is tolerated or even in certain circumstances required. The international society described by the international lawyers and the theorists of balance of power is one in which war has a permanent and perhaps even a necessary place. The argument for proceeding from anarchy to government may therefore be stated, as Kant states it, in terms of the possibility and desirability of perpetual peace.

It is a facile view according to which a universal state would abolish war because war is a relationship between sovereign states and sovereign states would have been abolished. Either we may take war to mean any kind of organized violence between large groups of human beings, in which case the statement is false. Or we may understand the term in the narrow sense of a contention between sovereign states, in which case although the statement is true it is misleading. War in this latter sense comprises only one area of the spectrum of possible violence; if the elimination of war in this special sense of public war were to occasion the re-establishment of the various forms of private war, this could not necessarily be counted a gain.

If, however, a universal state should be understood as providing, just as does the system of sovereign states, a particular solution to the problem of the management of violence, rather than a means of transcending it, this is not to say that it is an inferior solution. It may be argued that the propensities for violence that are inherent in any form of political organization on a world-scale, will be better managed through the medium of a single authority entrusted with the legitimate exercise of force, than through many such authorities; just as this is

D

the case in the smaller geographical context of the nation-state. Such an argument might well be sustained; yet the traditional arguments upholding international society against universal government would first have to be met.

[These arguments have often rested on a preference for liberty in international relations over order or security: the liberty of states and nations from domination by a central power, and of individuals from the reach of a tyrannical government whose ubiquitous authority must deny them the right of foreign asylum. It may well be replied to this that order or security is the prime need of international society, and that liberty should if necessary be sacrificed to it. International anarchy, however, may be preferred on grounds of order also.]

[Government, involving as it does a legal monopoly of the use of force, provides a means for maintaining order; but it is also a source of dissension among conflicting groups in society, which compete for its control. If government authority, once it is captured, may be wielded so as to deny the resort to force by private individuals or groups, it is also the case that the existence of the governmental mechanism constitutes a prize in political conflict, which raises the stakes in such conflict to a level above that it would otherwise be. In the typical modern nation-state order is best preserved when conflict takes the form of a competition between the contending forces for control of a single government, rather than that of competition among governments. Yet the political community is also familiar in which the reverse is the case; in which the dangers to order arising from the coexistence of sovereign governments are less than those involved in the attempt to hold hostile communities in the framework of a single polity. The partition of India in 1947 had this *rationale*. It is possible also to view the problem of order in the world community in this way. Formidable though the classic dangers are of a plurality of sovereign states, these have to be reckoned against those inherent in the attempt to contain disparate communities within the framework of a single government. It is an entirely reasonable view of world order at the present time that it is best served by living with the former dangers rather than by attempting to face the latter.

CHAPTER 3

THE GROTIAN CONCEPTION OF INTERNATIONAL SOCIETY

HEDLEY BULL

I

Underlying a great deal of the theory and practice of international relations since the First World War there is a certain conception of international society, whose imprint may be traced in the Covenant of the League of Nations, the Paris Pact, the United Nations Charter and the Charter of the International Military Tribunal at Nuremberg. It is widely taken to contain within itself an adequate formula for orderly and just international conduct, such that the disparity between it and the actual course of events since 1919 may be ascribed to the failure of states or statesmen to behave in accordance with it, rather than to its own inherent defects. The purpose of this essay is, at the risk of losing sight of its many varieties and nuances, to state the essence of this doctrine; and to consider the adequacy of its prescriptions.

The conception of international society I have in mind may be called the Grotian conception. The reason for giving it this name does not lie in the part which the writings of Grotius have played in bringing about this twentieth century doctrine, although this has been by no means negligible; but simply in the measure of identity that exists between the one and the other. We shall have occasion to consider the difference as well as the resemblances between Grotius himself and the twentieth century neo-Grotians; but the resemblances are remarkable enough to warrant our treatment of *De Jure Belli ac Pacis* as containing the classical presentation of the same view. Two important studies, to which reference will be made, have discerned a return to Grotius in this century, and along with it a reversal of the previous trend of international legal thought, which from the seventeenth century to the early twentieth, had been away from him. The first of these studies, by Cornelius van Vollenhoven, was written in the summer of 1918 and looked forward to the resuscitation of Grotian doctrines, for which the World War seemed to have set the stage.[1] The second was published by the late Sir Hersch Lauterpacht

[1] Cornelius van Vollenhoven, *The Three Stages in the Evolution of the Law of Nations* (The Hague, Nijhoff, 1919). See also his 'Grotius and Geneva', *Bibliotheca Visseriana*, vol. vi, 1926.

in 1946, by which time he was able to record the penetration by these doctrines into positive international law.[1] Both these writers are concerned to contrast the position shared by Grotius and the twentieth century neo-Grotians with representative thinkers of the intervening period, Vollenhoven taking Vattel to exemplify a position contrary to that of Grotius, and Lauterpacht referring in this connection to the work of the nineteenth century international legal positivists. Vollenhoven and Lauterpacht, it should be noted, themselves embrace the broad Grotian position. It shall be our purpose, while exploring the conflict between this position and that alternative conception of international society to which Vattel and the nineteenth century positivists may be said to have contributed, to consider whether the return to Grotius does indeed constitute that advance which Vollenhoven and Lauterpacht take it to be.

The central Grotian assumption is that of the solidarity, or potential solidarity, of the states comprising international society, with respect to the enforcement of the law. This assumption is not explicitly adopted and defended by Grotius, but, it will be argued, the rules which he propounds for international conduct are such as to presuppose that it is made. In the conception of international society which stands opposed to the Grotian doctrine the contrary assumption is made that states do not exhibit solidarity of this kind, but are capable of agreeing only for certain minimum purposes which fall short of that of the enforcement of the law. In the view it takes of the area of actual or potential agreement among the member states of international society it may be called pluralist where the Grotian doctrine is solidarist; and the rules it prescribes for relations among them are such as to reflect this difference.

The issues which divide the Grotian or solidarist conception from the pluralists one may be stated with greater precision by contrasting the doctrine of Grotius himself with that of a particular representative of the latter school, Lassa Oppenheim, the first edition of whose *International Law* was published in 1905 and 1906.[2] Three aspects of the disagreement between them are especially relevant to our inquiry. The first concerns the place of war in international society. The second is about the sources of the law by which the member states of international society are bound. And the third turns upon the status in the society of states of individual human beings.

---

[1] Sir Hersch Lauterpacht, 'The Grotian Tradition in International Law', *British Yearbook of International Law*, 1946.

[2] L. Oppenheim, *International Law*, vol. i, *Peace* (Longmans, 1905), vol. ii, *War and Neutrality* (Longmans, 1906). All subsequent references are to this first edition.

II

On what is perhaps the most fundamental question of the theory of international relations Grotius and Oppenheim (and indeed, the two schools of thought they illustrate) are at one. Both assert the existence of an international society and of laws which are binding on its member states in their relations with one another. Both are opposed to the tradition of *Realpolitik*, according to which there is no international society but rather an international state of nature in which states are without binding obligations in their relations with one another. And both are hostile also to that doctrine according to which the standards to which appeal may be made in international politics enjoin not the preservation of international society, but its subversion and replacement by a universal empire or cosmopolitan society.[1]

For anyone who upholds, as Grotius and Oppenheim do, the idea of international society, the fact of war presents a difficulty. In domestic society the private use of force, apart from certain residual rights of self-defence, is proscribed; and the legitimate exercise of violence is the monopoly of the community. If the private use of force has the same significance in relations among states that it has within them, then the fact of war must be taken to indicate that international society does not exist. If their theories are to take account of war and not merely ignore it, those who seek to show that there is a society of states must therefore demonstrate that in international relations the private use of force has a meaning altogether different from that which attaches to it within the confines of the state. They must present international society as a society of a different sort from that formed by individual men; as one with whose functioning the private use of force may be consistent. It is a point of departure common to Grotius and Oppenheim that war of a certain sort plays a part in international society; and that so far from indicating its absence, it provides evidence of its working. They are concerned to show, therefore, that while some kinds of war are contrary to the law of international society, other kinds may be sanctioned by it.

On the question of the legitimacy of war there are three possible positions. There is first the view of the pacifist that no war or act of war is legitimate. There is secondly the view, sometimes called that of the militarist, that any war or act of war is legitimate. And there is

[1] However, one way of describing the difference between Grotius and Oppenheim would be to say that while Grotius, in his conception of international society, leans toward the doctrine that would replace it with a universal state, Oppenheim leans toward the position of *Realpolitik*.

the view that a distinction should be drawn between some wars, or acts of war, and others; that some are legitimate while others are not. It is upon this third position that Grotius and Oppenheim both take their stand. The pacifist and militarist positions are alike inimical to the idea of international society: the former because it rejects that violence which is necessary to uphold the international order against attempts to subvert it; the latter because it admits violence of a sort that must destroy the international order; and both because, in asserting that war stands beyond the reach of law, they are denying the relevance of international law to a large area of international experience. Grotius is expressing a doctrine common to all those who embrace the conception of an international society when he writes: 'For both extremes, then, a remedy must be found, that men may not believe either that nothing is allowable or that anything is.'[1]

Here, however, the agreement between Grotius and Oppenheim ends. There are two ways in which the attempt may be made to distinguish just war from unjust. Either we may say that a just war is one fought for a just cause. Or we may say that it is one conducted in a just or lawful way. Whereas Oppenheim holds the law to be concerned exclusively with determining what constitutes lawful conduct in war, Grotius believes it also to distinguish just from unjust causes of war, and to insist that war be waged only for the former.

According to Oppenheim, although it is a part of ethics to distinguish just from unjust causes of war it is no part of international law. War, on his view, is the prerogative right of sovereign states; and the law is concerned simply to take account of the fact of war when it occurs, and to regulate the way in which it is conducted. Before 1919 the international law arising from custom and treaty was wholly in accord with Oppenheim's view. It had evolved certain rules concerning the observance of due form in beginning and ending a war; the legal consequences for states and individuals of the existence of a state of war; the proper limits of violence in war; and the relations between belligerent and non-belligerent states. But it did not seek to infringe the right of states to undertake war.

Grotius, by contrast, insists that it is the province of the law to determine the proper causes for which war may be fought. His basic criterion of just war is that it be fought in order to enforce rights: 'No other cause for undertaking war can there be excepting injury received.'[2] In elaborating this doctrine Grotius confines the just

---

[1] *De Jure Belli ac Pacis*, translated by Francis W. Kelsey (Oxford, Clarendon Press, 1925), Prolegomena, para. 29. Cf. below, p. 91.

[2] *Op. cit.*, book II, ch. i, section i. 4.

causes of war to three: defence, the recovery of property and the infliction of punishment. Since the First World War the Grotian doctrine of a distinction between just and unjust causes of war, and of the limitation of lawful causes of war to the former, has been written into positive international law. The League of Nations Covenant, the Paris Pact and the United Nations Charter all reject the older doctrine of an unqualified prerogative of states to resort to war; and all present war as something which can be legitimate only when it is the means by which the law is upheld, whether such war is undertaken on the independent decision of particular states or on the authority of bodies, such as the United Nations Security Council, deemed to represent the society of nations as a whole.

The drawing of a distinction between just and unjust causes of war may be said to have two effects. It excludes one kind of war; but at the same time it sanctifies another and enhances its dignity. Grotius was clearly intent that his doctrine should have the first effect, of excluding occasions of war. It is worth remarking how restrictionist he is in defining the boundaries of what is permissible. His proposition that 'war ought not to be undertaken except to enforce rights' is one that permits war only the function of conserving a fixed system of rights, of responding to infringements of them; it does not admit of war to change the system of rights.[1] He devotes a chapter to enumerating unjust causes of war.[2] In elaborating the right of self-defence he rejects the claims of preventive war, insisting that we must be certain not only regarding the power of our neighbour but also regarding his intent. The desire for richer lands furnishes no just cause of war; nor the refusal of marriage, where there is an abundance of marriageable women; nor 'the desire to rule others against their will on the pretext that it is for their good';[3] nor 'the discovery of things previously taken over by others.'[4] Consistently with his acceptance of the legitimacy of a society of sovereign states he rejects the title of Emperor or Church to universal empire as providing a just cause of war. Wars cannot justly be waged, either against those who refuse to accept the Christian religion or who err in its interpretation. Not even the desire of a subject people for freedom furnishes them with a just cause of war.

Moreover, Grotius is hesitant to endorse resort to war even where there does exist a just cause. He devotes a chapter to the consideration of 'Doubtful Causes of War', and stipulates that in addition to a

[1] Prolegomena, para. 25.
[2] Book II, ch. xxii.
[3] Book II, ch. xxii, section xii.
[4] Book II, ch. xxii, section ix.

just causes there must exist a conviction in the mind of the doer of its justice; in cases of doubt we must refrain from war.[1] In another chapter of 'Warnings not to Undertake War Rashly' he urges that war ought not to be undertaken for every just cause, and in particular that 'war is not to be undertaken, unless of necessity.'[2] All these restrictions are consonant with the purpose Grotius states in the Prolegomena for undertaking to write on the subject: that he had observed throughout the Christian world 'a lack of restraint in relation to war, such as even barbarous races should be ashamed of; I observed that men rush to arms for slight causes, or no cause at all. . . .'[3]

At the same time Grotius is concerned that the distinction he has drawn will have the second effect also, that of sanctifying war which is waged on behalf of international society rather than against it or in disregard of it. War in the Grotian system derives its legitimacy from the service it renders to international society as a whole; the king or people going to war to redress an injury received are entitled to regard themselves as the instruments of a general purpose. Their aims in war include not merely reparation for the damage they have suffered, but also the infliction of punishment. Grotius rejects the view of Vitoria and others that punishment may be inflicted only by those who have civil jurisdiction over the wrongdoer. The natural law, he argues, does require that punishment be inflicted by one who is superior; but a state which has committed a crime has thereby made itself inferior to others, and may be punished by them, so long as they are not equally guilty of the same offence. The waging of just war to obtain reparation from the criminal king or people and inflict punishment upon it, moreover, is not confined to the state which is the victim of the crime. It is one of the central Grotian theses that 'The causes . . . which are just in relation to the person whose interest is at stake are just also in relation to those who give assistance to others.'[4] There is therefore a general right of participation in just war, conferred by 'the mutual tie of kinship among men, which of itself affords sufficient ground for rendering assistance.'[5] Grotius even goes so far as to say that it is more honourable to avenge the wrongs of others than one's own.

Thus, although Grotius and Oppenheim both contend that war may be conducted within the bounds of international law and

---

[1] Book II, ch. xxiii, especially section vi.
[2] Book II, ch. xxiv, section viii.
[3] Prolegomena, para. 28.
[4] Book II, ch. xxv, section i. 1.
[5] Book II, ch. xxv, section vi.

society, they differ as regards the place they assign to it. For Oppenheim war is a political act, and the attitude of the law towards the purposes for which it is waged is one of indifference. For Grotius war is either an infringement of the law or an act of law enforcement; and the interest of international society is not merely that the rules of war should be observed but also that the side upholding the law should triumph. It should be noted that each thinker, while stating his distinctive view, displays some awareness of the contrary position. Thus, Oppenheim does recognize that one of the reasons a state may have for going to war is the enforcement of its rights; and indeed his claim that the rules he is expounding have the status of law is founded upon the proposition that they are enforced by 'self-help and the help of other states which sympathize with the wronged one.'[1] He contends, however, that states also go to war for purely 'political causes' and that this is the fact of which the law needs to take account. Grotius appears to concede something to the position contrary to his own when he recognizes that, although a war cannot be just on both sides it can be just on neither side, so that there may exist a situation in which international society, as it were, is indifferent as to the outcome. Nevertheless there remains a fundamental contrast in their approaches; and it has important consequences for a wide range of their respective systems of thought.

III

The first of these concerns the rights and duties of belligerent states in relation to one another during the course of a war. The tendency of the Grotian doctrine that war be waged only for a just cause is to weaken the rules of customary and treaty law, requiring that it be conducted in a just way. For Oppenheim, who holds the law to make no distinction between just and unjust causes of war, it is a natural conclusion that the rules of war apply equally to both parties in a conflict. For Grotius, however, the question arises whether the party fighting for the law should suffer the same inhibitions as the side fighting against it.

There is no logical inconsistency in holding both that war should be fought only for a just cause and that it should be carried on in a just way. Yet in their application to social life there is clearly a certain tension between these two doctrines. If international society is to regard war as a contest in which one side is seeking to uphold the law and the other to undermine it, it would seem desirable that no obstacle be placed in the way of the former. On the other hand, if the

[1] Oppenheim, *op. cit.*, vol. i, p. 13.

prime consideration is to ensure that war, for whatever reason it breaks out, is conducted according to the rules, then the duty to abide by the laws of war must be made reciprocal, for it is only on the understanding of reciprocity that any prospect exists of their being observed.

Grotius does not reject the idea of laws of war; on the contrary *De Jure Belli ac Pacis* is as much concerned with upholding *jus in bello* as it is with defining *jus ad bellum*; and almost the whole of Book III is devoted to the former subject. What he rather does is attempt to reconcile the two conceptions. In asking himself what is permissible in war he begins by considering the matter from the standpoint of natural law, which he regards as the chief source of international law and in terms of which his theory of the just causes of war has been primarily worked out. From this viewpoint, Grotius considers just conduct in war to be something deriving from the justice of the cause for which it is fought: for 'in a moral question things which lead to an end receive their intrinsic value from the end itself.'[1] Moreover, given a right to self-defence, the recovery of property or the infliction of punishment, all use of force which is necessary to enforce that right is permissible. From such a viewpoint no rights are enjoyed by the unjust party and no obligations bind the just, apart from that of remaining within the bounds of necessity.

Grotius goes on, however, to consider the matter from the standpoint of the law of nations, the law arising from the will of nations or of many nations. From this viewpoint any war which is waged on behalf of a sovereign Power and is preceded by a declaration of war, is a lawful war; and whatever the cause for which it is undertaken, acts performed in it may be said to have 'a legal effect'. The laws of war of the early seventeenth century, which Grotius goes on to expound, were extremely permissive by comparison with what they had become by the time of Oppenheim. For example, according to Grotius' account the law of nations permitted belligerents to kill and injure all who are in enemy territory, including women and children; to destroy and pillage enemy property, even that which is held sacred; to kill captives and hostages; and to make slaves of prisoners of war (although it strictly forbade the use of poison). Grotius however, makes clear his dissent from the existing state of the law by saying that it prescribes merely what is permissive in the sense that it is done with impunity, even though it might 'deviate from the rule of right.'[2] He then adds a series of pleas for modernization in the exercise of what the law permits.

[1] Grotius, *op. cit.*, book III, ch. i, section ii. 1.
[2] Book III, ch. x, section i. 1.

It is noteworthy also that Grotius displays considerable understanding of the functions performed in international society by a system of law of war which disregard the causes for which a war is fought. He considers why it is that the law of nations insists upon a declaration of war, and concludes that it is so that 'the fact might be established with certainty that war was being waged not by private initiative but by the will of each of the two peoples.'[1] He asks why nations should have approved a rule allowing both belligerents the right to kill, and gives these reasons: 'To undertake to decide regarding the justice of a war has been dangerous for other peoples, who were on this account involved in a foreign war. . . . Furthermore, even in a lawful war, from external indications it can hardly be adequately known what is the just limit of self-defence, of recovering what is one's own, or of inflicting punishments; in consequence it has seemed altogether preferable to leave decisions in regard to such matters to the scruples of the belligerents rather than to have recourse to the judgments of others.'[2]

But although he admits the idea of laws for the conduct of war that do not discriminate among the belligerents with regard to the causes they pursue, Grotius weakens its force by stating alongside it the contrary doctrine he derives from natural law. If we treat *De Jure Belli ac Pacis* as the exposition of a system of law, rather than as a contribution to philosophy or political theory, it has the grave weakness which Lauterpacht has remarked, that while it tells us what is said about international relations by various laws (the Roman law, natural law, the law of nations, divine law, canon law, the moral law) it nowhere forges these into a system by stating unambiguously what is *the* law.[3] In his discussion of what is permissible in war Grotius states what the natural law and the law of nations each contains on this subject, and criticizes both from the standpoint of love and Christian charity; but he leaves us without guidance as to which of these constitutes the law in cases of conflict. It is difficult to decide, therefore, how the clash between the natural law and the law of nations with regard to what is permissible in war is reconciled in Grotius' account. Setting aside the question of the law, however, we can form some impressions of what he thought should be done and of what kind of rules he thought international society requires.

It is clearly not the view of Grotius that those who are fighting for an unjust cause thereby place themselves *outside* international

[1] Book III, ch. iii, section xi.
[2] Book III, ch. iv, section iv.
[3] Lauterpacht, *op. cit.*, p. 5.

society, where they enjoy no rights. Although it is suggested by some of his language, such a conception is foreign to Grotius' fundamental assertion of the universality of international society, the participation of all mankind in *magna communitas gentium*. It derives not from the theory of just war but from the doctrine of a holy war, the conception of a struggle between completely incompatible systems, against which the main thrust of the idea of international society was directed. To make war against a state in order to compel it to conform to the rules, even to punish it in the severest way for having broken them, is still to treat it as part of the system.

Moreover, Grotius urges that the party equipped with a just cause should practice moderation towards the enemy. There is a limit to vengence and punishment; punishment may often be justly remitted even to enemies who deserve death; women, children, farmers, merchants, prisoners, even the guilty, if their number is very great, should, if possible, be spared for 'the rules of love are broader than the rules of law.'[1] Good faith must always be observed with the enemy, not only with an unjust king or people, but even with tyrants and pirates and with those who are faithless.

Grotius, however, nowhere says that the privileged position afforded by natural law to the just party is overridden by the law of nations. And while he employs arguments drawn from the higher moral law to plead moderation in the exercise of these privileges, he also uses such arguments to show that the acts of a king or people fighting an unjust war, even if they conform to the laws of war, are morally wrong. Those with a just cause, moreover, are specifically afforded the privilege of violating neutral territory in case of necessity.[2] Those who have given others cause for just war are denied the right of self-defence against the just invader of the territory; the argument that 'few are satisfied with exacting vengeance in proportion to the injury suffered' Grotius dismisses on the ground that 'fear of an uncertainty cannot confer the right to resort to force.'[3]

The progress after 1919 of the doctrine that war should be fought only for a just cause has confronted the twentieth century neo-Grotians with the same problem of reconciling this with the tradition of laws of war, so much less permissive by this time as the result of changes brought about by both custom and treaty. Like Grotius they have not felt able to deny the unjust party all rights in war. The view

[1] Grotius, *op. cit.*, book III, ch. xiii, section iv. 1.
[2] Book II, ch. ii, section x.
[3] Book II, ch. i, section xviii. 1.

of the United States Military Tribunal at Nuremberg in the Weizsäcker case, that the Paris Pact 'implicitly authorized the other nations of the world to take such measures as they might deem proper or necessary to punish the aggressor', and that it 'placed the transgressor outside the society of nations', was untypical.[1] Lauterpacht [in his view that 'any application to the actual conduct of war of the principle *ex injuria jus non oritur* would transform the contest into a struggle which is subject to no regulation at all', is giving expression to the same hesitancy which Grotius experienced when faced with the implications of the just war doctrine.[2] At the same time, like Grotius, Lauterpacht seeks to salvage something of the idea of discrimination in favour of the just party, while shrinking before its full consequences.

The second important consequence of the disagreement between Grotius and Oppenheim about the just war concerns the relationship between the states immediately involved in the war and the remainder of international society. Oppenheim's theory, since it treats the causes for which the war is waged as irrelevant from the point of view of the law, extends no invitation to other states to enter the conflict on the side of the just party. Although in his system any state not immediately involved may, by exercising its prerogative of making war, decide to join in the conflict, it is also true that such a state is not encouraged by the law to regard the causes of other states as its own. Moreover, according to Oppenheim, having once embarked upon the policy of neutrality a state has, in return for enjoying the rights of this status, the duty of absolute impartiality as between the belligerents. Grotius, however, holds that when a war breaks out, one party may be seen to have a just cause; and it is his view also, as we have noted, that the causes which are just in relation to the person whose interest is at stake are just also when adopted by those who render him assistance.[3] In Grotius' view, therefore, if a war breaks out in which one party has a just cause, all other states have the right to join in the struggle. Moreover, if they choose instead to remain neutral, that status does not oblige them to adopt an attitude of impartiality but requires them instead to exercise a qualified discrimination in favour of the just party.

Grotius rejects the idea that third states have a *duty* to go to war

---

[1] Quoted by H. Lauterpacht in 'Rules of Law in an Unlawful War', in *Law and Politics in the World Community*, ed. G. A. Lipsky (University of California Press, 1953), p. 97.

[2] *Ibid.*, p. 92.

[3] See above, p. 56.

on the side of the just party.[1] He upholds the rights of 'those who are of neither side in war' against the tendency of belligerent states to infringe them. Indeed, he undoubtedly contributed to the development of the idea of neutrality as a regular status. Such a notion had no place in the systems of Vitoria and Suarez, and although Gentili among theorists of law had upheld it before him, Grotius was among the first to provide an analysis of it. But at the same time his concern for the victory of the just party in war leads him to subordinate the objective of limiting the number of participants in a conflict, which later writers such as Vattel were to regard as the chief object of a status of neutrality. In asserting the right of third states to enter the war on the side of the just party, and in reinforcing this with the idea of the nobility of fighting for causes in which one's own interests are not involved, Grotius was diluting the idea of a right to be neutral with the earlier (and later) notion of the solidarity of the community in relation to a struggle between right and wrong. His definition of the duties attaching to a status of neutrality, moreover, reflected the same kind of dilution. While those who wish not to participate in the war, and to have this wish respected by the belligerents, may do so, in Grotius' view they must also refrain from hindering the just party or from assisting the unjust party (what Grotius had in mind was especially the extension to belligerents of the right of passage across neutral territory and the supply to them of provisions).

The just war doctrines contained in the League Covenant, the Paris Pact and the United Nations Charter also have the consequence of weakening the right to remain neutral, and of transforming the duty of neutrals to be impartial into one of 'qualified neutrality' or 'non-belligerency.'

A third consequence of the disagreement between Grotius and Oppenheim concerning just war concerns the obligation of alliances. Oppenheim does insist that immoral obligations cannot be the object of a treaty; and that an alliance for the purpose of attacking a third state without provocation is not binding. But he does admit that 'the question as to what is immoral is often controversial';[2] and he does not insist that a state is obliged to assist its ally only if it has a just cause. Grotius, by contrast, insists that the principle that war be fought only for a just cause must override the obligations of a treaty of alliance.

The twentieth century equivalent of Grotius' doctrine is the

---

[1] Grotius, *op. cit.*, book II, ch. xxv, section vii.
[2] Oppenheim, *op. cit.*, vol. i, p. 528.

principle that the justice of the case, defined in relation to the purposes of international society as a whole, must override partial alliances. The disparagement of alliances, the international counterpart of Rousseau's disparagement of factions as coming between the individual and the general will, is a feature of the solidarist ideology, engendered by the League of Nations and the United Nations. According to this ideology alliances, since they come between the individual state and international society as a whole, distort its judgement of 'the merits of the issue'. They constitute in themselves a source of tension and discord; not a device for coping with it. Criticism of the French system of alliances in the inter-war years exemplified this solidarist view. After the Second World War the solidarist view itself became an important ingredient in the Indian doctrine of non-alignment.

A fourth consequence concerns the right of states to territorial sovereignty and their corresponding duty not to intervene in one's another's internal affairs. For Oppenheim the existence inside the boundaries of a state of a civil conflict in which one party may be said to have a just cause cannot be taken to qualify the duty of states to refrain from dictatorial intervention in foreign domestic conflicts. Oppenheim does recognize that intervention of this sort sometimes occurs in order to uphold minimum standards of humanity; and he concedes also that, as in the case of the intervention of the European Powers in Turkey so as to uphold the rights of Christian subjects, this may be accompanied by the support of public opinion. He is also able to conceive, furthermore, that a time may arise when the law of nations will provide for humanitarian intervention, so long as this takes the form of the collective intervention of the Powers (it is likely that he had in mind the collective European intervention in China at the time of the Boxer Rebellion). But he rejected any notion that a right of military intervention to enforce standards of conduct was already part of the law, his position being that the right of territorial and personal sovereignty and the duty of non-intervention were part of the constitution of international society; and that the only purposes for which they could be overridden were that of self-preservation and that of the maintenance of the balance of power. For Grotius, on the other hand, the right of a sovereign state to take up arms for a just cause applies to civil conflicts as well as international ones; kings, as well as being responsible for the safety and welfare of their subjects, are burdened with the guardianship of human rights everywhere. Although Grotius denies, along with Hobbes, that subjects may themselves justly rebel against their ruler, he holds that 'nevertheless it will not follow that others may not take up arms on their behalf.'[1]

It would not be possible to find much support at the present time for the view that international law confers upon international society a right of humanitarian intervention by war, still less that it bestows such a right upon particular states. Nor would there be general assent to the more general presupposition of Grotius, from which his right of humanitarian intervention is derived: that individual human beings are subjects of international law and members of international society in their own right. On the other hand a number of developments in international theory and practice in this century indicate the progress of such conceptions: on the one hand the assertion of human rights in the United Nations Charter, the Charter of the International Military Tribunal at Nuremberg and the Declaration of Human Rights; and on the other hand, the view of some international legal theorists that individual human beings are themselves subjects of international law, or even that international law conceived as a law regulating the relations of sovereign states is ceasing to exist and is in process of giving place to a universal law of mankind.[2]

A fifth and final consequence concerns the obligation of individual human beings to bear arms on behalf of their ruler or state. For Oppenheim, who takes the view that only states are members of international society and subjects of international law, the duty of the citizen to bear arms is something upon which international law cannot have anything to say. Grotius, however, contends that if an individual subject believes the cause of the war in which he is ordered to bear arms to be unjust, he should refuse. There is no ground for contending that such a principle has become part of international law in this century. At Nuremberg the view was rejected that German soldiers, apart from being charged with having committed unjust acts in the course of the war, could be held culpable merely for having taken part in an unjust war. Such a notion is tantamount to the equation of war with murder and to the obliteration of the whole convention that there exists a society of states.

IV

The disagreement between Grotius and Oppenheim concerning

---

[1] Grotius, *op. cit.*, book II, ch. xxv, section viii. 3. Cf. below, p. 119.
[2] For the former view see H. Lauterpacht, *International Law and Human Rights* (Stevens, 1950). For the latter view, C. Wilfred Jenks, *The Common Law of Mankind* (Stevens, 1958).

the place of war in international society may be characterized in a different way. Oppenheim's theory clearly rejects the view that international society is like domestic society; and it upholds the contrary doctrine that states form a society which is unique. The theory of Grotius, by contrast, hesitates between the one view and the other.

Within the modern state there exists a government exercising a virtual monopoly of force. Above states no such government exists. If the only kind of political society that obtains is that represented by the modern state, then it may be argued that states do not form a political society; and that such prospects as may exist for the establishment of a political society on a universal scale depend upon the dismantling of the system of states and its replacement by a single, universal state. Those who have maintained that sovereign states *do* constitute a political society have done so by rejecting the model of the modern state and demonstrating that the society formed by states is one with its own special institutions and ways of working. Grotius and Oppenheim both contend that there is an international society, and they are both concerned to reject the domestic analogy. But while Oppenheim's system is free of the domestic analogy, the Grotian system makes important concessions to it.

In domestic society when violence is legitimately exercised it is as an act of law enforcement; and the rules which are recognized in relation to the use of force are calculated to place no obstacle in the path of the victory of the side representing the law. When the champions of the law clash with criminals, it is not expected that rules for the conduct of violent conflict will be observed, applying equally to both parties. Bystanders have the right to assist the victim of the crime, and the duty not to aid the criminal or to hinder the police. The chief loyalty of the citizen is to the state; in the event of a conflict between loyalty to the state and some more partial allegiance, the former must take priority. In international society as conceived by Oppenheim, however, the analogy with police action and crime is rejected. Since war is taken to be a legitimate political act of states, the consideration which informs the rules governing its conduct is not that of ensuring the victory of a just party but that of limiting the dimensions of the conflict so that the international order is not destroyed by it. The duty to observe the laws of war, the right of neutrality, the obligation of alliances, the right of sovereignty and duty of non-intervention, the silence of international law concerning the private duty to bear arms, are devices for the limitation of conflict.

E

The position of Grotius is one of hesitancy between the domestic model and the international one. On the one hand Grotius embraces the notion that war is an act of law enforcement, substituting the idea of enforcement by particular members of society for that of enforcement by a central authority. But on the other hand he recognizes that war is a recurrent phenomenon; and that international society may be threatened by the way in which it is conducted as well as by the failure of the side representing the law to achieve victory. Thus he recognizes such institutions as the laws of war, neutrality, alliances and non-intervention, but at the same time seeks to circumscribe their operation with qualifying clauses drawn from his doctrine of the just war.

However, although Grotius' view of international relations concedes so much more to the domestic analogy than does that of Oppenheim, it may be argued that his own originality, his 'contribution', was to have assisted the movement of thought in a direction opposite to this. The place of the domestic model in *De Jure Belli ac Pacis* may be seen as a medieval residue; its novelty as lying in the stirrings it contains towards the conception of international society as a unique society, that is fully defined only by the writers of the eighteenth and nineteenth centuries. From this perspective what is remarkable in Grotius is not that he 'qualified' such notions as those of the laws of war, neutrality, alliances and sovereignty with the solidarist doctrine of just war which he inherited and adapted from the Catholic tradition. What is noteworthy is rather that he recognized these notions at all, at a time when their position had not yet become assured.

In this respect the positions of Grotius and of the twentieth century neo-Grotians are quite distinct. Grotius stands at the birth of international society and is rightly regarded as one of its midwives. For him the terminology of a universal state is what is still normal, and the language of international relations can be spoken only with an effort. The neo-Grotians, however, have three more centuries of the theory and practice of international society behind them; their novelty lies not in moving away from the domestic model in international relations, but in moving back towards it.

A second aspect of the disagreement between Grotius and Oppenheim which may be briefly mentioned concerns the sources from which the law of nations is derived. For Oppenheim international law is the law arising from custom and treaty, and may be equated with what Grotius called the law of nations in the sense of the law arising from the will of nations or of many nations.[1] Natural

[1] Grotius uses the term *ius gentium* in two senses. The first or broad sense com-

law, in Oppenheim's view, forms no part of international law; and indeed he holds in addition that it does not exist. For Grotius, however, natural law is not merely a source of the law governing relations between states, alongside divine law and voluntary law; it is even taken to have a kind of primacy among the sources of the law of nations. He does not adopt the position of Pufendorf that natural law alone governs the relations between states. But he places it in a central position by arguing, on the one hand, that natural law is valid independently of divine law and cannot be overruled by it; and on the other hand that natural law is the ultimate source of the validity of voluntary law, and is itself a direct source of international law, when the positive law is silent.

For Oppenheim, then, the law judged to be binding in international society may be gauged empirically by ascertaining the rules to which the states members of that society have given their express or their tacit consent. The prescriptions of international law in the positivist view display a certain broad conformity with the movement of historical events. It is for this reason that Oppenheim takes states to be united in international society only for certain minimum purposes; and that he considers international society not to be universal, but to be limited to those states which share a certain civilization whose standards are in origin Christian and European. But for Grotius the ascertaining of the law is not merely a matter of empirical observation but, in so far as it involves the natural law, a matter of 'certain fundamental conceptions which are beyond question, so that no one can deny them without doing violence to himself. For the principles of that law, if only you pay strict heed to them, are in themselves manifest and clear, almost as evident as are the things which we perceive by the external senses.'[1] In the understanding of Grotius, therefore, international law need not be in conformity with the movement of events but may utter a protest against them. Thus Grotius may prescribe rules for an international society united by an area of agreement much wider than any to which it has given its consent; and he may take international society to be universal in scope, denying the distinction drawn by the expositors of the positive international law between relations among member states of international society and relations between these and barbarians. Whereas for Oppenheim the question whether or not the law distinguishes

prises all the laws governing relations between sovereigns or peoples, from whatever source they are derived. The second, narrow sense entails the law arising from the will of nations or of many nations, and may be roughly equated with what is now called positive international law.

[1] Grotius, *op. cit.*, Prolegomena, para. 39.

just from unjust causes of war is a matter to be determined by observation, for Grotius it is a matter settled in advance by the dictates of right reason. Moreover, whereas for Oppenheim it is an empirical question whether in any given case agreement exists as to which is the just party in a war, for Grotius the results of such an inquiry cannot alter the principle that each individual is equipped for the making of such a distinction.

A third aspect of the disagreement we have been considering concerns the membership of international society. For Oppenheim international society is composed of states, and only states possess rights and duties in international law. Individuals, in his view, may be regarded as objects of international law, as when rights and duties are conferred upon them by international agreements regarding diplomatic immunities or extradition; but these are rights and duties in the domestic law of the country concerned and do not render the recipients of them members of international society in their own right. Individuals can and do have rights and duties in other systems of rules; but in the conversation among the Powers there is a convention of silence about the place in their society of their human subjects, any interruption of which is a kind of subversion. In Grotius' system, however, the members of international society are ultimately not states but individuals. The conception of a society formed by states and sovereigns is present in his thought; but its position is secondary to that of the universal community of mankind, and its legitimacy derivative from it. Grotius states in the Prolegomena that he wishes to expound that body of law 'which is concerned with the mutual relations among states or rulers of states';[1] but the natural law, to which he affords primacy as a source of this law, is one which binds all human beings. The rights and duties of individuals may therefore be directly asserted in transactions between states, as we have noted in connection with the right of humanitarian intervention and the right to bear arms. Grotius' use of the conception *magna communitas humani generis* is one calculated to buttress the idea of a society of states. By asserting the bonds of natural law binding the persons who ruled states and the communities of persons of whom they are composed he sought to fill the vacuum left by the declining force of divine or ecclesiastical law and the rudimentary character of existing voluntary or positive law. At the same time the conception of a universal community of mankind is potentially destructive of the society of sovereign states, for it may be employed not only to support the rules of international society but also to assert others that undermine it.

[1] Para. 1.

V

The Grotian conception of international society is upheld by Vollenhoven and Lauterpacht on the ground that sovereign states cannot permit one another an unrestricted right to undertake war. According to these writers international society, different though it is from domestic, can and should be modelled upon it at least to this extent: that in it, violence is regarded as either police action or crime The pluralist conception, which we have taken Oppenheim to exemplify and which Vattel did a great deal to establish, they dismiss as one which amounts to the admission that international society does not exist; or as one which, while asserting the existence of international society, does not allow it to be capable of that further development which in the twentieth century it can and must undergo.[1] If the Grotian conception is said to be a scheme set over and against the facts, then the reply of its defenders is that the pluralist doctrine is a cowardly submission to them. 'For what is the nature of Vattel's success?' ask Vollenhoven, seeking to account for popularity of *Le Droit des Gens*. 'The success of a mother who suffers herself to be bullied by her children; of a schoolmaster who abolished homework; of a cabinet minister who grants and puts down in the Estimates whatever the members of parliament come to ask of him.'[2] 'In the assertion of "reason of State" and of the double standard of morality,' Lauterpacht writes, 'the claim to an unrestricted right of war is the most important. It is not the dagger or the poison of the hired assassin or the sharp practice of the realistic politician which expresses most truly, upon final analysis, the ideas of *"raison d'état"*. It is the infliction, without a shadow of a specific right and without a claim to any particular right, of the calamities and indignities of war and of the territorial mutilation and the very annihilation of statehood following upon defeat in war. Prior to the changes introduced by the Covenant of the League of Nations, the Pact of Paris of 1928, and the Charter of the United Nations, that central idea of "reason of State" formed part of international law. States claimed—and had— the right to resort to war not only in order to defend their legal rights but in order to destroy the legal rights of other states.'[3]

The question at issue between the Grotians and the pluralists is not

---

[1] Vattel's theory bears superficial resemblances to that of Grotius but in spirit is closer to that of Oppenheim. Thus although he held the law to insist that war be fought only for a just cause, he holds that what constitutes a just cause for a particular state it alone can decide.

[2] Vollenhoven, *Three Stages in the Evolution of the Law of Nations*, p. 33.

[3] Lauterpacht, 'The Grotian Tradition in International Law', *British Yearbook of International Law*, 1946, p. 36.

one as to what is contained in the law. It is a question as to what kind of legal rules are most appropriate to the working of the international order; a matter not of international law but of international political science. The central assumption of the Grotians, as was mentioned at the outset of our inquiry, is that there exists solidarity in international society with regard to the enforcement of the law. If in fact a consensus may be reached as to the nature of the distinction between just and unjust causes of war; if the international community can be brought to agree in a particular case as to which side is engaging in police action and which in crime; if the claims of the former to represent international society as a whole are in fact given credence by the active or passive support of a preponderance of states, then it may well be that it is upon Grotian principles that the international order should be shaped. But if, on the other hand, no solidarity on these matters obtains; if international society finds itself unable to agree as to the criterion of just war; if the outbreak of war typically finds international society at large, as well as the belligerents themselves, divided as to which side embodies the just cause, then our conclusion must be a different one. It may be argued of the Grotian conception in this event not merely that it is unworkable but that it is positively damaging to the international order; that by imposing upon international society a strain which it cannot bear, it has the effect of undermining those structures of the system which might otherwise be secure. And it may be said of the pluralist doctrine that so far from constituting a disguised form of *Realpolitik*, it presents a set of prescriptions more conducive to the working of the international order than those of the Grotians.

International society will be able to enforce its law only if it can mobilize superior power in its support. The existence of a system of rules favouring the victory of the just party may facilitate the imposition of the law, as the work of the police within a modern state is assisted by the legal principles we have discussed.[1] But they will not suffice to call into being a coalition with will and force sufficient to ensure victory, where these elements are lacking. That they have been lacking in the years since the First World War, and that the provisions of the Covenant, the Paris Pact and the Charter facilitating the victory of the just party in war have not been acted upon by an international community with solidarity enough to make a reality of them, is today well enough understood.

What is less appreciated is that the Grotian doctrine may have, and perhaps has had, an influence positively detrimental to international order. For to the extent that it influences the course of events, the

[1] See above, p. 65.

doctrine that war should be fought only for a just cause is injurious to the institutions with which international society had equipped itself for the limitation of war. The qualifications that the Grotian doctrine attaches to its endorsement of institutions are such as to impede their working. If one side in an armed conflict regards itself as specially privileged by the laws of war, then reciprocal observance of these laws, which is a basic condition of their efficacy, is undermined. If a state which wishes to remain neutral nevertheless discriminates in favour of one party, then unless it does so from a position of superior strength, as did the United States when it pursued a policy of 'qualified neutrality' in 1940–41, it cannot expect to have the belligerent which suffers discrimination respect its wish. If the obligations of an alliance are to be qualified by the justice of the cause, this latter being something subjectively or arbitrarily determined, then an impediment exists to the conclusion or to the maintenance of alliances, which in the absence of a system of collective law enforcement may be held to be essential devices for the maintenance of security and order. If a right of intervention is proclaimed for the purpose of enforcing standards of conduct, and yet no consensus exists in the international community governing its use, then the door is open to interventions by particular states using such a right as a pretext, and the principle of territorial sovereignty is placed in jeopardy.

To show how in the twentieth century the influence of Grotian conceptions has in fact impeded the working of these institutions for the limitation of conflict would take us far afield. Three episodes may be mentioned, however, as having been especially influenced by the neo-Grotian doctrine. The first is the action of the League of Nations in imposing economic sanctions against Italy in 1935. The second is the trial and punishment of German and Japanese citizens by the International Military Tribunal of Nuremberg and that of the Far East, on charges of having begun an unjust war. The third is the war conducted in the name of the United Nations in Korea. None of these events could be regarded as having been brought about by the neo-Grotian doctrine; but each assumed the particular character it did in part because of that influence. The effects of these three episodes on the structure of international order were manifold and even contradictory; and it is possible to derive all sorts of lessons from them. But it might be argued in each case that the Grotian influence served to weaken devices for the limitation of conflict.

The view of the pluralists is not to be dismissed as a mere rationalization of state practice; it is a conception of international society founded upon the observation of the actual area of agreement between states and informed by a sense of the limitations within which in this situation rules may be usefully made rules of law. It seeks not to burden international law with a weight it cannot carry; and to have it leave room for the operation of those political forces, beyond the control of law, on which the existence of international society also depends. Thus although Oppenheim's exposition of the law allows war to be fought for any cause whatever, the political theory he presents does include a doctrine of just war; and it is partly in deference to this that he rejects the Grotian position. 'The assertion that whereas all wars waged for political causes are unjust, all wars waged for international delinquencies are just, if there be no other way of getting reparation and satisfaction, is certainly incorrect in its generality. The evils of war are so great that, even when caused by an international delinquency, war cannot be justified if the delinquency was comparatively unimportant and trifling. And, on the other hand, under certain circumstances and conditions many political causes of war may correctly be called just causes. Only such individuals as lack insight into history and human nature can, for instance, defend the opinion that a war is unjust which has been caused by the desire for national unity or by the desire to maintain the balance of power which is the basis of all International Law.'[1] It may be held one of the weaknesses of the Grotian and neo-Grotian doctrines that they do not take account of the theory of the balance of power, nor face up to the question of the relationship between the prescriptions emanating from this theory and the prescriptions of international law.

Grotius is, I believe, fundamentally correct in his perception that international society cannot survive if it is to tolerate resort to war for any purpose whatever. The difference between Grotius and Oppenheim is partly explicable in terms of the fact that during the Thirty Years' War all sorts of claims were being advanced, hostile to the emergence of a society of sovereign states and a reality to its first great theoretician, that in the opening years of the twentieth century seemed remote and improbable. War to enforce the right to universal empire and war to impose a religion cannot be comprehended under the heading of 'war for political causes' which Oppenheim thought international society could tolerate; and if these dangers did not seem real enough in 1905 to be worthy targets of protest, it was nevertheless still true that international society rested on the rejection of them. There is in Grotius also an awareness of a threat to international society more deadly even than these, and seeming still more remote within the confines of European international society in 1905: the war of barbarians. Grotius recognizes in addition to causes for war

[1] Oppenheim, *op. cit.*, vol. ii, p. 71.

which are justifiable and causes which are merely persuasive (in the sense that though just causes are stated for them, these are only pretexts) a third category of causes of war which are neither justifiable nor persuasive but 'wars of savages' fought without a cause of any sort.[1] Vattel also is conscious of this possible dimension of international experience and speaks of those who begin war without pretext of any kind as 'monsters unworthy of the name of men,' whom nations may unite to suppress.[2] If Oppenheim is correct in taking the divisions in international society to be too great to warrant an attempt to write a theory of just war into international law, it is also true that international society in his own time displayed on more fundamental matters a solidarity so great that it did not occur to him to call it in question.

But it is one thing to appreciate that international society presupposes abstention from war directed at certain ends and another to say that rules enjoining such abstention can usefully be made rules of law. Oppenheim's approach to the question of the place of law in international society was accompanied by an attitude of complacency about war and its use as an instrument of national policy which is rightly rejected today. But it may still be held that the method he employed, of gauging the role of law in international society in relation to the actual area of agreement between states is superior to one which sets up the law over and against the facts. And although the solidarity exhibited by international society may increase in the future, just as it may decrease, it can still be argued that in the twentieth century the Grotian conception has proved premature.

---

[1] Grotius, *op. cit.*, book II, ch. xxii, section ii.
[2] *Le Droit des Gens*, book III, ch. iii, section 34.

CHAPTER 4

NATURAL LAW

D. M. MACKINNON

The subject of this paper is a notion very much canvassed in the history of ethics and of political theory and one may question whether much that is new can be usefully said of it. The purpose of what I have set down is tentative and exploratory and may indeed seem to be largely devoted to throwing into clear relief some distinctions which a study of the history of the idea compels us to acknowledge.

I

Professor A. P. d'Entrèves in his book *Natural Law* distinguishes the 'natural law' of the medieval schoolmen from the 'natural rights' of the Enlightenment. Mr Rohan d'O. Butler in *The Roots of National Socialism* stressed the opposition between what he calls the teaching of the 'school of natural law' and that of the so-called German school of political thought, making his own and elaborating a distinction associated with the name of Ernst Troeltsch. But in Butler's 'school of natural law' the distinction emphasized by d'Entrèves went unrecognized. It is as if the student of Hooker's *Ecclesiastical Polity* and of Locke's frequent praise of the 'judicious Mr Hooker' into forgetting the great gulf that yawned between them. Again, the reader of D. G. Ritchie's essay on *Natural Rights* might be misled into supposing that however the followers of the tradition of Jeremy Bentham might differ from those who stood in the following of the German idealists, especially Hegel (as glossed in Ritchie's idiosyncratic essay by some hardly assimilated Darwinian ideas), for all alike the notion of natural rights, 'inalienable, imprescriptible, universal' was *vieux jeu*. Yet Edmund Burke, whose *Reflections* had provoked Tom Paine's *Rights of Man*, and whom none could call friend of those 'natural rights' of the French Revolutionaries which Bentham dismissed as 'nonsense on stilts', none the less himself wrote essays, pamphlets, speeches and letters on issues of political theory, suffused by the idea of 'natural law'. It is certainly a different 'natural law', very different at once in context and in style from that defended by Thomas Aquinas and invoked, with no little effect at the time, by Pius XII in his encyclical *Summi Pontificatus* of the autumn of 1939;

yet there are also similarities in pedigree and in content.

What then of the fundamental differences between 'natural law' and 'natural rights'?

(a) Where 'natural law' is concerned, we have to do with an order in our nature, whether we are concerned with the domain of personal morality or with that of collective behaviour, with which we have to reckon. It is an inaccurate commonplace of the class-room that the man who walks over the cliff edge does not break the law of gravity; he merely illustrates it. Similarly in human life the man who e.g. habitually neglects one side of his nature is sooner or later compelled to reckon with the malaise of that which he has allowed to atrophy or decay. One thinks of Darwin's sacrifice of the power to appreciate beautiful things; one thinks of D. H. Lawrence's vehement polemics against falsely spiritual religiosity in the account of the visit to Lincoln Cathedral in *The Rainbow*; one thinks even of his return to this theme in *The Man who Died*. One thinks also of Joseph Butler's subtle and perceptive vindication of the complementarity of resentment and compassion in human life. The roots of both these propensions are passional; without resentment expressed in sudden fierce bouts of anger against her gaolers, Edith Bone found she could not survive as a human being in Rakosi's prisons;[1] without compassion men are easily hardened into the remorseless, indifferent profession of an exact standard of behaviour, intolerant of all transgression. Yet these two springs of our actions must balance each other. Pity without resentment, called into play by knowledge of injustice, is sentimental self-indulgence; resentment carried over beyond the grave can withdraw a man from sympathetic patience with the frailty of his friends. For Butler, our nature, not least at the passional level, is inherently complex. The law of that nature is therefore for him found in the principle of reflection within us, a matter of our own promulgation; yet it is a law which we neglect always at the peril of dwarfing our stature to something less than human.

(b) Similarly where government is concerned, theologically its very existence may be regarded as a concession to the sinful condition of men. To use the jargon of the schools, it may belong to the sphere of 'relative' as distinct from 'absolute natural law'. But it too stands under the sovereign sway of a law that defines its end and nature. Those who bear rule can transgress the norms of their office. The tyrant is an historically familiar phenomenon. The state, for instance, which claims for its own life as an effective *Machtstaat* complete self-justification, is transgressing the norm of the state's proper nature. Similarly the state, which deliberately determines its policies,

[1] See Edith Bone, *Seven Years Solitary* (Hamish Hamilton, 1957).

and employs all the means at its disposal for enforcing these policies, in the interest of a class or section of society, and not of the society as a whole, violates its character as a state. Thus radical Catholics in these islands pointed to the policies adopted and pursued by the so-called 'National Government' of 1931 as policies calculated to safeguard the interests of the rentier class as against e.g. the interests of those living on unemployment assistance, and claimed that such definite class-bias in legislative and executive action, impugned the state's character as a state; it was revealed not as an institution seeking a common good, but as something for which the claims of the middle classes of Bournemouth and Orpington counted for more than those of the unemployed steel workers of Ebbw Vale, and the shipyard men of Hebburn-on-Tyne.

(c) In contemporary discussion the notion is most before our attention in connection with controversies in the West and the Far East between Roman Catholic and other Christian bodies concerning the legitimacy of the use of artificial means of contraception, an issue sharply pointed at by contemporary concern over the rise in population. For the Catholic, artificial means of contraception are unnatural; their use violates the proper form and structure of the sexual act. This form and structure is regarded as something God-given; it is not something that men and women can alter at choice or under pressure of the peculiar needs of a particular age. Mention must be made of this issue, as it is much under discussion; but the mention is purely illustrative.

Now in all of these three examples (valid or invalid) it is clear that what belongs to 'natural law' is presented as something found and discovered, something acknowledged and accepted. This *is* the way of human life, individual and collective; these are the orders which men and women must accept. If a partial legitimacy is allowed to the function of government, that legitimacy is only acknowledged as a protest against the totalitarian claim to make the sphere of the state's effective power coterminous with human life itself. Government is a task and work that has its own laws no less than the life of the individual. The apologist of 'natural law' is the apologist of the constitutional state, which (in terms of Dr C. H. McIlwain's important distinction, drawn in his book *Constitutionalism: Ancient and Modern*) exalts the element of *jurisdictio* above *gubernatio*. If sovereignty is conceded in such a state, efforts will be made theoretically to lodge it in the constitution itself, finding that alone unquestionably supreme, which in its impersonality assigns to all alike their place, their role and their power.

One can trace the sources of these ideas in Greek thought: in

Aristotle's conviction that a man who could dispense with the ordered life of the city state must be either a beast or a god; in Antigone's appeal against Creon's self-obsessed preoccupation with the political dignity of government, to the unwritten laws before which she bows, affirming them in tragically costly action; in the elusive, pervasive idea of *hubris*, of limits which men transgress, in their self-confidence, at their utmost peril.

To mention Plato and Plato's evaluation of the sophistic method is to invite every sort of criticism. But for Plato, at once preoccupied as he was by the characteristically human function of education, and ready to go a-whoring after the philosopher's fantasy of a final solution of all the problems that beset mankind, there was a continually recurring question of the frontiers between the natural on the one side and, on the other, the artificial, including the devices men fashion to ease the burden of living, and, in fact, the historical itself. At his profoundest, e.g. in the second book of the *Republic*, where Socrates allows the young men Glaucon and Adeimantus to set the problem of the whole work, he gives truly classical expression to the inexpugnable human belief (however precarious) that the life of the saint, broken and utterly unsuccessful, compelled to rebut evidence against its claim more grievous than the career of Alcibiades itself provided in the trial of Socrates, is in accordance with the nature of things; while the career of the supremely competent statesman, the man of Periclean genius who with unscrupulous energy bends the immense opportunities that come his way to write new chapters in the history of human achievement, has yet turned aside from that pattern of living which alone corresponds to what is. Adeimantus supplements his brother's exquisitely formulated perplexity by pointing out how the bias of a young man's education, including under that name the whole process by which a society transmits to its members the standards whereby it would have them live, encourages the young man to esteem success and achievement, dignity and reputation above justice, and therefore to esteem the Periclean archetype above the Socratic.

Plato's argument here seems a long way removed from the more commonplace deliverances of 'natural law'. Yet it belongs to the same universe of discourse. For even as our nature is something that we have to accept, to find, not to invent, so for Plato that transcendent *Form of the Good* in whose light the way of the saint is revealed as the ground of that of the true scientists, is the eternal source of being and essence in the intelligible realm, and in consequence that on which all the furniture alike of the eternal and the temporal world depends. Apart from its vision, we do not know where we are, nor of what stuff we are made. Thus the distinguished French Platonic scholar, M. Léon Robin, is right to speak of Plato's ethics as 'une morale naturaliste, mais d'un type assurément peu commun'.[1]

With Plato's speculations (and for Whitehead, all subsequent Western philosophy is a 'footnote to Plato') we are in the presence of the work of an extraordinary, if unbalanced genius, who had the supreme merit of raising for his readers, in subsequent generations, the question of how this supposed 'natural law' was discovered and established, how indeed the vague, fleeting impressions men had of its over-arching, wide-embracing authority, related to other precarious, yet persistent acknowledgements of a vantage point from which the obscure and fragmentary circumstances of human life might be reviewed, in the light of a vision of the origin and source, the sense and sanction of all. 'We are not our own.' If Jean Paul Sartre argues that men alone in their freedom give sense to the world, he has to reckon with those who claim that the idiom of discovery, finding, acceptance belongs to the vocabulary of the moralist, as essentially as inescapably that of invention, devising and even sometimes deciding.

A man for whom the true order of human life is something to be accepted, to be admitted as something continually tugging him and beckoning him, sustaining him with the promise of a vision in which what he now sees as a reflection cast in a mirror, he will see for what it actually is, will not feel himself circumscribed; rather he may acknowledge himself pressed upon, even visited, by the eternal in the most ordinary occasion of life.

(d) One can say, Burke apart, that such thinking is curiously indifferent to historical change. If it is conservative in its admission of reverence, even of *pietas* in human life (this note is clearly sounded in discussions e.g. of the morality of euthanasia), it is also radical. Wilful declension from the norm is as clearly visible in the gimcrack *Machtstaat* of Mussolini, even in the Western German impotence before the Krupp empire, as in the more familiar, more often advertised signs of its presence, e.g. in the dissemination of a mandate theory of representation. But it seems at once to neglect the reality of novelty, preferring to emphasize the element of threat rather than of promise in the Promethean age into which we move, and to turn aside (a little impatiently) from the concretes of historical change and of the diversity of cultures.

In Plato the pattern of a proper way of human living was something which men only made their own securely in the light of a vision

[1] Léon Robin, *La Morale Antique* (Paris, Alcan, Nouvelle Encyclopédie Philosophique, 1938), p. 42.

of transcendent reality. So in the Christian tradition the element of a 'natural law' has always been complemented in practice by the tradition of a *unum necessarium*, of a union with God in Christ from whose achieved summit the believer saw, not indeed as he would see when his knowledge was commensurate with God's knowledge of him, but at least (in fragments) the constituents of a truly human dignity, from whose pieces indeed Christ fashioned the manifold imagery of those parables whereby he pressed upon men the urgent, even tragic quality of God's questing after them. But again there has been fear of novelty, retreat from enlarged horizons, nostalgia for the more manageable frontiers of a fabled 'Europe', even sentimental, romantic flirtation with the fantasy of a supposed normative 'peasant-culture'. Yet there *has* also been acknowledgement of the ethical import of a human norm, even an unexpected admission of the great difficulty of understanding how men can lay hold of such a norm. Perhaps even as for Plato, his extraordinary, and in parts horrifying ethic, derives its significance from the deep perception he enjoyed of the problems of finding a metaphysical basis for the good life, indeed of understanding what one sought in seeking such a basis, so in the post-Christian ages the very difficulty of understanding the nature of faith, and its relation to hope and to love, supposed the greatest of the triad, has enabled men to use on occasion the idea of 'natural law' without finding themselves quite at home with it, alive more to its corrective power than to its positive content. Thus its very elusiveness makes the notion less epistemologically vulnerable than that of 'natural rights'.

II

With 'natural rights' we are no longer concerned with constraints and limitations, but rather with demands and permissions.

(a) Let us take *permissions* first in order more or less to have done with this sense of the notion. The late T. H. Green's hostility to the language of 'natural rights' was not simply expressive of his meta-physical rejection of the theory to which the notion seemed to belong. It was the language of entrenched, seemingly sacrosanct permissions that invited his ire. 'I am within my rights.' And if these rights were invested not only with the authority of positive law, but with the metaphysical quality of 'inalienable, imprescriptible, natural rights', those who claimed sancrosanctity for their right to do what they will with their own were able to infuse, with nearly religious dignity, their claim for immunity from any sort of control.

(b) But it is on 'rights' as 'claims' that I shall largely concentrate.

If the notion of natural rights is to be distinguished from that of natural law, it can be argued that the former notion is parasitic upon the latter. The idea of a right is the idea of something that can be enforced or sustained or even if necessary, overridden by the process of law. A natural right is a right that men claim to be theirs as men; they demand recognition of their right to subsistence or freedom to associate, not as citizens of the United Kingdom or as Frenchmen or as Ghanaians, but as *men*.

(1) It is not accident that in some of the classical statements of the idea of natural rights, evidence is claimed for them akin to that claimed (in the traditional view) for the axioms and demonstrations of Euclidean geometry. Although the parallels postulate has been under fire since Proclus, the actual development of non-Euclidean systems of geometry had to await the work of such men as Lobachevsky and Bolyai in the 1800s; and the rationalist philosophers of the Enlightenment were able to find in the system of Euclidean geometry a body of universal and necessary truths concerning the properties of configurations in actual space, timeless and unquestionable, a veritable paradigm of knowledge in any field, lying somehow outside the reach of sensuous observation. Thus for John Locke himself, 'the proposition, where there is no property, there is no injustice, is as evident as any demonstration in Euclid'.[1] To the modern there is something almost fantastic in the implied claim that principles relating to distributive and commutative justice can be conceived as being of the same order as, e.g., the theorem that the internal angles of a triangle are equal to two right angles. But the advocate of an ethic resting upon rational intuition, whether John Locke, or the later Richard Price (whose address to the Revolution Society provoked Burke's *Reflections*) found in the supposed insight of the geometer, the paradigm of that inviolable apprehension of universal, necessary and immutable principles which he sought. The universality of the rights men enjoyed as men was conceived as akin to the universality of the property of congruence enjoyed by two triangles with two sides and the included angle equal.

(2) The doctrine was also in implication strongly individualist. No authority gave a man these rights; none could take them away. Here one can trace a clear continuity with certain Stoic arguments, for instance, the sort of arguments adduced by Seneca in his *Epistulae Morales* against the doctrine that some men are by nature slaves and against the punishment of murderers by compelling them to fight in the arena. Thus in letter XLVII, Seneca points out that persons as distinguished as Hecuba, Croesus, Sisigambis (the mother of Darius

---

[1] *An Essay concerning Human Understanding*, book IV, ch. iii.

of Persia), and Plato all at some state of their lives, by misfortune, found themselves slaves; moreover the arrogant well-to-do man of yesterday cringes today before his former freedman, seeking as an obsequious 'client 'a pittance on which to subsist. Again in letter VII Seneca protests against the idea that guilt of the crime of murder makes legitimate our treating the criminal as one who may rightly be butchered for our entertainment. In the criticism of the doctrine that some men are by nature slaves, one can trace the influence of the Stoic image of time as cyclical; but the astringent empiricism of the argument is unmistakable. Likewise the emphasis on men as individuals. The temper of Seneca's letters and teaching is anything but egalitarian; he addressed Lucilius as, with him, a member of a small élite, capable, by disciplined study, of building for themselves an enclave immune from the corruptions and distractions of Neronian Rome. But what in many places in these often very tedious letters shows itself as a contemptuous disdain for the common run of contemporary mankind, is also an insistence that men can, as men, rise superior to the institutions under which they live, and the environment that hems them in. They have in fact their own nature as men.

(3) Enough has been said already to indicate that the doctrine of natural rights is by implication, cosmopolitan, and (in one sense) anti-historical. Emphasis on the rights of men as men diminishes sharply any sense of an individual's indebtedness to the traditions of the society in which he has been born and educated. Its institutions do not provide in any sense a framework for his *paideia*; rather he will come to regard them as mechanisms, effective or ineffective as the case may be, for ensuring his enjoyment of those rights that belong to him as man. The Stoic disdain for the whole apparatus of the Neronian principate is extended by the believer in natural rights to all forms of human association; those things which are private are significant, those that touch public order must be judged by the extent to which they secure men in their unfettered enjoyment of their private dignity.

It is not accident that the theorist of natural rights speaks easily in terms of the analogy of alleged geometrical self-evidence. For him history, in the sense of the field which the historian studies, is never a realm in which we can learn wisdom, let alone trace the workings of Providence. He will oppose the authority of universal truth, discernible by the individual, to that of the essentially relative circumstance of the tradition and manners of the society into which he was born. There is little or nothing, e.g., in the Prussian military tradition, in Bonapartism, even in the '43 (the Scottish Church disruption, wherein the Free Church of Scotland was born), or in the spirit of

F

Cromwell's Ironsides, to commend his reverence. The historian's study often touches only the periphery of the human reality, where too often the human essence has been obscured by the wilful folly of men who have mistaken what they call glory or truth for the immutable core of their being. Of course, just as in books VIII and IX of the *Republic*, Plato ranged timocracy, oligarchy, democracy and tyranny as increasingly grave divagations from the norm of his *kallipolis*, so the professor of natural rights will order societies and moments of historical decision by reference to their more or less effective affirmation of those rights in such societies and at such moments. If he accepts a belief in progress, in the increasing enlightenment of the mass of human kind concerning their nature and the circumstances of their existence and the gradual embodiment of this enlightenment in their manner of life, this belief is logically separable from the conviction of the reality of human rights. (Indeed the Stoic Seneca clearly combined belief in the reality of the rights of men with a cyclical view of the order of human history.)

(4) As a matter of historical fact, it would seem that the idea of natural rights took hold of men's imagination (I choose the word advisedly) when the struggles between Protestant and Catholic, and between Anglican and Puritan, together with the eagerness of the devout to make themselves the apologists of absolute monarchy, drove men to find in their actual nature, an alternative and religiously neutral foundation for human culture. 'A man's a man for a' that.' Such sentiment at once cut across the seemingly sterile and certainly internecine debates of Reform and Counter-Reform, and at the same time put a question to anyone who claimed in his own person, as anointed king, to embody and realize his whole community. The temper of rebellious scepticism can be discerned in the invocation of the idea of natural rights: a scepticism concerning the pretentions of priests, presbyters and monarchs to hold in their keeping the secrets of the ways of mankind, which was all the more sturdy in that for its principles was claimed the irrefutable self-evidence of Euclid's axioms.

(5) The modern student (especially if he has had occasion to work even as a mathematical amateur, upon the foundations of geometry, and the distinction between pure and applied geometry) finds the effort sympathetically to assimilate the underlying conception of knowledge of universal truths, on which the idea of natural rights rests, hard to achieve. He is predisposed, even if he is not a conservative, to endorse the somewhat cynical comment of Professor Michael Oakeshott that the hard-won rights of Englishmen in common law crossed the Channel to become the Rights of Man of the Enlighten-

ment.[1] Out of what belongs to the empirical contingencies of constitutional history, men have fashioned a mythology for which they have sought to claim the unqualified necessity supposedly residing in the truths of geometry. But alas! their understanding of the nature of mathematics was as wide of the mark as their appreciation of the sources from which their ideas were coined.

Moreover, the historian of political theory well knows that Locke's successors, the so-called 'philosophical radicals', abandoned altogether the notion of natural rights, substituting for them the 'greatest happiness principle'. In Bentham's voluminous writings the student can trace an oscillation between treating the idea of the 'rights of man' as a confused formulation of the principle of utility, and treating it as a piece of metaphysical lumber to be discarded in favour of Bentham's own more precise and empirically based yardstick for the evaluation of laws, institutions and traditions of behaviour. Newton's conception of the proper method of physics had displaced Descartes' conception of that science as an extension of geometry; and the theory of political obligation of the men in whose forbidding school John Stuart Mill was educated, setting out what they supposed to be the empirically established laws of human behaviour, and the sanctions whereby that behaviour could be directed (through the operation of the 'association of ideas') into channels profitable to all Bentham's hedonistic calculus, displays in distorted caricature the Newtonian fusion of empirical observation with insistence on the ultimately dynamical form of natural laws. In the history of the development of utilitarian political ideas, with the principle of utility invoked alternately as a justification for *laissez-faire* and the unfettered operation of the market economy, and as a fully adequate ground for drastic state regulation of economic affairs, one can perhaps trace a parallel between emphasis on rights as 'permissions' and rights as 'claims'. The kinship between the school of natural right and that of utility is discerned in their common universalism, in their indifference to national and cultural particularities, and in their underlying temper of rationalism: this last clearly discernible in both, although the former is Cartesian and the latter empiricist in ethos.

(6) Finally, as if enough had not already been said to discredit the notion of natural rights, one has to recall the variety of those rights that have from time to time been accounted natural. One recalls the right to assemble together whether for the purposes of discussion or of worship; one recalls also the right freely to express by word of mouth or writing considered opinion; one recalls the right to criticize

[1] *Rationalism in Politics* (Methuen, 1962), p. 120.

established authority; but in more recent years, one has seen in new tables of alleged 'rights of man' the right to work, and this to be guaranteed by public policy of full employment, adopted and enforced by the state. The element of protest against the usurped authority of priest and king has been replaced by eager demand that public authority shall not abdicate the responsibility which it alone can fulfil, of guaranteeing for men (if need be, by the most drastic intervention with the working of the economy) at once the financial security and the functional status that only employment can give them. The traumatic experience of the years following the slump of 1929 (an experience which Mr Alan Bullock in his life of Hitler has said bit deeper into memory than the war itself) added a new item to the supposedly universal, yet ever flexibly receptive, table of the 'rights of man'.

We come now to the evaluation of the ideas of 'natural law' and 'natural rights' in relation to international theory.

The late Professor C. C. J. Webb, discussing the relation of reason and revelation, urged that 'We could not allow the name of God to a being on whose privacy an Actaeon could intrude, or whose secrets a Prometheus could snatch from him without his assent'.[1] In a very valuable essay entitled 'La Recherche d'un Homme Nouveau', the distinguished Jesuit theologian Père Henri de Lubac points out (impressive language in a member of his Society if one recalls the controversies of the seventeenth century between Jesuit and Jansenist) that the God whose secrets Prometheus sought to steal was Zeus, not the God of Abraham, Isaac and Jacob.[2] The traditionalist protest against the supposed irreverence or *hubris* of the Promethean spirit, may be sometimes complaint at the loss of an ill-defined spirit of reverence, more than expression of a serious moral judgment. Where the problems of international relations and the methods of warfare are concerned, we merely darken council if we indulge in vague and generalized denigration of the technological revolutions through which we are living.

But granted the proviso that any significant ethic of law must do full justice to the vast enlargement of human horizons both in respect of understanding and of achievement which marks the age we live in, there are certain points which require emphasis.

(a) Any teacher of moral philosophy is familiar with the necessity of helping the student at the elementary level to distinguish between

[1] C. C. J. Webb, *Problems in the Relations of God and Man* (Nisbet, 1911), pp. 25–6.
[2] H. de Lubac, *Affrontements Mystiques* (Paris, Témoignage Chrétien, 1949), p. 39.

an action and an event. The Lisbon earthquake of 1 November 1755 was an event; its impact on European thought was tremendous, reflecting in works as different as Kant's three *Kritiks* and Voltaire's *Candide*. Men had to live in a world in which such things had happened, and whose claim therefore to be 'the best of all possible worlds' had been impugned. When we are however told that we must 'live with the atomic or hydrogen bomb', what we are being told we must 'live with' is not something that has happened like the Lisbon earthquake or the great storm of January 30, 1953. Men decided to do what was done at Hiroshima and Nagasaki. The sense in which the word 'decided' is here used is obscure; we are not speaking of decision in the sense in which I speak of a decision to learn Hebrew, to reduce my consumption of cigarettes, or to change my job, or in which we speak of a committee's decision (to be recommended to that body whose committee it is) to do such and such. There is something at once highly subtle, and at the same time almost haphazard, in the way the decision to act on August 6, 1945, was taken.

No doubt there are certain sorts of determinist who would argue that the decision to use the bomb is explicable in a way akin to that in which a natural event, say a seismic tremor in the 'Great Glen' is explicable. (The sense in which the historian's assumptions are deterministic, if they are so at all, is a very controversial one.) Yet still it is a decision, not a natural happening; if our world can never be the same again, it is so by reason of the action which men have taken. If we are not determinists, we can significantly say (we may be wrong) that they acted wrongly, that they did what they ought not to have done. We do say such things, referring e.g. to persons who have murdered deliberately by use of poison, for gain. We do indeed say such things concerning so-called statesmen; for instance, if we say of Eden's behaviour over Suez that it was both wicked and stupid. But the development illustrated by the Sandys policy (so astringently criticized by the fascinating, if indiscreet, speech of General Cowley[1]) is something so pervasive in its effects that we are told in fact that scruples in respect of its implications are a mark both of irresponsibility and indeed of disrespect towards the devoted and responsible men whose decisions have helped to bring us where we are. No one who has read such documents as the recent report of a committee of the British Council of Churches concerning the ethical problems of nuclear warfare can escape the strong atmosphere of quasi-determinism that suffused them, or rather fail to discern in

[1] Sir John Cowley, lecture on 'Future Trends in Warfare' to the Royal United Service Institution, November 4, 1959 (*Journal of the Royal United Service Institution*, 1960, vol. 105, pp. 4–16).

such documents what can only be described as a marriage between a curious sort of determinism and an equally curious sort of religiosity.[1] We are told we must accept certain changes because they have happened, and in fact refrain under the compelling rubric 'Judge not', as well as in recollection of our ignorance, from passing any kind of ultimately adverse comment on those who have brought us where we are.

Now it is precisely at this point that the notion of 'natural law' begins to show itself, begins I might say to intrude upon our consciousness. Indeed it is only through the acknowledgement of its authority that we find ourselves confident enough to assume our elementary democratic duty of criticizing our rulers. Thus in the name of 'natural law' we can argue that there are risks which men have no right to take with their world. There is indeed a quality of the sheerly frivolous in the smooth manner whereby the claims for information concerning the control of H-bomb, nuclear-headed rockets, etc., are brushed aside, with the inevitable appeal to national security. Those who are in government, are inevitably caught up in the running of a machine which they find running in one way, and whose history they feel themselves bound to defend.

(b) Questioning there must be, and questioning of a peculiar sort in that it sees the whole issue of human life and the 'posture befitting men under the sun' thrust upon us anew by the powers we have acquired, and the seeming indiscipline in our use of them to which we have yielded. The issue of a 'natural law' ethic, raised at a place where practical and theoretical perplexity meet, is that in fact of the possibility of metaphysics. To say this is not to retreat from the problems of international politics into abstract philosophy; it is rather to advertise the former as raising for us the issues of the latter. The practical man will, of course, be eager to stress the urgent primacy of his concerns; but the Western world has need maybe of finding new ways to redress the balance of action and contemplation.

(c) To write in this way is not to ignore the extraordinary resilience of the idiom of 'natural rights' as an idiom of protest. In situations where constitutional means of redress of grievance and of social reform are whittled away or rendered nugatory, this language is a virtually indispensable *argot* of protest. To remove it from the vocabulary of mankind would be to diminish human capacity for revolt and protest on the one hand, and for establishing a kind of communication between past, present and future on the other, which keeps alight men's sense of the authority of a truly human universal.

[1] *Christians and Atomic War: a Discussion of the Moral Aspects of Defence and Disarmament in the Nuclear Age* (British Council of Churches, 1959).

(d) It is in the ethics of Kant that as a matter of historical fact the tradition of 'natural right' rejoined that of 'natural law'. And it is with a brief indication of the manner of that rejoining that I will conclude this paper.

In Kant's theory of knowledge the notion of communication is central. It is through the categories of understanding, working by way of imagination upon the presentations of sense, that a common world, whose laws men may confidently probe and frame, is achieved. So in his ethics it is in the egoism, whether individual or collective, that prohibits communication between men, and thus the affirmation of a human universe, that we must discern the essential quality of moral evil. And if it is through the demand upon us of the moral law that we know freedom, the central mystery of our existence, yet the denial of freedom, the sacrifice of its ultimacy in the name of a supposed vision of the world as it ultimately is, violates as much as anything the character of that law.

Kant's philosophy is emphatically anti-ontological, in the sense in which Aristotle's is ontological. Indeed for him in all ontology (if we refuse to treat his doctrine of categories as ontology) there is implicit a threat to the primacy of freedom. Yet his ideas rejoin the characteristic emphasis of the school of 'natural law' as distinct from that of 'natural right'. The claims we make for the ultimate dignity of our human nature we make not in mere protestation, but in affirmation of that which (through critical reflection) we discern ourselves to be. If we are only free in affirming our freedom, yet that freedom which is ours through the moral law within us, is something found; wven though we cannot represent the character of that finding to ourselves except in terms of the sort of vision of the world which would, by its very nature, contradict the character of what we find when we come upon the reality of our freedom.

(e) It is at least possible that further thought along lines *suggested by* Kant, particularly in his *Perpetual Peace*, may do something toward suggesting how we may achieve a proper balance between hope and fear in the way in which we approach the human future; it will not, in my view, take us the whole way. Perhaps nothing but a renewed and transformed religious imagination can do that. But there are lessons in the reconciliation of contradictory attitudes which we can still learn from Kant. And this is because, of all modern philosphers, Kant frequently succeeds most effectively in striking a balance between alternatives that are totally unacceptable. Thus for instance he recognized that human moral excellence was irreducible, shining by its own light, in the most diverse situations. The course of history was itself not the judgment-seat from which a final verdict could be sought on the ultimacies of human achievement. For Kant to speak of *die Weltgeschichte* as *der Weltgericht* was to blaspheme the first principle of his ethics, namely that moral excellence was the sum of the universe of value, by which men must judge the worth of all else, including any imaginable constitutional or juridical institution they might conceive. Yet Kant's profound reflection on the teleological compelled him to recognize that an absolute ethic, which simply prised the moral realm apart from that of nature and of history, failed to do justice to men's need for assurance that the field in which they had to act somehow 'co-operated' with their effort to affirm in the springs of their conduct those principles whose authority they could not gainsay. *What is could not in the last resort be positively inimical to what ought to be.* So we have Kant's masterly delineation of the 'idea of progress', free from the facile optimism that ignored the reality of the evils whose contemplation had provoked Voltaire's *Candide*, and yet innocent of the moral enormity present in Hegel's doctrine of the 'cunning of the Idea'.

Kant's ethic and metaphysic (if I may use the latter term) are a long way removed from the relatively naive world of Hooker and Aquinas. But they are also both individually, and together, wrought on a deeper plane of moral and intellectual awareness than the 'natural rights' conceptions of the Enlightenment. Kant leaves his readers with the issue of the status of the individual person, whose moral dignity he deploys as something poised between achievement and receptivity; an issue which he has, by his self-critical awareness of the limitations of metaphysical thought, done much to clarify; making his readers, if not to see their way through impossible alternatives, at least to believe that a path may be found.

CHAPTER 5

WESTERN VALUES IN INTERNATIONAL RELATIONS

MARTIN WIGHT

Western values are commonly identified with the freedom and self-fulfilment of the individual. The history of Western Civilization is thus seen as primarily the development and organization of liberty, especially in the form of the tradition of constitutional government which descends from Aristotle through Aquinas to Locke and the Founding Fathers of the United States. The aim of the present paper is not to trench upon this familiar ground, but to follow some of its lines of thought into the fields of diplomacy and international relations.

Two assumptions may be remarked at the outset. 'Western values' is an awkward phrase because it is bound up with the Cold War. I assume that it is *not* our present purpose to define 'what we are fighting for in the Cold War'. By Western values we shall not mean, what all Western men believe in or ought to believe in. Western men are perhaps more various in their range of beliefs than the men of any other culture. They may be pacifists, Roman Catholics, scientific humanists, or Marxists. It is likely that the more definite a man's beliefs, the less satisfied will he be to hear them described as 'Western values'. At best, Western values are the highest common factor of the range of beliefs by which Western men live. At worst, the phrase is the label of the undifferentiated, the waste-paper basket for half-believers in casual creeds, like 'C. of E.' for British Army recruits. I assume, then, that we discuss Western value without the impulses of personal commitment: that even if we were able to agree completely on a description of Western values, some of us might say 'My values are different from this': that our concern is detached analysis, not to hammer out a creed.

A deeper question may be asked. Is the capacity for detached self-scrutiny itself a Western quality, the fruit of a 'Western value'? Is there a correlation between Western values and toleration, self-analysis, the scientific outlook? There are those who argue that the West will not be able to resist the attack from Communism unless the West discovers or rediscovers a creed as powerful as Communism; that only ideas can destroy ideas, that if Marx is to be beaten at all, he will be beaten by Thomas Jefferson, or Thomas Aquinas. But it is

difficult, perhaps impossible, to formulate a creed that will be sub-
scribed by a Dulles, a Maritain, a Croce, a Russell, a Waddington
and a Sartre. Any such creed will exclude some of them, thereby
stamping them arbitrarily as un-Western. There are those, on the
other hand, who argue that the common ground in the West is the
very agreement to differ, the critical spirit, the tradition of questioning what is traditional; and that this liberal scepticism is both less
dangerous to mankind than Communist dogma, and has greater
intrinsic vitality. The present paper will not try to say anything on
this profound issue, but we may recognize that it is at our elbow.

Secondly, it is assumed that there is no simple way of deducing
Western values from Western practice. For example, the tradition of
British diplomacy is by itself a weak authority for Western values.
This tradition is likely to be construed less favourably by non-
British Westerners than it may be by ourselves. And there are other
traditions of diplomacy—the French or the American—which have
as much right as the British to be regarded as the bearers of Western
values. Is the traditional American doctrine of recognition and non-
recognition in international law less Western than the traditional
British doctrine? There is not a simple answer.

We can perhaps discern the values of a society, not so much in the
record of its practice, nor even in the simple doctrines which, like
those of international law, are mainly a codification of practice, as
in the history of its ideas. This paper will try to indicate a certain
coherent pattern of ideas that may be detected from time to time in
Western statesmen, political philosophers and jurists. For preliminary identification it may be described as the Whig or 'constitutional'
tradition in diplomacy, and it is exemplified in different ways by
Suarez, Grotius, Locke, Halifax, Callières, Montesquieu, Burke,
Gentz, Coleridge, Castlereagh, Tocqueville, Lincoln, Gladstone,
Cecil of Chelwood, Ferrero, Brierly, Harold Nicolson, Churchill,
Spaak. The names are merely illustrative. It is ideas and assumptions
we are concerned with, and their logical interdependence; and this
commits us to the dangerous method of tracing ideas through a
variety of writers and politicians without dwelling on their place in
each's complex aggregate of doctrine. We are not primarily concerned
with the gulf between Hooker and Locke, or the problem of the
development or contradiction in Burke's political philosophy, or
whether Gladstone's radicalism is a matter more of his language or
his thought.

This pattern of ideas is persistent and recurrent. Sometimes eclipsed
and distorted, it has constantly reappeared and reasserted its authority, so that it may even seem something like a consensus of Western

diplomatic opinion. As Guizot said, 'C'est aussi une majorité que celle qui se compte par générations'. It is likewise a coherent pattern. It will be necessary to try to break it up into what Lovejoy (in *The Great Chain of Being*) calls its unit-ideas; but these unit-ideas are generally found in mutual association, the reason perhaps being that diplomatic theory is among the least profound and individual branches of political philosophy. Nevertheless, there are other patterns of ideas in international history for which persistence, recurrence and coherence can be claimed. But there may be reasons for thinking that the tradition we are at present considering is specially representative of Western values. One is its explicit connection with the political philosophy of constitutional government. The other is its quality of a *via media*. This pattern of ideas usually appears as the *juste milieu* between definable extremes, whether it is Grotius saying: 'A remedy must be found for those that believe that in war nothing is lawful, and for those for whom all things are lawful in war'[1] or Halifax's classic exposition of the balance of power in *The Character of a Trimmer*, or Gladstone's conception of the European Concert seen as a middle way between the radical non-interventionism of Cobden and Bright and the *Realpolitik* of Beaconsfield and Bismarck, or the policy of collective security between the World Wars as a middle way between the pacifists and disarmers on the one side and the imperialists turned appeasers on the other. The golden mean can be an overcautious and ignoble principle as a guide to action, but it may also be an index to the accumulated experience of a civilization which has valued disciplined scepticism and canonized prudence as a political virtue. The disposition to think of true policy as a difficult path between seductive but simplified alternatives is a likely, though not of course an infallible, sign of the tradition we are concerned with. 'We must neither count upon its immediate efficacy, nor reject the hopes that it awakens.'[2]

This paper will try to outline the following figures in the pattern:

1. International Society
2. The Maintenance of Order
3. Intervention
4. International Morality.

---

[1] *De Jure Belli ac Pacis*, Prolegomena, para. 29.

[2] Charles de Visscher, *Theory and Reality in Public International Law* (Princeton University Press, 1957), p. 129. The configuration of thought may be seen in John Strachey's last book, *On the Prevention of War* (Macmillan, 1962). 'It would however be a disastrous error to suppose that there is nothing between leaving things as they are and the creation of a fully-developed world authority. It will be suggested below that what may yet be possible is the gradual emer-

1. INTERNATIONAL SOCIETY

The primary questions of international theory concern the nature of international society and of international law. (Sociologists have not agreed on a satisfactory distinction in usage between the words 'society' and 'community', and in this paper, as in most of the literature of international law, they will be used interchangeably.)

Ever since Machiavelli and Hobbes there have been those who take the view that there is no such thing as international society: that international relations constitute an anarchy whose social elements are negligible. The doctrine that the state is the ultimate unit of political society entails the doctrine that there is no wider society to embrace states. In this conclusion, in the nineteenth century, the separate influences of Hegel, of Social Darwinism and of legal positivism converged. It is true that there exists, empirically, a network of relationships which used to be called 'the diplomatic community': a system of resident ambassadors reciprocally recognized which antedates the formulation of the question whether international society exists. To the diplomatic system was added, in the nineteenth century, the network of functional international organizations beginning with the Telegraphic and Postal Unions. But it is possible to deny that the diplomatic system and the international organizations constitute a society. Some, perhaps most, of the greatest diplomatists have made this denial. 'Qui parle Europe a tort, notion géographique: *Who is Europe?*' Bismarck noted irritably on a memorandum by Gorchakov.[1] 'Some one has said before me,' wrote Saburov to Jomini: ' "The European Concert is only a dream of the idealists. There is no Europe; there is a Russia, a Germany, a France, an England". In order that there may be a Europe, there must be a Confederation obeying a single will. But there are five of them (sc. the Great Powers).'[2] Many diplomatists have written with similar scepticism of the notion that the League of Nations or the United Nations afford evidence of an international society. Indeed, an interesting development in international theory since the Second World War has been the spread of this scepticism among those who have hitherto been the professional supporters of the notion of an international community, the international lawyers themselves. The American jurist P. E. Corbett may be quoted:

gence of an elementary sense of common purpose, in a strictly limited field, between the Russian and American Governments.' (p. 195).

[1] *Die Grosse Politik*, vol. ii, p. 87.

[2] J. Y. Simpson, *The Saburov Memoirs* (Cambridge University Press, 1929), p. 136.

'Consensus is the life of society, and the dominant characteristics of our world is conflict, not consensus. The question may of course be asked whether it has ever been otherwise. The vaunted unity of medieval Europe was a unity of culture among intellectuals, not a unity of purpose or of action among the powerful. The vaunted peace of the nineteenth century was kept in anxious suspense by the manoeuvers of competing alliances, when it was not interrupted by bloody wars. At the present time, the spectacle presented is not that of one society but of two great power-concentrations struggling by every means short of declared general war to increase their strength for a feared battle to the death. Over the contest hovers, as in all ages, a concept of society formulated and fostered by intellectuals. This is not a reflection of reality, but a goal and hope of good men. To present the hope as a reality renders no service to humanity, because it obscures the complex obstacles that still stand in the way of realization.'[1]

If international society is a fiction or an illusion, then international law is radically different from municipal law, law as generally understood. It is only the sum of the principles and rules which states—the *real* political units—have agreed to regard as obligatory; and the basis of international obligation is purely contractual. This is the doctrine of legal positivism. It follows that the subjects of international law can only be independent states. The only international persons are these collective persons, of whom it is postulated that they have a moral nature analogous with that of individuals, making them capable of enjoying rights and assuming obligations. It might even be said of legal positivism (which it must be added has been for two centuries the orthodoxy of international legal philosophy) that by recognizing no international society except the society of sovereign states, it denies the existence of an effective international society.

At the opposite extreme, the nature of the international community is conceived in a different way by those who believe that the society of states is the *unreal* thing—a complex of legal fictions and obsolescent diplomatic forms which conceals, obstructs and oppresses the *real* society of individual men and women, the *civitas maxima*. On this view, international society is none other than the community of mankind. If the community of mankind is not yet manifested, yet it is latent, half glimpsed and groping for its necessary fulfilment. The prototypal *a priori* argument is provided by Dante. The specific

[1] P. E. Corbett, *Law and Society in the Relations of States* (New York, Harcourt, Brace, 1951), pp. 51–2.

capacity of man consists in his possible intellect; the task of mankind is to fulfil the total capacity of the possible intellect all the time; universal peace is the best condition for fulfilling this task. The argument of Kant's *Idee zu einer allgemeinen Geschichte in weltbuergerlicher Absicht* is curiously similar. Man is the only rational animal; nature intends the full development of his rational faculties in the species, not the individual; nature accomplishes the development of all the faculties by means of the antagonism of men in society, which in the end becomes the cause of a lawful order in society. The difference lies between Dante's 'proprium *opus* humani generis' and Kant's 'Naturabsicht, die ihnen selbst unbekannt ist'.[1] Like Turgot before him and like most thinkers since, Kant clarified or simplified the mysteries of Providence into a perceptible linear movement of history that would bring about, irrespective of individual human strivings, the fruition of collective human aims. Hence the belief, common in varying degrees to the Huguenots, the Jacobins, Mazzini, President Wilson and the Communists, that the whole of diplomatic history has groaned and travailed together until now, and that the community of mankind, like the kingdom of God, is the glory that shall be revealed, is within reach, is at hand.

Such beliefs mean that the existing society of states is to dissolve and merge into the world community, cosmopolis. There are various elements in the expected transformation, some complementary, some alternative. Either the society of states will become co-operative and homogeneous through the universal acceptance of some standard of legitimacy, so that all states will become Catholic, or Communist, or national, or republican. Or the society of states will federate and form a world government. Or the principles of transformation will establish themselves first, in accordance with the law of uneven development, in a single country, whether an insignificant city-state like sixteenth-century Geneva or in a Great Power like eighteen-century France or 20th-century Russia. This state thus becomes the bearer and exemplar of the new order, and its relations with the unregenerate society of states will reproduce the relations of the Church militant with the secular and infidel world. There follows no single or simple notion of international law. One set of beliefs is governed by the idea that the whole is prior to the part, that the greater includes the less, and that the state is or ought to be subordinate to the international community. This will tend to minimize the difference between international and municipal law. The word 'law' denotes a system of rules which is created and modified by a legislature, interpreted and

[1] Dante, *De Monarchia*, book i, ch. 4 *ad init*; Kant, *Idee*, first paragraph (*Werke*, Academy edition, vol. viii, p. 17).

applied by a judiciary, and enforced by an executive; and if these organs appear rudimentary or non-existent in diplomatic life, the task is to create them, since the urgent need of international relations is to establish the rule of law. Another set of beliefs is governed by the idea of the impassable gulf between believers and infidels, the elect and the reprobate, and the impossibility of co-operation between them. Therefore the revolutionary state opts out of the existing law of nations because it is defective and unjust, or observes it as a matter of expediency not of legal obligation. A true international law awaits the final transformation of international society; meanwhile it is adumbrated by the diplomatic principles of the revolutionary state itself. When President Washington's administration in 1793 accused Genêt, the French Convention's ambassador to the United States, of proceedings contrary to the spirit of the doctrines of Grotius and Vattel, Genêt replied that he knew nothing of Grotius and Vattel and that his conduct was conformable to the doctrines of the French constitution. 'This was either ignorance, or design; if the one, it can form no case; but if the other, it was almost a direct notice, that the French meant to retire from the obedience they had paid to the Code of the European Law.'[1]

Between the belief that the society of states is non-existent or at best a polite fiction, and the belief that it is the chrysalis for the community of mankind, lies a more complex conception of international society. It does not derogate from the moral claims of states, conceding that they are, in Suarez's phrase, *communitates perfectae* (exercising valid political authority);[2] but it sees them as relatively, not absolutely perfect, and as parts of a greater whole. It does not see international society as ready to supersede domestic society; but it notes that international society actually exercises restraints upon its members. Such a conception lacks intellectual conciseness and emotional appeal. The language in which it is stated is necessarily full of qualifications and imprecision. Thus, the famous and noble description of international society in Suarez:

'The human race, though divided into no matter how many different peoples and nations, has for all that a certain unity, a unity not merely physical, but also in a sense political and moral. This is shown by the natural precept of mutual love and mercy, which extends to all men, including foreigners of every way of thinking. Wherefore, though

[1] Robert Ward, *An Enquiry into the Foundation and History of the Law of Nations in Europe* (1795), vol. i, p. 161 n.
[2] *De Legibus*, book I, ch. vi, section 19, following Aquinas, *Summa Theologica*, 1ª2ae, qu. 90, art. 2, and Aristotle, *Politics*, book I, ch. i, section 8.

any one state, republic or kingdom be in itself a perfect community and constant in its members, nevertheless each of the states is also a member, in a certain manner, of the world, so far as the human race is concerned.'[1]

'Aliquid unitas . . . quasi politica et moralis.'[2] Tocqueville has similar language of half-lights and indefinition: 'Cette societé des nations où chaque peuple est un citoyen, societé toujours un peu barbare, mêmes dans les siècles les plus civilisés, quelque effort que l'on fasse pour adoucir et régler les rapports de ceux qui la composent.'[3] Compare the Belgian jurist de Visscher:

'If the international community, or more accurately the sense of such a community, finds so little echo in individual consciences, this is less because power obstructs it than because the immense majority of men are still infinitely less accessible to the doubtless real but certainly remote solidarities that it invokes than to the immediate and tangible solidarities that impose themselves upon them in the framework of national life.'[4]

Language so indefinite, and embodying such tension between opposites, is likely to be unsatisfactory to the political and legal scientist: but the school of thought we are considering may claim that it corresponds more accurately to the intractable anomalies and anfractuosities of international experience.

International society, then, on this view, can be properly described only in historical and sociological depth. It is the habitual intercourse of independent communities, beginning in the Christendom of Western Europe and gradually extending throughout the world. It is manifest in the diplomatic system; in the conscious maintenance of the balance of power to preserve the independence of the member-communities; in the regular operations of international law, whose binding force is accepted over a wide though politically unimportant

---

[1] *De Legibus*, book II, ch. xix, section 9.
[2] Cf. Vitoria, *De Potestate Civili*, section xxi, para. 4: 'totus orbis, qui aliquo modo est una respublica' (*Relecciones Teológicas*, ed. Fr. Luis G. Alonso Getino (Madrid, La Rafa, 1933–35), vol ii, p. 207). Brierly, following Professor Barcia Trelles, has suggested that in Suarez the quasi-political and moral unity of mankind, and the state as a *communitas perfecta*, are really two irreconcilable concepts (*The Basis of Obligation in International Law* (Clarendon Press, 1958), p. 362).
[3] Address to the Académie des Sciences Morales et Politiques, April 3, 1852 (*Oeuvres*, vol. ix, pp. 120–1).
[4] *Theory and Reality in Public International Law*, p. 92.

range of subjects; in economic, social and technical interdependence and the functional international institutions established latterly to regulate it. All these presuppose an international social consciousness, a world-wide community-sentiment. The language in which these 'doubtless real but certainly remote solidarities' have been asserted deserves note, both for its strength and its weakness. Two famous examples may be given. One is from Gladstone's speech in the Don Pacifico debate:

'There is a further appeal from this House of Parliament to the people of England; but, lastly, there is also an appeal from the people of England to the general sentiment of the civilized world; and I, for my part, am of opinion that England will stand shorn of a chief part of her glory and her pride if she shall be found to have separated herself, through the policy she pursues abroad, from the moral supports which the general and fixed convictions of mankind afford—if the day shall come in which she may continue to excite the wonder and fear of other nations, but in which she shall have no part in their affections and regard.'[1]

The other is from the first *Letter on a Regicide Peace:*

'In the intercourse between nations,' wrote Burke, 'we are apt to rely too much on the instrumental part ... Men are not tied to one another by paper and seals. They are led to associate by resemblances, by conformities, by sympathies. It is with nations as with individuals. Nothing is so strong a tie of amity between nation and nation as correspondence in laws, customs, manners, and habits of life ... The secret, unseen, but irrefragable bond of habitual intercourse holds them together, even when their perverse and litigious nature sets them to equivocate, scuffle, and fight, about the terms of their written obligations.'[2]

What E. H. Carr calls the realist critique of such doctrines is easiest when they are translated into statements of fact. Brierly in 1936 could adduce in support of the international social consciousness the evidence of the mandates system, the minorities treatises, the Nansen Office, the International Red Cross, the ILO, the effort of the great majority of states to enforce the rule of law on Italy when she violated the Covenant, as well as the regional sense of community that binds together severally the Scandinavians, the English-

[1] House of Commons, June 27, 1850 (Hansard, 3rd Series, vol. cxii, col. 589).
[2] Burke, *Works*, ed. H. Rogers (Holdsworth, 1842), vol. ii, pp. 298–9.

G

speaking and the Spanish-speaking peoples.[1] But every undergraduate who has taken a course in international relations thinks he can debunk the irrefragability of these bonds. Were not the age of Gladstone and of the League of Nations exceptional and illusory periods of international lull? Did not Brierly's vision overlook the secession from the international community of Russia and Germany? Has not the Cold War swept the whole argument into limbo? Is it not sufficient comment on Burke's picture of the 'commonwealth of Europe' that it was prompted by the need to denounce France for having torn herself from its communion with studied violence?

Yet it might be answered that in the long run Burke's conception of the European community was vindicated, rather than his emotional reaction against the threat to it. European society was more resilient than he feared, more capable of development than he imagined. It withstood French aggression, it tamed the French Revolution, it digested French principles. War does not disprove the existence of international society, because war is followed by peace. Nor even does ideological conflict, because it is followed at a longer interval by ideological accommodation. And this is implied in Burke's own treatment, in *Thoughts on French Affairs*, of the previous international 'revolution of doctrine and theoretick dogma', the Reformation. The Religious Wars, like the French Revolutionary, had been 'a real crisis in the politicks of Europe', but he does not suggest that they had dissolved European society. They had in the end only introduced a little diversity into 'the similitude throughout Europe of religion, laws and manners'.[2] Two elements must be distinguished in Burke's doctrine of international society. One is a broad description of its nature and origin. The other is his linking it with the social and political structure of the Europe he knew, so as to find its indefeasible principle of legitimacy in Christianity and prescription. It was the second theme that made him construe the French Revolution as a wilful act of secession from international society followed by an assault upon it from the outside, instead of a debate within international society which would in the end produce a modified principle of legitimacy. But a hundred years later Westlake, who in fundamental matters was in the tradition of Burke, could put in a striking sentence what had by them become accepted doctrine: 'The international society to which we belong is not one for the mutual insurance of established governments.'[3]

[1] *Basis of Obligation in International Law*, pp. 251–3.
[2] *Works*, vol. i, p. 564; vol. ii, p. 299.
[3] *The Collected Papers of John Westlake on Public International Law*, ed. L. Oppenheim (Cambridge University Press, 1914), p. 124.

But the case of Burke is not quite disposed of. To speak of the principle of legitimacy being modified, as if the international social consciousness has a changing content, runs the danger of a certain kind of historicism. Is it indefinitely modifiable? Is it the random deposit of wars and settlements, informed by no rational theme? Is there no change or modification conceivable where we could say that international society has abandoned its essential principles, has become wholly other than what it was? In the pattern of ideas we are considering Westlake's principle is complementary to, not inconsistent with, another, which was put in this way by Phillimore:

'The first Limitation of the general right, incident to every State, of adopting whatever form of government, whatever political and civil institutions, and whatever rules she may please, is this:

'No State has a right to establish a form of government which is built upon professed principles of hostility to the government of other nations.'[1]

The force of this principle has been unintentionally illustrated by George Kennan. No contemporary writer has argued more persuasively and consistently than Kennan for moral non-interventionism—that one nation cannot judge the interests of another, and one nation has no right to judge the affairs of another. But when he comes to consider the conditions on which we can live in peace with Russia, he writes thus:

'What attributes are we, as responsible members of the world community, entitled to look for in the personality of a foreign state, and of Russia in particular?

'We may look, in the first place, for a Russian government which, in contrast to the one we know today, would be tolerant, communicative and forthright in its relations with other states and peoples. It would not take the ideological position that its own purposes cannot finally prosper unless all systems of government not under its control are subverted and eventually destroyed . . .

'Secondly, while recognizing that the internal system of government is in all essential respects Russia's own business and may well depart drastically from our own, we are entitled to expect that the exercise of governmental authority will stop short of that fairly plain line beyond which lies totalitarianism. Specifically, we may expect that any regime which claims to contrast favourably with that which

[1] Robert Phillimore, *Commentaries upon International Law* (Benning, 1854), vol. i, p. 435.

we have before us today will refrain from enslaving its own labour—
industrial and agricultural . . . In this way, excess of internal authority leads inevitably to unsocial and aggressive conduct as a government among governments, and is a matter of concern to the international community . . .

'The third thing we may hope from a new Russia is that it will
refrain from pinning an oppressive yoke on other peoples who have
the instinct and the capacity for national self-assertion . . .

'These, then, are the things for which an American well-wisher
may hope from the Russia of the future: that she lift for ever the Iron
Curtain, that she recognize certain limitations to the internal authority of government, and that she abandon, as ruinous and unworthy,
the ancient game of imperialist expansion and oppression . . . If she
is prepared to do these things, then Americans will not need to concern themselves more deeply with her nature and purposes; the basic
needs of a more stable world order will than have been met, and the
area in which a foreign people can usefully have thoughts and
suggestions will have been filled.'[1]

This is simply an application of Phillimore's principle. The modest
and conciliatory tone cannot disguise the extent of the demand. Nor
does it alter the implication of these words that they were written
before the death of Stalin. A Russian of the new dispensation would
equally reply: 'Imperialist expansion is not in question: this is your
sort of activity. We are agreed on peaceful coexistence. But you ask
us to allow the free circulation of corrupting bourgeois influences
and imperialist spies among our people; to dismantle the dictator-
ship of the proletariat; and to cease to believe that Communism is
the only road for mankind.' Is it fair to say that Burke's writings
against the French Revolution illustrate a central paradox of the
view of international society he propounded, that its principles of
legitimacy have been modified instead of being dissolved, only
because men have been ready to fight that they should undergo no

---

[1] G. F. Kennan, 'America and the Russian Future', *Foreign Affairs*, April 1951,
reprinted in his *American Diplomacy 1900-1950* (University of Chicago Press,
1952), pp. 136–7, 138–40, 143. Macmillan held the same doctrine in his speech
to the South African Parliament at Cape Town on February 3, 1960: 'It is the
basic principle for our modern Commonwealth that we respect each other's
sovereignty in matters of internal policy. At the same time, we must recognize
that in this shrinking world in which we live today, the internal policies of each
nation may have effects outside it. We may sometimes be tempted to say to each
other, "Mind your own business." But in these days I would myself expand the
old saying so that it runs: "Mind your own business but mind how it affects my
business too" ' (*Guardian*, February 4, 1960).

change at all? It is those who have died to prevent modification who have made possible a modification within limits that posterity can accept.

There is one further element in the picture of international society that we are considering. It does not easily accommodate the strict doctrine that the only international persons, the only subjects of international law, are states. In international legal practice there have always been anomalies, and it has seemed that the law of diplomatic privilege, of extradition, of piracy, of prize, have regarded the individual as the subject of rights and duties, enforceable by or against him. Explaining or reconciling these anomalies with the orthodox doctrine has been a useful field for examination questions. Breaches in the doctrine have multiplied as the doctrine has hardened. Not only certain individuals but certain institutions other than states have attained a rudimentary international personality, reminiscent of the crusading Orders of the Middle Ages. The great chartered corporations, like the East India Company and the British South Africa Company, seemed, although subject in relation to their own government, to be sovereign in relation to the barbarians they treated with. The status of the Pope from 1870 to 1929 was an interesting problem, when the only generally accepted definition of his position was the Italian Law of Guarantees. 'An Italian statute,' wrote T. J. Lawrence, 'cannot confer international personality; but the tacit consent of a large number of states to treat a given prelate as if he possessed some of the attributes of an international person puts him in a very different position from that of an ordinary individual.'[1] The public international unions that multiplied from the end of the nineteenth century were accorded by treaties what seemed a quasi-personality in international law. The Central American Court of Justice instituted in 1907 had jurisdiction to hear a claim by an individual against a state. The League of Nations possessed rights and duties and appeared to be an international person *sui generis*.[2] The United Nations and its organs, the partial recognition of individuals by the Declaration on Human Rights, and the urgent problem of stateless persons, have multiplied such confusions and emphasized the defects of the doctrine of exclusive state-personality.

But this doctrine only became definite with Wolff and Vattel in the eighteenth century, in whose writings the idea of the *jus gentium* as the

---

[1] *The Principles of International Law* (Macmillan, 7th edition, 1925), pp. 76–7. Cf. A. Pearce Higgins, *Studies in International Law and Relations* (Cambridge University Press, 1928), ch. iv.

[2] Oppenheim, *International Law*, vol. i, para. 167c; W. E. Hall, *A Treatise on International Law* (8th edition, 1924), pp. 32, 72.

basis of international law fades and is replaced by the notion of the abstract personality of the state as the sole titulary of rights. An earlier tradition saw the princes and subjects of different states as all bound together by the obligations of the *jus gentium*. Such doctrine was less clear-cut and intellectually satisfactory than that which superseded it, but more loose, flexible and true to the variety of international life. In Grotius's description of international society there is a fruitful imprecision. *Communis societas generis humani, communis illa ex humano genere constans societas, humana societas, magna illa communitas, magna illa universitas, magna illa gentium societas, mutua gentium inter se societas, illa mundi civitas, societas orbis*—such is his range of language. Are kings or peoples or individuals the members of this ambiguous society? exclaims the positivist in irritation. All were. Nor was this tradition entirely eclipsed by the orthodox doctrine of state-personality. Perhaps it might be said that it survived among the lawyers who saw international law rather as a legitimate child of political philosophy than as a recalcitrant vassal of legal science. It may be traced in the attempt to develop an *a priori* jurisprudence by James Lorimer, who held the Chair of the Law of Nature and of Nations at Edinburgh from 1865 to 1890. It is seen in the doctrine of T. J. Lawrence that 'there are grades and degrees among the subjects of International Law'.[1] It was admirably expressed by Westlake as the first of his principles of international law:

'1. The society of states, having European civilization, or the international society, is the most comprehensive form of society among men, but it is among men that it exists. States are its immediate, men its ultimate members. The duties and rights of states are only the duties and rights of the men who compose them.'[2]

It is represented more recently by those like Brierly and Philip Jessup, who have argued that a broadening of the notion of international personality is needed both to bring international law into closer relation with political experience, and to develop and strengthen the effectiveness of the law itself.

2. THE MAINTENANCE OF ORDER

If there is no international society, then international relations are not only the state of nature, but also the state of nature Hobbes described. There is no call to maintain order, there is only a struggle

---

[1] *Principles of International Law*, p. 47.
[2] *Collected Papers*, p. 78.

for survival—which may lead in the end to the *creation* of an order through the survival of a single strongest Power which has subordinated its rivals. Security, on these premises, is necessarily exclusive, and your security is my insecurity. Foreign policy is essentially self-regarding, and all international action is to be explained as self-help.

If there is an international society, however, then there is an order of some kind to be maintained, or even developed. It is not fallacious to speak of a collective interest, and security acquires a broadened meaning: it can be enjoyed or pursued in common. Foreign policy will take some account of the common interest. It becomes possible to transfer to international politics some of the categories of constitutionalism.

How is this international order to be conceived? Is it an even distribution of power? Is it, as Burke and Metternich and Bismarck believed and as many Americans today believe, a distinct international social order? Is it a distinct moral or ideological order? The two last conceptions are probably bound up with the notion of international society as a *civitas maxima*, with the assimilation of international society to domestic society; and the second is the conservatives' inversion of the third. The Holy Alliance and the Dreikaiserbund displayed the pattern of ideas of the Jacobins, but in a counter-revolutionary key. Perhaps the distribution of power is the central preoccupation of those whom we are considering, but it is not possible to say that concern for the social and moral order are excluded.

The postulate that there is an international society generally entails the following beliefs:

1. That international society exists and survives by virtue of some core of common standards and common custom, difficult to define, but having its partial embodiment in international law.

2. That the tranquillity of international society and the freedom of its members require an even distribution of power. This presupposes a belief that some degree of objectivity and disinterestedness are possible in international politics: that the majority of states can agree on a broad comparative estimate of international power, and can co-operate in a common policy to maintain it.

3. That international society has a right of self-defence and of coercion. If its common standards are challenged, they may be defended and reimposed by force; and if the distribution of power is threatened it may be restored by force.

4. That the exercise of this right of self-defence and coercion is most fully justified when it is undertaken by the members of international society collectively, or by the majority of them, or by one of them

with the authorization of the others. But this does not exclude the possibility of separate action by an individual Power deserving the approval of the rest.

The interdependence of the core of common standards and the even distribution of power is illustrated in the notion of aggression. Aggression is both a violation of the legal and moral order, and a threat to the balance of power. It is a classic test of statesmanship to keep both evils of aggression in view, and not to remedy one by neglecting the other; and around this much diplomatic controversy and historical interpretation ranges. Thus the diplomacy of Harley and St John from 1711 to the Peace of Utrecht is generally justified as having avoided a vindication of the moral and legal order at the expense of acquiescing in a derangement of the balance of power (the succession of the Emperor Charles VI to the Spanish inheritance) as dangerous as that which had occasioned the war; Roosevelt's policy in the Second World War is condemned for having failed to do the same; and the strongest case against the attempt by the League of Nations to coerce Italy by sanctions in 1935–6 is that it tended to break down one of the obstacles to German predominance in Europe. On the other hand, criticisms of the Peace of Vienna in 1815 usually take the form of asserting that it restored a balance of power at the expense of the legal order (e.g. by confirming the extinction of Polish sovereignty and by not allowing the doctrine of legitimacy to extend to Venice, Genoa and many German states) or at the expense of the moral order (which was now developing in the direction of recognizing the claims of nationality).

The word 'aggression' places the weight of moral approval on the side of the order which aggression violates. The notion that there could be a lawless or delinquent state has been integral to this conception of international society. In 1602, in the course of the long-drawn war in the East Indies, the Dutch naval commander in the Malacca Straits captured the Portuguese carack *Catharine* with a cargo of merchandise. A prize court in Amsterdam considered the legality of the seizure, declared the captured property a good prize, and awarded the proceeds to the Dutch East India Company. Some of the shareholders, however, especially the Mennonites, had conscientious scruples, withdrew from the Company, and controversy continued. 'A situation has arisen that is truly novel, and scarcely credible to foreign observers, namely: that these men who have been so long at war with the Spaniards and who have further-more suffered the most grievous personal injuries, are debating as to whether or not, in a just war and with public authorization, they can rightfully despoil an exceedingly cruel enemy who had already

violated the rules of international commerce.' These are the opening
words of Grotius's *De Jure Praedae*.[1] At the very beginning of the
classical literature of international law there is this dramatic confrontation between the state that is law-abiding even in war and the
delinquent state (it is also a confrontation between the state with
constitutional processes and the despotic state). The *De Jure Praedae*
argued that in international society there could be a robber or
bandit, *praedo* or *latro*, whose crime even according to the established
law of nations deserved punishment; that it was in the interest of the
international community and of unconcerned nations that violation
of the law should not pass unnoticed; that a penal code for states
was as indispensable as a penal code for citizens. This was the
central doctrine of Grotius's bigger and more famous book, published twenty-one years later, when he was no longer pleading the
cause of the Seven Provinces against Portugal, but of international
society at large against all the Great Powers. If there is an international society at all, then its members have duties, and the duties
are enforceable.

In the later nineteenth century, the same argument inspired the
international coercion of a Turkey that was reluctant to conform to
the changing standards of domestic government required by international society. Between the World Wars, it inspired the doctrine
of collective security, the demand for effective sanctions against any
aggressor, the conception of the League of Nations as 'a potential
alliance against the *unknown* enemy'.[2] After 1919 the Grotians
discovered, with a kind of messianic wonder, that the doctrines of the
master had at last, after three hundred years, been embodied in the
first written constitution of international society. Here, it may seem,
is the point of closest approximation between the pattern of ideas
under consideration (which at this point has generated a theory of
international constitutionalism) and theories of world government.
Those who propounded the sincere milk of the League Covenant saw
the establishment of the rule of law in international society not only
as necessary for the continuance of orderly social relations but as a
path to a more orderly future, where international law might
progressively acquire the coercive jurisdiction of municipal law. But
this was to be achieved, not through the creation or imposition of an
international government, but by the collective action of the members
of international society inspired by a clearer recognition of their
legal duties. The same idea is buried in the obsolete articles of the

---

[1] *De Jure Praedae Commentarius* (Clarendon Press, 1950), ch. i.
[2] Sir Arthur Salter, *Security* (Macmillan, 1939), p. 155.

United Nations Charter which prescribe the duties of the Security Council.

Underlying this theme is the insistent question of the relation between order and justice, or more precisely, between the moral order, legal order, and the balance of power. For Grotius this was not a problem. The moral and the legal order were the same; there was no general demand of unsatisfied justice, such as oppressed nationality, to create a cleavage. The threat to the moral and legal order was occasional and particular, the criminal state. Punishment of the criminal state restored order by vindicating justice. With the balance of power he was not concerned at all. After Westphalia, the moral and legal order became increasingly identified with the balance of power, a development that strict Grotians like the Dutch jurist Vollenhoven regard as a dilution, even a perversion of the gospel.[1] After 1815, a cleavage appeared between the legal and moral orders, as the Vienna Settlement fell into disrespect for obstructing the rightful claims of nationality. But the balance of power was sufficiently stable (and the consequences of its overthrow were sufficiently uncalamitous if this had to be contemplated) to allow the revision of the legal order. In the key case of Italy it was possible to indulge a moral condemnation of the legal order because this would not seriously endanger the balance of power. Hence the paradox noted by A. J. P. Taylor about the war of 1859; 'though the war lacked justification on any basis of international law, no war has been so unanimously approved by posterity. . . . The historian cannot be expected to explain this paradox; while himself approving of the war, he can only record that it was incompatible with any known system of international morality'.[2] Cavour and Palmerston would have answered that a new legal and moral order was coming to birth, in which states would be based on the consent of the governed. The liberation of the Balkan nations, from the rising in the Morea in 1821 down to the Treaty of Bucarest in 1913, was a more delicate process, but here, too, far-sighted policy could pursue national justice without allowing the balance of power to be deranged. Order, in fact, did not preclude a peaceful advance towards greater justice, until the rising tide drove Austria to desperation; and then the Grotian theorem seemed to become fact, and punishment of the criminal state restored order by vindicating justice.

[1] Cf. C. van Vollenhoven, *The Three Stages in the Evolution of the Law of Nations* (The Hague, Nijhoff, 1919), pp. 17–22.
[2] *The Struggle for Mastery in Europe 1848-1918* (Clarendon Press, 1954), p. 112. Cf. H. Temperley and L. M. Penson, *Foundations of British Policy* (Cambridge University Press, 1938), pp. 226–9.

After 1919 the question appears in a new light. The League of Nations seemed to combine the Grotian doctrine about the enforcement of law against a delinquent state with the system of the balance of power. The balance of power was now institutionalized, and would work against any state that resorted to war in defiance of its obligation to observe the procedures of the Covenant. At the root of the argument about collective security preceding peaceful change lay the principle that order precedes justice; that the prevention of violence is prior to the redress of grievances, that law can only function within a frame-work of order. Acknowledgment of this principle grew slowly, with growing acknowledgment of the nature of the threat to international order. It might be found, variously expressed in the writings of Brierly, Hancock, Salter and Zimmern.[1] What distinguished this doctrine was not the premise that the breakdown of order was so calamitous that peace must be preserved, because everybody agreed on this and the argument was about what might preserve it. Nor was it the premise that order was precarious, that the victory of 1918 had been hardly won, that the doctrine of national self-determination left Germany potential master of the Continent, and that time and prudent exercise were needed for the new legal order created by the Covenant to become habitual; because in the 1920s the balance of power was all in favour of the upholders of the Versailles settlement. The premise lay rather in the hard-won recognition that the Versailles Settlement, the existing order, embodied no substantial injustice, when compared to what had come to challenge it. The majority of the inhabitants of Europe enjoyed the right of self-determination on which the existing order claimed to be based. The exceptions were marginal and explicable by reference to the needs of the balance of power. The advocates of collective security had become unhappily involved by their opponents in bewailing the injustices of the peace settlement, the lack of provision for peaceful change, the inefficacy of Article 19 of the Covenant. It might have made for intellectual clarity if they had early taken the ground roundly defended by Headlam-Morley in a Foreign Office memorandum of 1925, that the fabric of the continent depended on the maintenance of the peace settlement just because

---

[1] See for example J. L. Brierly, *The Basis of Obligation in International Law*, pp. 262–3 and ch. 20, and *The Outlook for International Law* (Oxford University Press, 1944), pp. 73–4; W. K. Hancock, *Survey of British Commonwealth Affairs*, vol. i (Oxford University Press, 1937), pp. 314–15, 492–3; Salter, *Security*, p. 135; Sir Alfred Zimmern, *Spiritual Values and World Affairs* (Clarendon Press, 1939), pp. 112–13.

it represented, in broad outline, a peace of reason and justice.[1]

Since 1945 the doctrine that order precedes justice has been maintained by Reinhold Niebuhr, a writer perhaps with a different configuration of thought, and whose views were not quite the same in earlier days when the United States admitted no responsibility for upholding world order. In 1932 he wrote: 'A society of nations has not really proved itself until it is able to grant justice to those who have been worsted in battle without requiring them to engage in new wars to redress their wrongs'.[2] In his books reflecting the beginnings of the United Nations, in the last years of the Second World War and the brief interval before the Cold War was acknowledged, the emphasis falls differently. 'Order precedes justice in the strategy of government; but only an order which implicates justice can achieve a stable peace.'[3] 'The first task of government is to create order. The second task is to create justice.'[4] But more generally, since 1945, the relationship between order and justice has undergone a new transformation. It has now seemed that there is a direct and positive relation between national justice and the maintenance of order: that if the Western Powers could not free their colonies quickly enough the colonies would secede morally to the opposing camp, that the West must run at top speed in order to remain in its existing position, that peaceful change is no longer the antithesis of security but its condition. Order now requires justice. The premise here is that security is not seriously endangered. It is assumed that the balance of power is frozen into the balance of terror, and that the apparent delinquency of states is only their striving for national justice. Perhaps this premise is as ill-founded, this assumption as delusory, as those of the preceding epoch.

Aggression in the extreme case evokes the traditional instrument of the grand alliance, which prevents international society from being subverted and transformed into a universal empire. The archetypal example is the Grand Alliance of 1701 between England, the United Provinces and the Emperor, though it is neither the earliest example nor even the first to which the name 'grand alliance' has been applied. But it seems to be the only grand alliance concluded in advance of a general war, and with the partial aim of averting the war. The treaty was contingent on further negotiations with France, and the three Powers did not declare war on her until eight months later. More-

[1] J. W. Headlam-Morley, *Studies in Diplomatic History* (Methuen, 1930), pp. 184–5.
[2] *Moral Man and Immoral Society* (Scribner, 1932), p. 111.
[3] *The Children of Light and the Children of Darkness* (Nisbet, 1945), p. 123.
[4] *Discerning the Signs of the Times* (S.C.M. Press, 1946), p. 46.

over, the treaty concerted the interests of the three Powers who were to prosecute the war if war became necessary, and partly for this reason its provisions were strikingly similar to those of the peace settlement twelve years afterwards. In the wars against Revolutionary France, Imperial Germany and Nazi Germany, by contrast, the grand alliance did not come about until after the event, by a process of undignified muddle and compulsion, and its war aims were only slowly hammered out in the course of the fighting. The Grand Alliance of 1701, therefore, might be regarded as marking a high point of rational international politics, and has been appealed to by generations of statesmen as a model of political sagacity. It was recalled by the Dutch Government in 1793 as the great paradigm for co-ordinating resistance to France (it had the incidental advantage for the Dutch of placing them on an equal footing with the Great Powers). It was large in Churchill's mind when, after the remilitariza-tion of the Rhineland, rather belatedly, he tried to conjure a grand alliance out of the dying League of Nations, for he was fresh from the biography of the English plenipotentiary in the negotiations at The Hague of 1701.

Two notions are prominent in this view of the grand alliance. One is that of collective action. When Powers become aware of an over-riding common interest, they can co-ordinate and even subordinate their parochial interests, and pursue a common policy. The external expression of such common policy, only gradually arrived at in diplomatic history, is the multilateral treaty. 'Separate conventions between each power will not answer the end', said the Grand Pensionary to Malmesbury in 1793, 'and such necessarily will create separate operations, and in the result perhaps separate interests; they must all be circled by one strong and common political chain for one common and distinct cause'.[1] Perhaps the most subtle and sophistic-ated theory of collective action is found in Gladstone's doctrine of the Concert of Europe. Gladstone reflected on how Canning, in the Greek question, and Palmerston, in the Eastern crisis of 1839–40, had developed a tradition of working with the Power whose independent action they most feared, and he concluded that when two Great Powers co-operate for a common object, they not only assist one another but also act as a check upon each other.

'By keeping all in union together', he said in one of the Midlothian speeches, 'you neutralize and fetter and bind up the selfish aims of each. . . . They have selfish aims as, unfortunately, we in late years

[1] *Diaries and Correspondence of the First Earl of Malmesbury* (2nd edition, Bentley, 1845), vol. iii, p. 11.

have too sadly shown that we, too, have had selfish aims; but then, common action is fatal to selfish aims. Common action means common objects; and the only objects for which you can unite together the Powers of Europe are objects connected with the common good of them all.'[1]

But there are instances where the Great Powers (or a number of them) have united in order to pursue by agreement their selfish aims, by partitioning weaker Powers; and it is not clear whether Gladstone would have regarded these as illustrating moral perversion or an imperfect conception of the common good.

The second notion is that of anticipating and thereby controlling events. Collective action, prepared in advance, can coerce the unruly and regulate the general consequences. If we reflect upon the general correspondence of the peace terms of 1713 with the aims of the Allies of 1701, and mark the growing degree of unpredictability in subsequent general wars, we might believe that the Spanish Succession War marked the nearest point that international society has come to directing its own destiny. (Observers with different premises will not fail to comment that essential to this happy result was the unscrupulousness of Bolingbroke and Britain's desertion of her Allies in the field; the strongest Ally coercing her indignant partners into accepting peace on terms that suited her.) And connected with the notion of forestalling events is that of averting them. It lurked in the Treaty of the Hague, 1701, though such a hope was not seriously entertained by the signatories, and all of them looked to profit if the war was not averted. It was laid down by Gentz as the second of the three essential maxims of the balance of power,

'that to escape the alternate danger of an uninterrupted series of wars, or of an arbitrary oppression of the weaker members in every short interval of peace; *the fear* of awakening common opposition, or of drawing down common vengeance, must of itself be sufficient to keep every one within the bounds of moderation.'[2]

And as, in the next century, the common interest in averting war seemed to grow greater, so did the logical step between anticipating events and preventing them from happening seem to grow clearer. Now the argument is heard that collective action, prepared suffici-

[1] Speech at West Calder, November 27, 1879 (*Selected Speeches on British Foreign Policy* (World's Classics, 1914), p. 372).
[2] *Fragments upon the Balance of Power in Europe*, p. 62.

ently in advance, can prevent a crisis from reaching the point of danger. 'The coercion was recommended', said Gladstone, 'was coercion by the united authority of Europe, and we always contended that in the case where the united authority of Europe was brought into action there was no fear of having to proceed to actual coercion.'[1] This became the central, most intellectualized doctrine of orthodox collective security between the World Wars, easy to ridicule and misrepresent, yet expressing a possibility, in Ranke's phrase, 'at the glimmering boundaries of experience': that if each Member of the League regarded its obligations under the Covenant with as much seriousness as it did its own vital interests, then an overwhelming preponderance of power would always be capable of being mobilized against an aggressor, and consequently aggression would not take place. 'The collective authority behind the prohibition of war', wrote Salter, 'would prevent it from either occurring or being seriously threatened'.[2] Intelligent precaution and common action would regulate the balance of power without war being necessary at all. Deterrence would be perfected.

3. INTERVENTION

One of the most notable means of coercion for upholding standards and maintaining order in international society is intervention. Intervention perhaps gives rise to more controversy than any other international conduct. Violating the assumption of the equal independence of all members of the society of states, it is *prima facie* a hostile act. Yet it is so habitual and regular that it is impossible to imagine international relations without it; and international law can only make a system out of it by losing touch with diplomatic facts.

The very usage of the word intervention is fluid and imprecise. We say that Charles VIII intervened in Italy in 1494; that the United States intervened in the First World War in 1917; that Russia, Germany and France by the Triple Intervention in 1895 compelled

[1] Speech at Edinburgh, November 25, 1879 (*Political Speeches in Scotland* (Elliot, 1880), vol. i, p. 53).

[2] Sir Arthur Salter, *Recovery* (Bell, 1932), p. 278; cf. *Security*, pp. 106, 128. The same idea is present in John Strachey's argument for a rudimentary world condominium by the two nuclear Great Powers: 'What, it may be asked, would an American and a Russian Government actually *do* to enforce their will . . . upon a recalcitrant nation-state? I should not have thought that once the all-important, and so far unfulfilled, condition of their having a *joint* will, had been achieved, they would have much difficulty. . . . It is most unlikely that they would actually have even to rattle the terrible sword of ultimate nuclear power in its scabbard. No, the difficulty lies in the achievement of a joint will, not in its implementation once achieved.' (*On the Prevention of War*, p. 167 n. Cf. pp. 282–3, 314–15.)

Japan to relinquish the Liaotung Peninsula which she proposed to annex from China; that Britain in 1961 at the request of the Ruler of Kuwait intervened in the dispute between Kuwait and Iraq; that Hitler and Mussolini intervened in the Spanish Civil War; that the United States tried with no success to intervene in Cuba for the purpose of overthrowing Castro in April 1961; that it is improper for a British Minister to intervene in an American presidential election by publicly expressing a wish about the outcome. Here the meaning ranges from a campaign of conquest among weaker Powers, through taking part in a war or a dispute between other Powers, and taking part in a civil war, to attempts to overthrow the regime or influence the domestic affairs of another country. Winfield has distinguished usefully between (1) *internal* intervention: interference in the domestic affairs of another state; (2) *external* intervention: interference in the relations, usually hostile, of two or more other Powers; and (3) *punitive* intervention: measures such as pacific blockade adopted by one state against another to compel observance of treaty engagements or redress a breach of law.[1] But the distinction between internal and external intervention constantly breaks down. Russell's despatch of 27 October 1860, recognizing the Garibaldian revolution in Naples and the Papal States, was argued as an intervention on the side of the rebellious subjects against their rulers, but it was also an intervention against the King of the Two Sicilies and the Pope on the side of the King of Sardinia. Anglo-American intervention in Lebanon and Jordan in 1958 was designed to protect those countries from external dangers in Iraq and the UAR, but it also gave their regimes another lease of life against the internal pressure of Arab nationalism.

We may try to confine attention here to internal intervention, and understand it as unwelcome interference by one member of international society in the domestic affairs of another. Intervention is always unwelcome, because it implies coercion. If intervention is solicited from within the country intervened in, it shows that the country is divided, and the intervention will be unwelcome to one party or faction. If it is solicited by a faction out of power, as was regularly the case in Balkan states in the nineteenth century, and has been in Middle Eastern states in the twentieth, it is in order to get into power. In many cases the initiative probably lies with the intervener rather than with the nominal inviter, as it did in Hitler's relations with the Sudeten Germans. In some cases it is difficult to tell where the initiative lies, because intervener and inviters are united in a common loyalty and a common purpose; and these cases

[1] P. H. Winfield, in Lawrence, *Principles of International Law*, pp. 119–20.

illustrate a world in which intervention is the norm and the independence and frontiers of states are an irrelevance. The Greek government intervened regularly in Cyprus by propagandist inflammation of the Enosis movement, but who can say whether the Cypriots asked for this help or had it thrust upon them? There is the same uncertainty about the relationship between Soviet Russia and local Communist parties.

On the one side are statesmen and publicists who deny the right of intervention. Wolff in the mid-eighteenth century was apparently the first jurist absolutely to prohibit intervention, as violating the natural liberty of nations.[1] Canning in 1823, at the time of the French intervention in Spain, laid down the doctrine that no ground for intervention is given by disturbances confined within the territory of a state, and not leading (as the French Revolution had done) to subversion or conquest abroad.[2] The tradition of positivist international law is represented by the classic treatise of W. E. Hall: 'No intervention is legal, except for the purpose of self-preservation, unless a breach of the law as between states has taken place, or unless the whole body of civilized states have concurred in authorizing it.'[3] But the ambiguities of Canning's own policy towards Latin America, Portugal and Greece, and the exceptions given by Hall, are enough to show the difficulties of denying absolutely a right of intervention. Cobden's political non-interventionism probably attained a more perfect consistency, but then it was the obverse of a gospel of unrestricted commercial interventionism.

On the other side are statesmen and publicists who consider intervention, in principle, as a continuing and universal duty. This duty can be derived from two opposite grounds: either the belief that the society of states ought to be revolutionized and made uniform, or the belief that it ought to be preserved as it is and kept uniform. In both views, the independence and separateness of states is less important than the homogeneity of international society, and the inviolability of frontiers is subordinated to the illimitability of truth. Thus the doctrine of the *Vindiciae contra Tyrannos*, that the Church is recommended and given in charge to all Christian princes in general, and to every one of them in particular, 'insomuch that if a prince who has undertaken the care of a portion of the church, as

---

[1] *Jus Gentium Methodo Scientifica Pertractatum* (first published 1749), sections 255–7.
[2] E.g. memorandum of March 31, 1823 (*British and Foreign State Papers*, vol. x, p. 66).
[3] *International Law*, pp. 343–4.

H

that of Germany and England, and, notwithstanding, neglect and forsake another part that is oppressed, and which he might succour, he doubtless abandons the church, Christ having but only one spouse, which the prince is so bound to preserve and defend, that she be not violated or corrupted in any part, if it be possible'.[1] Thus, Mazzini's argument that the principle of non-intervention could only be justified if the international system that is not to be intervened against is itself already perfectly just, which it isn't.

'What does this non-intervention principle in real fact now mean? It means precisely this—Intervention on the wrong side; Intervention by all who choose, and are strong enough, to put down free movements of peoples against corrupt governments. It means co-operation of despots against peoples, but no co-operation of peoples against despots.'[2]

Mazzini's doctrine has become the doctrine of the anti-colonialist campaign in the United Nations. The Latin American states have every reason to fear intervention in one form from the United States, but they have never abandoned a general theory of intervention, in earlier days *inter se*, and latterly in respect of the world at large.

'On the one hand we have the clear danger of intervention', said the Costa Rican delegate in the General Assembly in 1953; 'on the other, international indifference in the face of tyranny, genocide, the violation of rights, the fact that sovereignty is being snatched out of the hands of the people. . . . Non-intervention, in that extreme form, sometimes assumes the attributes of intervention against the people. . . . My country believes in collective surveillance.'[3]

The doctrine of the Troppau Protocol of 1820, which proclaimed a general right of the Holy Alliance to intervene anywhere to put down revolutionary manifestations, is the obverse of this, and illustrates a corresponding theory of international right. Similar ideas were expressed in the resolution entitled 'The Preservation and Defence of Democracy in America' adopted by the Bogota Conference of the Organization of American States in 1948, and found a

---

[1] Junius Brutus, *A Defence of Liberty against Tyrants*, ed. H. J. Laski (Bell, 1924), p. 217.
[2] 'Non-Intervention', *Life and Writings of Joseph Mazzini* (Smith, Elder, 1870), vol. vi, pp. 305–6.
[3] U.N. General Assembly, 469th meeting, December 8, 1953 (*Plenary Meetings*, 8th session, p. 438).

more definite form in the provisions for intervening to prevent subversion in the Manila Treaty of 1954 setting up SEATO. These ideas were clearly if unfortunately expressed by Spruille Braden, a former US ambassador to Argentina, in a speech in 1953:

'I should like to underscore that because Communism is so blatantly an international and not an internal affair, its suppression, even by force, in an American country, by one or more of the other republics, would not constitute an intervention in the internal affairs of the former.'[1]

At the Caracas Conference of the OAS, in March 1954, there was embarrassed discussion of the supposed inalienable right of each American state to set up its own form of government, and whether non-intervention logically followed if an American state chose Communism. Dulles replied: 'The slogan of non-intervention can plausibly be invoked and twisted to give immunity to what is in reality flagrant intervention'.[2] Three months late, the United States intervened or non-intervened to overthrow the government of Guatemala: intervening in substance by arming the rebels and the countries which gave them a base, non-intervening in form by pretending it was a simple revolt of Guatemalans against Guatemalans. The Guatemalan government appealed to the Security Council. The United States proposed that the matter should be referred to the appropriate regional organization, the OAS. The USSR vetoed the proposal, arguing that wherever aggression occurred it was the Security Council's responsibility to deal with it and that Central America was no exception. Colombia replied that the power of veto should not be accepted in the western hemisphere because it meant intervention by Communism. When Talleyrand was asked in 1832 to explain the real meaning of the word non-intervention, he replied: 'C'est un mot métaphysique, et politique, qui signifie à peu près le même chose qu'intervention.'[3] This was the practical judgment of a diplomatist in a generation which had explored the problems of intervention and non-intervention with more conscious thoroughness than any before or since. Without adopting the tacit premises of the remark, one may recognize that it is very difficult to give precision to the terms intervention and non-intervention, and very difficult to erect either of them into a theoretical norm of international conduct.

[1] Speech at Dartmouth College, March 12, 1953 (*New York Times*, March 13, 1953).
[2] Speech of March 8, 1954 (*New York Times*, March 9, 1954).
[3] Thomas Raikes, *A Portion of the Journal* (Longmans, 1856), vol. i, p. 106.

Between the opposing positions of non-interventionism and inter-ventionism, there is a central doctrine of what might be called the moral interdependence of peoples, which its holders would claim to be based on the requirements of social existence and true to the constant experience of diplomatic life. 'States are not isolated bodies,' as Webster has put it simply, 'but part of an international community and the events which take place in each of them must be of interest and concern to all the rest.'[1] The doctrine might for convenience be reduced to the following points:

1. That intervention, in the sense of unwelcome interference by one member of the community of states in the internal affairs of another, is an occasional necessity in international relations, because of the permanent instability of the balance of power and the permanent inequality in the moral development of its members.

2. That it is an unfortunate necessity, because it conflicts with the right of independence; and it should be the exception rather than the rule.

3. That in a moral scale, to maintain the balance of power is a better reason for intervening than to uphold civilized standards, but to uphold civilized standards is a better reason than to maintain existing governments.

These principles postulate the existence of an international society of which states are the immediate but men the ultimate members. In such a society, there will be social duties not only towards the states but also towards the individuals whom the states represent and for whom they exist. Moreover, the members will have the capacity in some degree to reconcile their own interests with those of others and to attain to the idea of a common interest. 'Kings,' said Grotius, 'in addition to the particular care of their own state, are also burdened with a general responsibility for human society',[2] and the idea has been repeated in many ways. Intervention, therefore, may present itself as an exercise, not simply of the right of self-preservation, but of the duty of fellow-feeling and co-operation. Seen in this light, the theory of the rightful occasions for intervention falls at once into the same pattern as the theory of the just causes of war.

If the existence of international society is conceded, it might indeed be supposed, *prima facie*, that intervention would play a greater part internationally than domestically, simply because the organization of international society is more rudimentary than that of domestic society. It is often argued that international society is in a condition analogous to that of English society at any time before the

[1] Sir Charles Webster, *The Foreign Policy of Palmerston* (Bell, 1951), vol. i, p. 99.
[2] *De Jure Belli ac Pacis*, book II, ch. xx, section xliv.1.

legal innovations of Henry II, with customary law, great local con-
centrations of power, no effective executive, no legislature in the
modern sense, and a rudimentary judiciary. But the frankpledge
system, and the duty of pursuing felons from hundred to hundred by
hue and cry (if it ever existed), were in modern terms intolerable
invasions of the independence of individuals. It might be true to say
that the possibility of non-intervention among the members of any
society varies with the effectiveness of its police system.

After the decline of intervention on religious pretexts (except in the
relations between Russia and Turkey) two broad grounds of intervention remained generally accepted: the interests of the balance of
power and the interests of humanity. From the middle of the seventeenth century it was a maxim of European diplomacy that intervention to uphold the balance of power was necessary and just. But
ambiguity arose, inasmuch as it has always been universally conceded that the duty of self-preservation can confer a right of intervention, and most states seek their preservation by pursuing the
balance of power. The various eighteenth century examples of intervention—the Partition Treaties for settling the Spanish succession,
and the repeated interference of the Great Powers in the affairs of
Sweden, Poland, Geneva or Holland—were in the last resort
justified by reference to the balance of power, but the franker language would be that of commercial and political interest. Thus
Vergennes wrote:

'Les insurgents que je chasse de Genève sont les agents de l'Angle-
terre, tandis que les insurgents américains sont nos amis pour long-
temps. J'ai traité les uns et les autres, non en raison de leurs systèmes
politiques, mais en raison de leurs dispositions pour la France.
Voilà ma raison d'Etat.'[1]

When one compares the rather loftier language of Castlereagh, the
greater sense he gives of being aware of the interests of the community of nations as a whole, it is impossible not to connect it with
the conception of the balance of power that pervaded all his thought.
When Castlereagh came to formulate a British doctrine of intervention against the interventionism of the Holy Alliance, it was the
maintenance of the balance of power as against a guarantee of
regimes that provided implicitly his point of difference. 'The only safe
Principle is that of the Law of Nations—That no State has a right
to endanger its neighbours by its internal Proceedings, and that if it
does, provided they exercise a sound discretion, their right of inter-

[1] Sorel, *L'Europe et la Révolution Française*, vol. i, p. 66.

ference is clear.'[1] In later statements he threw the emphasis the other way, not on the existence of the right but on the rarity of the occasions for exercising it.

'It should be clearly understood,' he wrote in the Circular of January 19, 1821, 'that no Government can be more prepared than the British Government is, to uphold the right of any State or States to interfere, where their own immediate security, or essential interest, are seriously endangered by the internal transactions of another State. But, as they regard the assumption of such right, as only to be justified by the strongest necessity, and to be limited and regulated thereby; they cannot admit that this right can receive a general and indiscriminate application to all revolutionary movements, without reference to their immediate bearing upon some particular State of States, or be made prospectively the basis of an Alliance. They regard its exercise as an exception to general principles, of the greatest value and importance, and as one that only properly grows out of the circumstances of the special case; but they, at the same time, consider, that exceptions of this description never can, without the utmost danger, be so far reduced to rule, as to be incorporated into the ordinary diplomacy of States, or into the institutes of the law of nations.'[2]

This language has been criticized from the one side as lacking in generous sympathy and readiness to offer help to the constitutional cause abroad; it has been criticized from the other side, as by Westlake, in that it failed sufficiently to repudiate, as Canning afterwards did, 'intervention for self-preservation against the mere contagion of principles'.[3] Castlereagh was trying to minimize the breach with Britain's allies which Canning delighted to widen; he had a greater sense than Canning of the interdependence of states and greater experience in reconciling their interests. The collective interventions of the Concert of Europe to maintain the balance of power, in the Belgian question and repeatedly in Turkey, were in the spirit of Castlereagh rather than Canning.[4]

[1] Memorandum of October 19, 1818: Temperley and Penson, *Foundations of British Policy*, p. 44. 'It was a private document, never intended for formal communication, far less for publication, and may be taken as expressing Castlereagh's most sincere views' (*ibid.*, p. 38).

[2] Sir Charles Webster, *The Foreign Policy of Castlereagh 1815-1822* (Bell, 2nd edition, 1934), pp. 322-3.

[3] *Collected Papers*, p. 125.

[4] In the editions of Oppenheim's *International Law* issued after 1919, the sections dealing with the balance of power as a ground for intervention have been replaced by others treating of collective intervention under the Covenant of the League, and later the U.N. Charter.

Humanitarian grounds for intervention were conceived first of all in terms of protection against tyranny, and the right of intervention followed the right of rebellion. Here is one of the explicit links between constitutionalist political theory and the tradition of international theory under present consideration. Grotius was surprisingly cautious about the right of rebellion (perhaps, as Carlyle suggested,[1] because he was a Roman lawyer and a political refugee in the French monarchy): he refused to allow oppressed subjects to take up arms in their own behalf, but permitted a foreign Power to intervene for them, as an application of the principle of trusteeship: 'quod uni non licet, alteri pro eodem liceri potest.'[2] Vattel's pattern of ideas is in many respects different, but it is part of his charm (and no doubt of his lasting influence) that he contains inconsistent arguments that can be used to support contradictory policies. He follows his master Wolff in a general condemnation of intervening, but then adds:

'Mais si le Prince, attaquant les Lois fondamentales, donne à son peuple un légitime sujet de lui résister; si la Tyrannie, devenue insupportable, soulève la Nation; toute Puissance étrangère est en droit de sécourir un peuple opprimé, qui lui demande son assistance . . . Quand un peuple prend avec raison les armes contre un oppresseur, il n'y a que justice et générosité à sécourir de braves gens, qui défendent leur Liberté. Toutes les fois donc que les choses en viennent à une Guerre Civile, les Puissances étrangères peuvent assister celui des deux partis, qui leur paroît fondé en justice.'[3]

Vattel was a quiet Neuchâtelois who admired England and the Glorious Revolution; but in these words he unintentionally foreshadowed much of the international experience of the nineteenth and twentieth centuries. This passage was quoted with some glee by Russell in his despatch of October 27, 1860, supporting the overthrow of the Neapolitan and Papal governments.[4]

In the history of nineteenth century intervention, humanitarianism became increasingly the prime motive, as the balance of power was always the limiting one. The joint intervention in 1827 by France, Britain and Russia in favour of the Greek insurgents was justified first by reference to the material damage to nationals of the intervening Powers, and only secondly by 'the sentiment of humanity and interest in the repose of Europe'.[5] But when Britain and France

---

[1] A. J. Carlyle, *Political Liberty* (Clarendon Press, 1941), p. 95.
[2] *De Jure Belli ac Pacis*, book II, ch. xxv, section viii.3.
[3] *Le Droit des Gens*, book II, ch. iv, section 56.
[4] Temperley and Penson, *Foundations of British Policy*, pp. 223–4.
[5] Treaty of London, 1827, preamble.

withdrew their ambassadors from Naples in 1856 and staged a naval demonstration, it was because Ferdinand II refused to listen to their advice about his prison system. The Russian Government remonstrated that, 'To endeavour to obtain from the King of Naples concessions concerning the internal government of his state by threats, or by a menacing demonstration, is a violent usurpation of his authority, an attempt to govern in his stead; it is an open declaration of the right of the strong over the weak'; and some jurists support the condemnation.[1] The collective intervention in the Lebanon in 1860 to stop the massacres of the Maronites by the Druses was a greater and longer exercise of force, but is described by Lawrence as 'destitute of technical legality, but . . . morally right and even praiseworthy to a high degree'.[2] Lansdowne's commission to Casement, a consular official, to enquire into the administration of the Congo Free State, and the publication of his report, is another example of humanitarian intervention that has received the general approval of posterity. In 1902 the persecution of the Jews in Rumania led the signatories of the Treaty of Berlin to enforce the articles protecting the Balkan minorities. The United States was not a signatory, but John Hay wrote that though not entitled to invoke the treaty, she 'must insist upon the principles therein set forth, because these are principles of law and eternal justice'.[3] It will be noted that all such historical examples of intervention show the powerful correcting the weak. The moral interdependence of peoples has never been so strong , nor the circumstances so favourable, that there has been collective intervention to suppress the iniquities of a Great Power. Hence one may possibly feel a certain satisfaction that the United Nations, for all the doctrinaire extravagances of its interventionism, has accidentally developed into the first international organization that has been able to subject the Great Powers to systematic nagging.

4. INTERNATIONAL MORALITY

The morality of international politics is a vast and embracing subject, but it is here that there will be perhaps more agreement on a pattern of ideas that represents Western values. In this paper it is only possible to comment briefly on two intertwined elements from that complex: the place of the individual conscience in international politics, and the notion of ethical limits to political action.

The school of American realists in political theory who acknow-

---

[1] Hall, *International Law*, p. 344, n. 2.
[2] *Principles of International Law*, p. 128.
[3] De Visscher, *Theory and Reality in Public International Law*, pp. 122–3.

ledge Reinhold Niebuhr as their patriarch are accustomed to argue that it is only in national life and institutions that ideals such as justice, freedom and equality have a concrete meaning.

'Since nations in the present anarchic world society tend to be repositories of their own morality,' says Kenneth Thompson, 'the ends-means formula has prevailed as an answer to the moral dilemma, for undeniably it is a concealed but essential truth that nations tend to create their own morality.'[1]

The argument has been used more trenchantly by Morgenthau in words that have caused some debate:

'There is a profound and neglected truth hidden in Hobbes's extreme dictum that the state creates morality as well as law and that there is neither morality nor law outside the state . . . For above the national societies there exists no international society so integrated as to be able to define for them the concrete meaning of justice or equality, as national societies do for their individual members.'[2]

Morgenthau has interpreted this passage against possible misunderstanding, and perhaps lessened its force, by saying that the operative words are 'Hobbes's *extreme* dictum' rather than 'a profound and neglected truth'.[3] Nevertheless it is clear that Hobbes's doctrine that effective social power is antecedent to morality and law has acquired a new cogency and relevance in our lifetime. E. H. Carr's *Twenty Years Crisis*, which has dominated the study of international relations in Britain since 1939, is essentially a brilliant restatement of the Hobbesian themes. The new kingdom of the fairies that seduces the intelligence of men is not the Roman Church but the League of Nations, which is none other than the ghost of the Pax Britannica, sitting crowned upon the grave thereof, and the principal old wives who circulate its fables are President Wilson, Lord Cecil, Professors Toynbee and Zimmern, and the Winston Churchill of *Arms and the Covenant*.

To the student who asks, where else can one look for the concrete meaning of ideals than in national institutions—or in the life and institutions of some single state which is seen to embody the movement of history and the destiny of mankind—the ultimate answer

---

[1] Kenneth W. Thompson, *Political Realism and the Crisis of World Politics* (Princeton University Press, 1960), p. 137.
[2] Hans J. Morgenthau, *In Defense of the National Interest* (Knopf, 1951), p. 34.
[3] See his letter in *International Affairs*, October 1959, p. 502.

seems to be 'In the individual who defies the state'. At its noblest, this defiance may be embodied in the just man who is thrown into prison, scourged and racked, and after every kind of torment is impaled; at its humblest, it may be in the man who, having watched the frenzy of the multitude, keeps his own way, like the traveller who takes shelter under a wall from a driving storm of dust, and seeing lawlessness spreading on all sides, is content if he can keep his hands clean from iniquity while his life lasts.[1] (There are some people, with experience of the storms of nationalist politics in the twentieth century, who find the latter passage the most profound and piercing in the *Republic* for the ordinary man.) Two ideas are bound up in this answer. There is a positive denial that ideals are concretely embodied in social institutions, and the strength of the denial grows in proportion to the strength and exclusiveness of the claim. And this denial is made, not in the name of some political or social institutions against others, but in the name of the non-political against them all. Thus the pretensions of existing states may be repudiated in the name of the aspirations of the multitude of individuals who are the ultimate (but disfranchised) members of international society; but this does not mean that if their aspirations were fulfilled in the establishment of a world state, the world state would become the concrete embodiment of justice. In its turn it would be subject to the same repudiation in the name of the non-political. A world state more than others might be likely to embody a fundamental lawlessness that impaled the absolutely just man and compelled others to behave like travellers in a duststorm.

It seems that these ideas cohere with the pattern of thought I have tried to sketch. They contain the paradox, that the health of the political realm is only maintained by conscientious objection to the political. While Tawney delivered the Burge Memorial Lecture in 1949, choosing as his subject 'The Western Political Tradition', he made this point in language of characterictically inspissated grandeur:

'That denial of the finality of human institutions is both for practice and for theory a key position. It makes it not a paradox to assert that the most significant characteristic of the western political tradition—its peril, but also its glory and salvation—consists in a quality which, from Socrates to the least of those who have resisted dictators, has drawn its nourishment from sources so profound as to cause the word 'political' to be an inadequate expression of the obligations felt to be imposed by it.'[2]

[1] *Republic*, 361–2, 496 C-E.
[2] R. H. Tawney, *The Western Political Tradition* (S.C.M. Press, 1949), p. 16.

It is clear that the natural law tradition is the soil out of which these ideas have sprung. In his paper on 'Natural Law', Donald Mackinnon found the continued vitality of the natural law ethic in the encouragement it may give to ordinary men to criticize or even disobey their rulers. But he has a sentence which it may be permissible to gloss. 'Those who are in government,' he says, with the supposed exigencies of defence policy in mind, 'are inevitably caught up in the running of a machine which they find running one way, and whose history they feel themselves bound to defend'.[1] He may not have intended to suggest that the distinction between governors and governed corresponds to the distinction between *raison d'état* and moral sensitivity. For it would be equally true to say that those who are in government are inevitably more aware of the practical complexities of every political decision than their constituents can be, and probably more aware of the moral ambiguities. The history of democratic government has as much evidence of enlightened governments hampered by the folly and ignorance of the public and the selfishness of vested interests, as it has of the plain people judging right on broad considerations of humanity and justice against narrow-minded governments. The public is still the greatest of all sophists, and by and large there is a congruity between peoples and governments. The individual defying the state is not to be identified with the Campaign for Nuclear Disarmament demonstrating against the government, although the CND may contain some who are potentially individuals defying the state. For the CND is not the repudiation of politics in the name of the non-political, so much as the assertion of an illusory or ill-considered alternative within the realm of the political; and to this extent it is itself but one of the heads of the many-headed beast.

The vitality of the natural law ethic might be looked for, not only in the encouragement it may give to ordinary men to criticize their rulers, but also in the encouragement it may give to rulers themselves to break free from political categories, to deny the finality of human institutions. The conscientious objection of politicians has perhaps been less studied by political philosophers than the conscientious objection of subjects, yet, on the view we are considering, it will not be less necessary to the health of society. What we are concerned with here is not so much the doctrine of natural law (whatever that is), as a certain ethical temper which may be regarded as its residue or hangover. Cicero's one eternal unchangeable law, the same at Athens as at Rome, the same in the future as now, may be an archaic fancy, or the archaic expression of something true.[2] But 'dis te minorem quod geris,

[1] See above, p. 86.
[2] *De Republica*, book iii, ch. 22.

imperas' has had more continuing power.[1] It is echoed in Burke's

'Among precautions against ambition, it may not be amiss to take one precaution against our *own*. I must fairly say, I dread our *own* power, and our *own* ambition; I dread our being too much dreaded'.[2]

It is echoed in Lincoln's Second Inaugural. It directly inspired Kipling's *Recessional*. It is reflected in the sense common to politicians as different as Bismarck, Gladstone, Salisbury and Churchill, of being in various modes and with varying degrees of humility the instruments of Providence.

It might be thought enough to say of the natural law ethic that it survives in an awareness of the moral significance and the moral context of all political action. But the moral context is focused more precisely where it is seen as imposing prohibitions on political action —at the point where the politically expedient and the morally permissible come into conflict. Thus the doctrine of the just war (which is essentially connected with the complex of ideas we are considering) includes the principle that military necessity is itself subject to moral limits. Is political necessity similarly limited, and if so can this limitation be illustrated in the concrete case? What is to be answered to the sceptic who crudely says, 'Show me a single example of your natural law ethic restraining a statesman from a course of action which was politically expedient'?

The question may be made more pointed by reference to antiquity. The moralistic repertoire of Roman education contained celebrated examples, supposedly historical, of the ethical veto on political action. There is the story Plutarch tells in the lives both of Themistocles and Aristides. After the withdrawal of Xerxes and the defeated Persians from Greece, the allied Greek fleet moved north to Pagasae on the Thessalian coast. Themistocles told the Athenians in the assembly that he had a proposal that would tend greatly to their interests and security, but of such a nature that it could not be made public. The assembly instructed him to tell it to Aristides, and if Aristides approved, to carry it out. Themistocles told Aristides that his project was to set fire to the allied fleet in harbour, which would give the Athenians the mastery of Greece. Aristides returned to the assembly and reported that Themistocles' plan was exceedingly advantageous and exceedingly dishonourable; 'on which the Athenians commanded

[1] Horace, *Odes*, iii, 6.
[2] *Remarks on the Policy of the Allies* (*Works*, vol. i, pp. 602–3). Cf. Wordsworth, letter to Captain Pasley, March 28, 1811, in *Tract on the Convention of Cintra*, ed. A. V. Dicey (Milford, 1915), p. 237.

Themistocles to think no farther or it'.[1] There is a similar story told of the Roman general Fabricius, who, as Cicero says, 'was to our city what Aristides was to Athens'. Fabricius disdainfully rejected a proposal for poisoning the invader Pyrrhus which was put to him by a deserter from Pyrrhus' camp, and handed the man over to Pyrrhus. Cicero comments that if we consult the vulgar conception of expediency, this one deserter would have put an end to a wasting invasion, but it would have been at the price of lasting disgrace.[2] Each of these tales has been subjected to realistic modern critique. Hume discusses the Themistoclean story, to illustrate how general ideas have less power over the imagination than particular ideas. If Themistocles' proposal had been made public, he argues, instead of being made known only under the general notion of advantage, it is difficult to conceive that the assembly would have rejected it.[3] Machiavelli comments on the Fabricius story with less subtlety, saying (quite unhistorically) that the revelation of Fabricius's generosity made Pyrrhus quit Italy, which Roman arms had not been able to do; so ethics paid off politically. He adds by contrast that the Romans hounded Hannibal to death, but they hated him more than they did Pyrrhus.[4]

Modern history does not seem to offer, even in legend, such copy-book examples of rectitude in international relations. Only two similar instances come to mind. One is Fox, when as Foreign Secretary in 1806 an approach was made to him for the assassination of Napoleon, instantly informing Talleyrand of it. There can be little doubt that Fabricius was in Fox's mind. The other is an incident at the Teheran Conference described in Churchill's Memoirs:

'Stalin, as Hopkins recounts, indulged in a great deal of "teasing" of me, which I did not at all resent until the Marshal entered in a genial manner upon a serious and even deadly aspect of the punishment to be inflicted upon the Germans. The German General Staff, he said, must be liquidated. The whole force of Hitler's mighty armies depended upon about fifty thousand officers and technicians. If these were rounded up and shot at the end of the war German military strength would be exterminated. On this I thought it right to say,

---

[1] Plutarch, *Vita Themistoclis*, ch. 20; cf. *Vita Aristidis*, ch. 22. The story may be a dramatizing of the trick by which Themistocles deceived Sparta over the fortification of Athens: Diodorus, book xi, ch. 42; Grote, *History of Greece*, ch. 44 (Everyman edition, vol. v, p. 346, n. 3); A. W. Gomme, *Historical Commentary on Thucydides*, vol. i (Clarendon Press, 1945), p. 260.
[2] *De Officiis*, book iii, ch. 22. Cf. Livy, book xiii.
[3] *A Treatise of Human Nature*, book II, part iii, section vi.
[4] *Discourses*, book iii, ch. 20.

"The British Parliament and public will never tolerate mass executions. Even if in war passion they allowed them to begin they would turn violently against those responsible after the first butchery had taken place. The Soviets must be under no delusion on this point".
'Stalin, however, perhaps only in mischief, pursued the subject. "Fifty thousand," he said, "must be shot." I was deeply angered. "I would rather," I said, "be taken out into the garden here and now and be shot myself than sully my own and my country's honour by such infamy."
'At this point the President intervened. He had a compromise to propose. Not fifty thousand should be shot, but only forty-nine thousand. By this he hoped, no doubt, to reduce the whole matter to ridicule. Eden also made signs and gestures intended to reassure me that it was all a joke. But now Elliot Roosevelt rose in his place at the end of the table and made a speech, saying how cordially he agreed with Marshal Stalin's plan and how sure he was that the United States Army would support it. At this intrusion I got up and left the table, walking off into the next room, which was in semi-darkness. I had not been there a minute before hands were clapped upon my shoulders from behind, and there was Stalin, with Molotov at his side, both grinning broadly, and eagerly declaring that they were only playing, and that nothing of a serious character had entered their heads. Stalin has a very captivating manner when he chooses to use it, and I never saw him do so to such an extent as at this moment. Although I was not then, and am not now, fully convinced that all was chaff and there was no serious intent lurking behind, I consented to return, and the rest of the evening passed pleasantly.'[1]

If it were true that modern history does not contain such clear-cut instances as classical antiquity of the moral veto on political action, the reason might be that the conception of policy has changed. Perhaps modern Europe has acquired a moral sensitiveness, and an awareness of the complexities of politics, denied to a simpler civilization. The Greeks and Romans gave small thought to political ethics, still less to international ethics. It is striking that the civilization which invented political philosophy and political science gave so little attention to the relations between states. In so far as it had a conception of an international society, it was much simpler than that of modern Europe. Hellas for the Greeks was a community of blood and language and religion and way of life;[2] but the Greeks never developed the theory of a society of states mutually bound by legal

[1] *The Second World War*, vol. v, ch. xx, *ad fin.*
[2] Herodotus, book viii, ch. 144.

rights and obligations. There was no Greek Grotius. And the international experience of Rome, first in the consolidating of Italy, and then in the Mediterranean world at large, was that of conqueror, aggressive ally and patron of clients—never of equal intercourse between states. The true 'international law' of the Roman Republic was the fetial law; but since its principles were defensive, it was early circumvented and superseded by the expansionist principle of *fides Romana* pledged to threatened client-states.[1] If the Roman Empire is dated by external hegemony, not by the ending of civil war, it begins (as Polybius saw) at Pydna not at Actium. For the last century and a half of the Republic Rome had no diplomatic equal, and her foreign policy was analogous to that of the British in India after 1798, not to that of any Great Power in modern Europe. The *jus gentium*, which became identified with the law of nature and then presided over the origins of modern international law, was a collection of rules and principles common to Rome and to the Italian tribes from whom Rome's immigrants came, and constantly growing with the acquisition of new provinces. It was mainly concerned with the sphere of commercial law and law of contract. It began as a body of what in modern terms is called *private* international law, and developed into the common law of a universal empire; public international law between states represents a stage it never went through.

Such thought as the ancients gave to international ethics found little middle ground between the statesman's personal honour on the one side, and on the other, the justification of what we should describe as humane action on grounds of pure expediency, such as the arguments Thucydides puts in the mouth of Diodotus against carrying out the Athenian decree for the destruction of Mytilene, the massacre of its men and the enslavement of its women and children.[2] Perhaps it is a characteristic of medieval and modern Europe that, in contrast to classical civilization, it has cultivated this middle ground, and developed the conception of a political morality distinct equally from personal morality and from *Realpolitik*. Cicero it is true reached the point of describing the administration of government as a trust, *tutela*, for the benefit of those entrusted to its care, not of these to whom it is entrusted;[3] but he was thinking of the class-struggles within the state, not of the field to which Burke extended the notion of trusteeship, still less of foreign relations. In the later Roman Empire the idea turns into paternalism, that the king must be a father to his subjects, consulting their interests and not living for himself. It

---

[1] E. Badian, *Foreign Clientelae* (Clarendon Press, 1958), pp. 31, 35, 68.
[2] Thucydides, book iii, chs. 42–8.
[3] *De Officiis*, book i, ch. 85.

might roughly be said that it was left for medieval thinkers to explore the doctrine that governments are stewards for their peoples and for future generations, having duties analogous to those of trustees; and for modern thinkers to explore the doctrine that these duties are owed, not only by each government to its subjects, but by one government to another, and by one people to another.

The cultivation of this middle ground, and the discovery of political morality, seem peculiarly related to Western values. Political morality is different from personal morality, as the moral duties of a trustee are different from those of one who acts on his own behalf. In the profoundest passage of the War Memoirs, Churchill reflects (like others before him) that the Sermon on the Mount is not the terms on which Ministers assume their responsibility of guiding states.[1] The incident in Teheran shows, however, that political ethics have their ultimate sanction in the personal ethics of the politician, and a nation's honour cannot rise higher than the personal honour of its representatives. But political morality is equally different from *raison d'état*, since it upholds the validity of the ethical in the realm of politics. It follows that the whole conception of policy is broadened and capable of being suffused with moral value. Political expedience itself has to consult the moral sense of those whom it will affect, and even combines with the moral sense of the politician himself. Thus it is softened into prudence, which is a moral virtue. The occasions for conscientious objection are diminished, since conscience has already had its say in the debate in which policy is shaped.

Therefore the characteristic fruit of the natural law ethic in modern politics is not so much the dramatic moral veto on political action (though this is always held, as it were, in reserve) as the discovery of an alternative positive policy which avoids the occasion of the veto— an *alternative* policy, because it embodies the notion of a middle course, of a permissible accommodation between moral necessity and practical demands. At the worst, the alternative rests on self-deception, and the search for it becomes the kind of supple casuistry that finds moral arguments to cover the dictates of interest of passion, of which their enemies accused the Jesuits or Cromwell or Gladstone. Thus Robert Dell's bitter description of Lord Halifax, when he attended the 101st session of the League Council in May 1938 to propose the recognition of Italian sovereignty over Ethiopia:

'Lord Halifax did not make a good impression at Geneva, where the tendency was to call him insincere. That, I am convinced, is unjust. He seems to me to be a mixture of the typical high-minded God-

---

[1] *The Second World War*, vol. i, ch. xvii, *ad fin.*

fearing English gentleman and a Jesuit moral theologian. He is, I should say, one of those over-scrupulous persons who never take any action without first having weighed the arguments for and against and convinced themselves that it is justified by the principles of moral theology, and usually succeed in finding a moral justification for any action they wish to take.'[1]

But at its best, the alternative policy is both a true alternative and a positive one, attaining justice or magnanimity or self-control. There are many examples in medieval and modern politics of restraint in the exercise of power, of refusal to exploit an advantage, where the motive seems to have been not the avoidance of moral self-condemnation, still less of awkward consequences, but the attainment of better relations. Such were St Louis' magnanimity to Henry III at the Treaty of Paris in 1259, or Castlereagh's and Wellington's magnanimity to France at the end of the Napoleonic War, or Gladstone's grant of independence to the Transvaal after Majuba, or perhaps Attlee's grant of independence to India. The moral evaluation of such policies requires, first of all, a careful examination of the language in which they were first privately formulated.[2] Thus it may appear that the arguments which Bismarck used against his king at Nikolsburg in 1866 for not imposing a severe peace on Austria did not spring from the natural law ethic but resembled those used by Diodotus in the Mytilenean debate.[3]

On the horizon of every discussion of the moral prohibition in politics there beckons the maxim, *Fiat justitia et pereat mundus*. If this is indeed first recorded as the motto of the Emperor Ferdinand I[4], it might be taken as one of the most profoundly paradoxical expressions of the modern international anarchy. The maxim has been applied in many different circumstances, and with many interpretations both of 'justice' and of 'the world perishing'. But on the whole it is not a formula that comes naturally to the representatives of the tradition we are considering. Robespierre in the debate on white supremacy in the French colonies in May 1791 crying 'Périssent les colonies si elles nous en coûtent l'honneur, la liberté'; George Hardinge, the Tory MP

---

[1] Robert Dell, *The Geneva Racket* (Hale, 1941), p. 137.
[2] It also requires, of course, consideration of the consequences of the policies, probably unforeseen and unforeseeable. But this raises different issues.
[3] *Gedanken und Erinnerungen*, ch. 20.
[4] Johannes Manlius, *Locorum Communium Collectanea* (Basel, 1563), vol. ii, p. 290; Julius Wilhelm Zincgref, *Der Teutschen Scharpfsinnige Kluge Sprüch, Apophthegmata genant* (Strassburg, 1628), p. 107. Rex Warner, in his two novels on the life of Julius Caesar, several times attributes this dictum to Cato the Younger, and calls it Stoic. For this attribution I can find no evidence.

for Old Sarum, saying 'Perish commerce, let the constitution live!' in the debate on the Traitorous Correspondence Bill in 1793; Milner's 'damn the consequences' speech in the Budget controversy of 1909— these belong to a different ethical style, perhaps because the criterion of repudiation is itself implicitly political. Or the maxim is used rhetorically, and without strict attention to the meaning of its second part. When the historian Freeman, at a public meeting in London in 1876 to express sympathy with the Balkan insurgents against Turkey, cried 'Perish the interests of England, perish our dominion in India, rather than that we should strike one blow or speak one word on behalf of the wrong against the right', it is not to be supposed that he envisaged these consequences, because he went on to argue that Constantinople was not on the path to India and that the Russians anyway were not threatening Constantinople.[1] No more did A. J. P. Taylor when he quoted Freeman's words and made them his own at a Caxton Hall meeting during the Suez crisis in August 1956; because he went on to argue that there was no need for the interests of England to perish because properly understood they did not conflict with the interests of Egypt.[2] It is indeed only since 1945 that it has been possible to imagine that the price of justice may literally be the ruin of the world. Sir Llewellyn Woodward referred to the translation of the maxim out of rhetoric into actuality in his Stevenson Memorial Lecture in London in 1955. 'What does this change signify? Does it mean that, for the rest of its poor duration, the human race must give up the attempt to establish and sustain justice, and must accept, century after century until the whole house crumbles in corruption, the triumph of wickedness in high places?'[3]

Fiat justitia et pereat mundus marks an extreme position. The opposite extreme has many landmarks, from the Athenian case in the Melian Dialogue to Fisher's dictum at the Hague Conference, 'If the welfare of England requires it, international agreements can go to the Devil', and Salandra's *sacro egoismo per l'Italia*. Between lies the moral sense we are considering. It can reach the point of uttering a moral prohibition in politics. But it assumes that moral standards can be upheld without the heavens falling. And it assumes that the fabric of social and political life will be maintained, without accepting the doctrine that to preserve it any measures are permissible. For it assumes that the upholding of moral standards will in itself tend to

[1] W. R. W. Stephens, *Life and Letters of Edward A. Freeman* (Macmillan, 1895), vol. ii, p. 113; cf. vol. i, p. 151.
[3] Speech of August 14, 1956 (*Arab News Letter*, Issue Nos. 12, 13, undated).
[2] E. L. Woodward, 'Some Reflections on British Policy, 1939-45', *International Affairs*, July 1955, p. 290.

strengthen the fabric of political life. These assumptions seem to lie within the province of philosophy of history, or belief in Providence, whither it is not the purpose of this paper to pursue them.

CHAPTER 6

THE BALANCE OF POWER

H. BUTTERFIELD

The idea of the balance of power is associated with the modern history of our part of the world, and envisages the political units of the Continent as forming what used to be called 'the European states-system'. On this theory, the whole order in Europe was a kind of terrestrial counterpart of the Newtonian system of astronomy. All the various bodies, the greater and the lesser powers, were poised against one another, each exercising a kind of gravitational pull on all the rest—and the pull of each would be proportionate to its mass, though its effect would be greatly reduced as it acted at a greater distance. When one of these bodies increased its mass, therefore—when, for some reason, France for example had an undue accession of strength—the rest could recover an equilibrium only by regrouping themselves, like sets of ballet dancers, making a necessary rectification in the distances, and producing new combinations. Otherwise, the overgrown power would swallow up the little ones near at hand, and become greater still—just as the moon would fall into the earth if there were no counteracting forces to offset the effect of gravity.

David Hume began his essay on 'The Balance of Power' with an imposing list of classical examples; and he has sometimes been taken as the authority for the assertion that the principle was familiar to the ancient world. He recognizes the fact that his view was seriously challenged in his own day, however; and it is clear to me that the examples often quoted to support his thesis do not quite meet the case. This is true of the passage of Polybius which Hume instances, and which, because it so excellently formulates one of the elements of the situation, is amongst the most famous historical texts on this subject. In it, Polybius applauds the ruler of Syracuse for helping the Carthaginians to resist the rise of Rome; and he puts forward the maxim: 'It is never right to help a power to acquire a predominance that will render it irresistible.'[1] I suppose that, if we to-day read our modern ideas into Polybius, we can say that in this thesis he is demanding, to say the least, that there shall be a distribution of power. But a passage of this kind would not (and historically it *did* not) suffice to communicate the idea of the balance of power to

[1] Polybius, book i, ch. 83, 4.

people unacquainted with the idea already.

In discussing the states of the ancient world, Hume makes reference to their way of 'shifting sides' sometimes in periods of conflict; but he knows that states change sides out of feelings of jealousy or a sense of emergency, and that it is merely our hindthought which so easily turns these policies into a doctrine of the balance of power. When people denied that the ancient world was aware of the doctrine, Hume replied that the Romans had never known of it, but the Greeks had possessed it, and the moderns had studied the history of the former while neglecting the latter. Rome, he says, had been helped in her rise to supremacy by the fact that the states of the Hellenistic World were unaware of the principle of the balance of power. What seems to surprise him is his discovery that the ancient writers had never called attention to this defect. From all this I should infer that the idea of the balance of power not only did not exist in the ancient world, but did not take its rise even from the modern study of ancient history. More than most of our basic political formulas, this one seems to come from the modern world's reflections on its own experience.

It is generally understood that the states of Renaissance Italy, like those of ancient Greece, formed a neat closed area in which the principle might be expected to develop. It provided an arena of limited size—something like a miniature states-system—a field of interacting forces such as can be envisaged for the most part in isolation. There is no doubt that, within such an arena, states will want to support the power of which they are less afraid against the power of which they are more afraid; so that interesting combinations are likely to be produced. At times, the governments in Renaissance Italy seemed to be playing with weights and counter-weights, and calculating, amongst their neighbours, the tipping of the scales. After the long struggle between Florence and Milan, it came to be seen (Hans Baron tells us) that the Venetians had been standing between the two belligerents, trying to secure first that the conflict should go on long enough to weaken both, and secondly that it should leave the two fairly equal in strength. We even meet with the word 'balance' on occasion, though we may wonder about the picture that was made of it, and the degree to which the notion was followed up. Since an idea can sometimes be illuminated by studying its negative, it may be useful to illustrate the effects of the absence of the doctrine of the balance of power. These can be seen even in the cases of Machiavelli and Guicciardini, who represent the crude beginnings of what might be called the science of international politics.

Machiavelli was shocked by the weakness of Italy's international position in his day. The tragedy of foreign invasion was one of his excuses for his enquiries into the science of politics. His own experience of public life is chiefly known to us by the records of his diplomatic missions. He devoted a great part of his study and reflection to problems connected with war. One would have expected his teachings about policy to be impressive, therefore, in the field of foreign affairs. But, though he is rightly famous for having established the beginnings of modern military science, his work seems to me to have been particularly weak on the diplomatic side. He always insisted on the importance of following the example of classical antiquity. Yet, for him as for other people, the ancient world proved a better quarry for military teaching than for maxims of international politics. He imagined that in his own day a kind of dictator might be needed to save Italy from the foreign invader; and I always feel that his friend Guicciardini had more diplomatic sense, and a better eye for the international scene. Guicciardini said that the way to save Italy from invasion was to take care that the powerful nation-states around her should be kept too busily occupied with one another elsewhere.

Machiavelli is weak in respect of the principle of the balance of power; and his weakness is all the more remarkable, his deficiency all the more clearly exposed, because his preoccupations ought to have drawn him to it. He had an unusual interest, even an obsessive interest, in one of the associated problems (an issue similar to that which Polybius was discussing in the passage to which I have referred), and he is responsible for awakening a wider interest in this particular problem—one which lasted throughout the sixteenth century. The point is worth examining, perhaps, because it illustrates the kind of thinking which men did before there was a current doctrine of the balance of power—a kind of thinking which was scarcely possible afterwards.

The problem and the controversy in question were ones which hung on the issue: what ought a state to do when its neighbours are at war, and one or other of these neighbours is going to increase its strength as a result of the war? It would hardly be possible in more recent times to approach this kind of theme without raising the whole issue of the balance of power. Neither Machiavelli nor his successors had any idea that the case could have any connection with a notion of the balance of power, and that the debate on the whole subject would ultimately be subsumed in discussions of the balance. Machiavelli, however, merely treats the topic as a question of the wisdom of remaining or not remaining neutral when one's neighbours are at war. In fact, in his most famous book he gives himself away in a still more significant manner. He deals with the matter under the curious chapter-heading: 'How a prince must act in order to gain reputation.'[1] Elsewhere, also, he tends repeatedly to treat this issue as one which primarily involves the mere question of prestige. On one occasion he says that you had better be sure to be on the winning side, though he knows that the victor may be ungrateful at the finish; but he holds (though it is unlike him to entertain such an illusion) that this will not usually be the case. What he is really sure about, really insistent about, is that both parties will hate or despise the neighbour who has merely remained neutral while they them-selves have been at war with one another. (There is one occasion on which he advises an alliance with France, because France is likely to win, at any rate if she secures this alliance; though he adds that France, even if she wins, will be more tolerable as a victor-Power than the other party can be expected to be.)[2] He comes nearest to Polybius when he says in one place that 'a prince ought never to make common cause with one more powerful than himself with the object of injuring another, unless necessity forces him to it'. I am not sure that these various ideas are very acute and I am very doubtful that they can be squared with one another. On the kind of issue which seems to me to distinguish ancient from modern discussions of foreign policy, I should regard Machiavelli as standing with both feet in the ancient world. I think, therefore, that we ought not to attach too much significance to the fact that, at least on one occasion, Machiavelli did make reference to the existence of a balance in Italy.

His younger contemporary, Guicciardini, has a similar interest in the question of the wisdom of remaining neutral when one's neighbour's are at war. He is more subtle than Machiavelli here, and as usual sees that there is a further range of considerations to be taken into account. He writes, for example:

'To remain neutral when others are at war is a good thing for a state that is powerful; for such a state need not be afraid, whichever side may win. It can preserve itself without difficulty and it is in a position to gain profit from the disorders afflicting the others.'

Neutrality is dangerous, however, for a power that is weak, he says. It merely results in your finding yourself ultimately at somebody else's mercy. Neutrality is most dangerous of all if it is the result of

[1] *The Prince*, ch. xxi.
[2] Letter to F. Vettori, December 1514 (*Opere* (Firenze, Conti, 1818-21), vol. x, pp. 199–211).

irresolution, and this is what often happens in the case of republics, where opinion tends to be divided. In this case, even the belligerent who was wanting you to be neutral, would be unable to feel sure of you, so that both parties would be left dissatisfied.[1] If you make alliance with either of the belligerents, he says in one place, your fears are at least reduced to one; for all that you have to worry about is the possible victory of the other party. Neither Machiavelli nor Guicciardini seems to me to be very interesting or profound on this issue; and I have the feeling that there is something archaic in their handling of the problem, because they are so constricted in regard to time and in regard to place. They are thinking of an *ad hoc* decision at the outbreak of a war, without reference to diplomatic action in its continuity, and in its long-term aspects. At the same time they fail to consider the overall international scene, the general disposition of forces in the world.

Yet it was Guicciardini, who ultimately made the crucial advance and gave the first vivid picture of the balance of power. He did it in an account of the political situation in Italy before the death of Lorenzo de' Medici in 1492; and the passage occurs in the very first pages of his *History of Italy*—a part of the work which only recently has been discovered to belong to a late date, that is to say, the year 1537. According to Guicciardini, Lorenzo de' Medici, the ruler of Florence, decided that his city would be endangered if any one of the major powers of Italy succeeded in achieving further aggrandizement. He determined therefore that the affairs of Italy should be kept in balance—one side not more weighted than another; and for this purpose, he saw that it was necessary to have peace. The King of Naples also wanted peace, and wanted to prevent changes in the Italian peninsula. The ruler of Milan knew that he, too, had more to fear than to gain by any disturbance of the existing situation. These important Italian powers came together, therefore, and formed a combination which proved strong enough to discourage foreign invaders, strong enough also to check the Venetians, who were greatly feared at this time. And, though it is important to note that they were not sincere in their friendship with one another, their system did achieve the object they had in view. Indeed, almost all the minor principalities of Italy came in to swell the alliance, we are told; and this makes us raise our eyebrows a little, provoking the question whether it really did represent a 'balance' of power. In a profound sense, it was genuinely a balance that Guicciardini set out to describe,

---

[1] *Ricordi politici e civili*, no. lxviii; cf. nos. ccxxxvii and ccxxxviii (*Opere Inedite di Francesco Guicciardini* (Firenze, Barbèra, Bianchi, 1857-58), vol. i, pp. 110–11, 170).

and the crucial evidence for this is a significant section of this descriptive piece. He wrote of these Powers:

'Since they were moved by mutual jealousy . . . they were unremitting in the watch that they kept on one another's movements, deranging one another's plans whenever they thought that a partner was going to increase his dominion or prestige. And all this did not make the peace any less stable, but rather made the powers more alert and more ready to bring about the immediate extinction of all those sparks that might start a fire. Everything was so disposed and counter-balanced that not only was there no fear of change in the present—it was difficult to imagine what counsels or dynasties or armaments could succeed in disturbing such a peaceful order in the future.'[1]

The historical accuracy of this particular picture of late fifteenth-century Italy is not the issue that concerns us at the moment. In this—perhaps the most famous of all literary passages on the subject of the balance of power—we have the distinct impression of a system of forces which has been brought to an equilibrium. It is not a perfect picture but it is remarkable for a reason which Francis Bacon particularly noted—namely, the suggestion of nervous tension throughout the system—the various principalities not really trusting one another, but jealously watching one another's every move, diplomacy being unremittingly awake, and the whole still serving the purpose of peace. Guicciardini insists on the point: he says that Florence could not have kept the system in balance if she had not 'shown the greatest diligence in watching every turn of events, however small.' At a later date, Francis Bacon particularly caught up this point. He talked of princes 'keeping due sentinel'.[2]

Guicciardini painted an interesting scene—a particular situation existing in Italy towards the end of the fifteenth century—but we must not imagine that he expounded a general theory of balance, or that the doctrine now became current in the world. In fact, from the time of the Renaissance, the reference to a 'balance' in international affairs generally shows that something was lacking—the real appreciation of the doctrine had just been missed or the formulation of it went wrong. At the time of the Renaissance the French diplomat and memoir-writer, Philip de Commynes, described France as confronted by England, England as set off against the Scots, Spain

[1] *Storia d'Italia*, book I, ch. i.
[2] 'Of Empire', first published 1612 in the second edition of *Essays* (*Works of Francis Bacon*, ed. J. Spedding, R. L. Ellis and D. D. Heath, vol. vi, p. 420).

as being the opposite number of Portugal, and Bavaria as competing with Austria. He speaks of each state or dynasty as having its eye on its opposite number, but what we miss here is the notion of a general field of forces, the idea of what we call a states-system. He says somewhere that, against each government or princely house in Italy, God has set up a 'contrary' to keep it humble—the Venetians against the Florentines; in Naples the house of Aragon against the House of Anjou; in Milan the family of Orleans against the Visconti.[1] Henry VIII, when he met Francis I of France at the Field of Cloth of Gold in 1520, had a device which represented him as holding a balance; but he was far from suggesting that the European states should be in equipoise. His motto merely promised 'Cui adhaereo prae est'—the one that I join is the one which will turn the scales. Even at a later stage than this, I get the impression that it was possible for people to have a negative idea of the balance without giving much thought to what constitutes the actual equipoise. It was an example of what used to be called the 'neglected positives'—the opposites of words like 'uncouth' and 'unkempt'—you knew when a preponderating Power had created a situation of imbalance, but you had not examined the notion of equilibrium itself. I think that it would be agreed nowadays that historians were once too ready to read back the doctrine of the balance of power into Tudor England. In any case the theory of the balance of power is to a great degree unachieved so long as people are thinking of a pair of scales and merely using it as a figure of speech.

Towards the end of the sixteenth century, there was a famous scholar, Justus Lipsius, who had an extraordinary influence as a teacher of statesmanship, whether you measure the influence by the number of translations and editions of his works, or by the way his teaching was taken up in universities, or by the fame of the monarchs and statesmen who sought his advice and tried to enlist his services. It was he who did so much to redeem the reputation of Machiavelli by separating the scientific aspect of his teaching from the maxims that were so obviously unethical; and it was important that he—a man palpably on the side of morality—insisted on recognizing Machiavelli's doctrine about the importance of force in international politics as well as his idea of learning politics from antiquity. But this man knew nothing of the balance of power, so far as I can see. He talked the language of Machiavelli and merely put forward the doctrine that it is a mistake to remain neutral when other Powers are at war. Francis Bacon comes nearer to the modern idea; for, when he talks about Henry VIII, Francis I and Charles V, he says that, if ever

[1] *Memoirs*, book V, ch. xviii; see below, p. 149.

any one of these rulers acquired a foot of earth, the other two would immediately set about to restore the balance.

It is my experience that if, as a general student of history, one collects references to the balance of power, or studies the ones that the experts have collected, they are comparatively few in the sixteenth century, but, after 1600, not only do they become more numerous— their meaning is less clouded by ambiguities. It is after about the middle of the seventeenth century, however, that the references begin to come in an amazing flood. And, so far as I can see, it is only at this point in the story, that the doctrine has its remarkable development.

There are references to the balance of power in the despatches of Mazarin in the 1640s, and in this period the idea was particularly associated with Venice—in both French literature and French diplomatic documents you find the Venetians described as the apostles of the doctrine.[1] But it is the course of events in the subsequent decades of Louis XIV's reign that gives the theory its extraordinary currency. Now that France had replaced Spain as the menace to Europe, it came to be seen that it had not been the peculiar wickedness of the Spaniards that had previously threatened the world—it was the disposition of forces that made the Spaniards the aggressors in one age and then the French in another age. The doctrine of balance was often deprecated in this new epoch by the French, for of course it became an important weapon against them as Louis XIV proceeded in his career of aggrandizement. And the significance of the whole theory was magnified because governments were paying attention to propaganda—Louis XIV's wars provoked in various countries great numbers of pamphlets and topical treatises. The War of the Spanish Succession was a remarkable example of the way in which the policies of European states came to be affected by the doctrine of balance. By this time the doctrine is repeatedly appearing in diplomatic despatches, state papers, treaties of alliance and treaties of peace.

[1] See a letter from Mazarin to the comte d'Avaux, in 1646: 'Le motif principal du Vénitien en cela est peut-être pour mettre les choses en cet équilibre que la République a si fort en tête' (quoted in G. Zeller, *Les Temps modernes, I. de Christophe Colomb à Cromwell* (*Histoire des Relations Internationales*, ed. P. Renouvin, vol. ii, Paris, Hachette, 1953), pp. 203–4). In another sphere, cf. the treaty of alliance between France and Denmark, November 25, 1645, art. xii: 'Comme la liberté du Commerce consiste principalement en ce que les choses soient maintenues, dans l'Ocean Occidental, dans la Mer Septentrional, et dans la Mer Baltique, au mesme estat qu'elles ont esté jusqu'à present, l'un et l'autre Roy travaillera et s'employera pour que cet ancien et salutaire équilibre qui a servi jusqu'à present de fondement à la Paix et à la tranquillité publique, soit conservé par tout sans aucune alteration' (J. Dumont, *Corps Universel Diplomatique* (Amsterdam, 1726–31), vol. vi, part i, p. 329).

Even in this new period, the idea was still rather rough at first; and some writers said that, between France and Spain, the Dutch represented the tongue of the balance—others said the English. It has been pointed out that this was a haphazard use of metaphor. Since the doctrine came to be directed against Louis XIV, official circles in France tended to dislike it, and support from that country came from critics of the government. In the ranks of these was the famous Fénelon who produces for the education of the Duke of Burgundy a work that showed a high degree of sophistication.[1] First he said that if once a Power was allowed to rise to a position of predominance, you would not be able to count on its good behaviour, however moderately it had hitherto behaved. Once it could act with impunity, it would not confine its ambitions within the accustomed channels. In fact, said Fénelon, you could not expect it to remain moderate for more than a single reign. Secondly, Fénelon pointed out that even a nation which at one time has been helping to check an aggressor will in the very course of those proceedings move imperceptibly into a career of conquest. In other words, it demands more and more securities against the old aggressor, and, suddenly, when you turn round, you see that it has been moving towards universal dominion itself. Thirdly, Fénelon is remarkable because he held that the balance of power should be regarded as an over-ruling law. The internal laws of a country—the law about the succession to the throne, for example—should give way to 'the right that so many nations had to security'.

Once things had reached this point and the idea had come to such conscious formulation, the balance of power not only became a diplomatic objective but was exalted into being the very highest of such objectives. The element of egotism in state policy was clearly recognized all the time; but in so far as you were not being egotistical, you were supposed now to aim at the preservation of the international order, the maintenance of the balance of power. The principle did in fact prescribe limits to egotism and ambition, and the check did actually operate. It operated because it involved a more enlightened view of your own interests—it was a case of limiting your short-term objects for the sake of your long-term advantage. I wonder whether, along with Bismarck, perhaps Frederick the Great is not a remarkable example of a conqueror who—unlike Napoleon—accepted a principle of self-limitation, seeing in the long

[1] 'Sur la nécessité de former des alliances, tant offensives que défensives, contre une puissance étrangère qui aspire manifestement à la monarchie universelle', Supplement à L'Examen de Conscience sur les Devoirs de la Royauté (Oeuvres, Paris, Lebel, 1824, vol. xxii, pp. 306–15).

run the importance of an international order, showing some solicitude for that order, and turning into something like a conservative statesman. And, of course, under this system you could be egotistical but at least even the egotist had to pretend to be following the principle of the balance of power, demonstrating that there, at any rate, was the accepted standard.

I do not think it can have been an accident that the doctrine of a European equilibrium became so fashionable, and proved so pregnant, just at the time when the world had become familiar with parallelograms of forces, and men were beginning to see the heavenly bodies beautifully equipoised. The expositions of the theory sometimes pressed mechanistic analogies and figures of speech in a remote way, and the sentences or the analyses come on occasion with a curiously Baconian ring. This was a general tendency, as the eighteenth century proceeded, and I recently read an unpublished essay which showed how important the idea of the balance was to Gibbon, whose particular predilection was the pendulum. Along with the idea of the balance of power, the notion of the balance of trade and the theory of equipoise in the British constitution seems to have been becoming fashionable in the seventeenth century. Francis Bacon has a rather different notion of the 'well-balancing' of trade, and returns at times to the idea of having the parts of society in equilibrium—the nobility in due proportion. Also he recognizes that a change in trade-relations can alter the balance of power.[1]

It is easy to see why the eighteenth century attached so much importance to the doctrine of balance. It constantly remembered the aggressions of Louis XIV as things that must never be allowed to happen again. It rejoiced that now there was no single Power which could be described as having the predominance, lording it over the continent. It remembered in the same way that in the seventeenth century a vast Swedish Empire had encircled the whole of the Baltic, and that, as this collapsed, the rise of Russia might bring another Power into the dominant position there. But for the time being all was well—the eighteenth century prided itself on the fact that the Baltic was now divided between five different states, no single one of which could be regarded as having the predominance. In the background of eighteenth-century thought there was the repeated remembrance of a past, still fairly recent, but darker than anything else—the cruel Wars of Religion, when one party fought to make all Europe Catholic, and the other to make it Protestant, without any regard for the balance of power. The eighteenth century did not set its heart on either a Catholic order in Europe or a Protestant order,

[1] 'Of Seditions and Troubles' and 'Of Empire' (*Works*, vol. vi, pp. 410, 420).

but on an international system which was to be defended for its own sake; a new kind of order because it comprised both Catholics and Protestants, just as it comprised both monarchies and republics.

But, more remotely still, the eighteenth century looked back to the Roman Empire as a thing that must never be allowed to happen again. They realized, what the twentieth century forgot sometimes, that there are only two alternatives: either a distribution of power to produce equilibrium or surrender to a single universal empire like that of ancient Rome. And this development in their theory became supremely relevant when Napoleon overthrew the balance and seemed to be creating a new Roman Empire. In other words, the theorists of the balance of power found it necessary to vindicate the idea of a Europe divided into separate states of only moderate size—a map of the continent which had the appearance of a patch-work quilt. Against the notion of a uniform Empire with a uniform culture, they promoted the idea of a civilization fundamentally one but broken into panes of many-coloured glass—achieving greater richness through the variety of its local manifestations. In general, and in a fundamental sense, it was their case that the distribution of power was the important thing, but that, apart from this, small states in themselves had an intrinsic value. The balance of power was a system—the only system—which, in a world so much at the mercy of force, made it possible for a considerable number of small states to remain in existence at all. Granted such a European order, it was not at all necessary—nor was it possible—that the various states should be equal or even roughly equal in power. In fact one writer, Gentz, asserted that, if Europe were divided up into states, that were absolutely equal squares, it would actually be harder, not easier, to establish between them anything like a balance of power.[1] Gentz pointed out that, even when one state increased its territory, it was by no means always necessary that the other should do so. The rectification of the balance might normally be brought about by a reshuffling of alliances. Furthermore, the balance not only guaranteed the existence of small states, but assured them of a certain autonomy, a power of independent action. It guaranteed their independence at its most crucial point, namely, in the realm of foreign policy. In other words, it made possible the existence of small states that should not merely be satellites. Richelieu had once pointed out that in the existing system, small states had greater freedom of action than larger states—in the case of an alliance it was the larger rather than the smaller power that was likely to be abandoned by its

[1] F. von Gentz, *Fragments upon the Balance of Power in Europe* (London, Peltier, 1806), p. 63 note.

partner.[1] And in fact the system of the balance of power even depended on the free action of the smaller states which, as an ally of theirs became too powerful, could shift their allegiance and throw their weight on the opposite side.

From all this you will see that the eighteenth century conceived of the balance of power in an imposing way and elaborated it into a whole theory of international relations. But there would be differences about the details of the system. There was a school of writers in Hanover who tended to regard Great Britain as the standing supporter and guardian of the balance of power. They took the line that a maritime state is never a danger to liberty. The French had a different point of view, and they sometimes argued that England was an offensive intruder—she really belonged outside the alliance-system. England, they said, talked about the balance of power in Europe but showed no respect for the principle in the rest of the world. The French complained in a similar way against any government that allied itself with Russia; and they affected to think of Russia as rather an Asiatic Power, that ought to be excluded by general assent. About Turkey there was bound to be much difference of opinion—in the 1790s the question was raised in the British parliament whether she was within the system or outside it. In some respects she had to be reckoned as being inside the balance-system, because she had a traditional alliance with France.

The mechanics of the European order—the design of the whole machine—was sometimes a complex affair; and some writers describe wheels within wheels. It was possible to conceive of many local systems of the balance of power, and then to comprehend all these in a wider system of European balance. One writer sees first an equilibrium between the south-western states, then another among the north-eastern states, and then a third within Germany, and finally a comprehensive one, embracing all these and spanning the whole continent. After 1763, when both Russia and Prussia had emerged to greatness, you had a curious triangle of forces in Eastern Europe—Austria, Russia and Prussia all poised against one another, all crouching like tigers ready for a spring. If one gained an advantage the other two would draw together to redress the balance and secure compensation—there was constant switching and interchange

---

[1] 'Bien que ce soit un dire commun que quiconque à la force a d'ordinaire la raison, il est vrai toutefois que deux puissances inégales, jointes par un traité, la plus grande court risque d'être plus abandonnée que l'autre,' Richelieu, *Testament politique*, ed. L. André (Paris, Laffont, 1947), p. 354. See Rudolf von Albertini, *Das politische Denken in Frankreich zur Zeit Richelieus* (Marburg, Simon, 1951), p. 188.

amongst the three ballet dancers—it is the most intensive application of the principle of the balance of power I have ever seen in history. But if those *three* Powers ever agreed on a policy, the Western states —England and France, for example—could never stop them in Eastern Europe. And that is how the Partition of Poland was able to take place—there might be a balance in Eastern Europe, but there was a defect in the overall European balance-system. On the other hand, for a long time the balance of power enabled the Turkish Empire to survive after it had become too weak to defend itself. Here the West was able to counter-balance the East—England and France were able to check Russia—partly no doubt through the existence of sea-communications.

The principle of the balance of power apparently tended to the preservation of the *status quo*, putting a brake on territorial changes. In one of his Political Testaments, Frederick the Great marked out a piece of territory for future acquisition but gave warning that such an attempt at aggrandizement was not feasible at the time.[1] However completely you took the world by surprise, he said, the other states would intervene, and sides would be too equally matched. The struggle would be a severe one, and, at the finish, the game was not worth the candle. Within a few years of this, Edmund Burke was writing in the *Annual Register*:

'The balance of power, the pride of modern policy, and originally invented to preserve the general peace as well as freedom of Europe, has only preserved its liberty. It has been the original of innumerable and fruitless wars. That political torture by which powers are to be enlarged or abridged, according to a standard, perhaps not very accurately imagined, ever has been, and it is to be feared will always continue a cause of infinite contention and bloodshed. The foreign ambassadors constantly residing in all courts, the negociations incessantly carrying on, spread both confederacies and quarrels so wide, that whenever hostilities commence, the theatre of war is always of a prodigious extent. All parties in those diffusive opera-

---

[1] *Politische Corespondenz Friedrich's des Grossen*, Erganzungsband, *Die Politischen Testamente Friedrich's des Grossen* (Berlin, Hobbing, 1920), p. 48. '*Voilà un équilibre de puissances qui s'établit et qui constitue une égalité de force entre l'agresseur et l'attaqué.* . . . *Cette politique, une fois établie en Europe, empêche les grandes conquêtes et rend les guerres infructueuses, à moins qu'elles ne soient conduites avec une grande supériorité et une fortune invariable.*' Cf. p. 49 which declares the '*coup d'éclat*', the surprise attack on Silesia, unrepeatable. Frederick's attitude to the problem of peace and war in this Political Testament of 1752 is discussed in E. Bosbach, *Die 'Rêveries Politiques' in Friedrichs des Grossen Politischem Testament von 1752* (Köln Graz, Böhlau, 1960), pp. 64–7.

tions have of necessity their strong and weak sides. What they gain in one part is lost in another; and in conclusion, their affairs become so balanced, that all the powers concerned are certain to lose a great deal; the most fortunate acquire little; and what they do acquire is never in any reasonable proportion to charge and loss. . . . (In) modern treaties of peace . . . none can properly be called conquerors or conquered.'[1]

Gibbon says much the same thing but puts a better face on the matter. He wrote: 'In war, the European forces are exercised by temperate and indecisive contests.'[2] But it was sometimes recognized by the theorists that the balance of power, precisely because it vindicated small states, operated to preserve freedom rather than peace. It corresponded to one of the peculiarities of the European order—an order in which freedom was more important than tranquillity. In other words, you have to choose between the principle of universal empire and the principle of the distribution of power.

An article in the *Edinburgh Review* in 1802 declared that the idea of the balance of power was the result of the progress of science and the peculiar circumstances of the modern world. It was as unknown to the ancient Greeks and Romans as the teaching of Kepler and Newton. The article emphasized the elasticity which the system required—constant vigilance, careful observation of little changes that take place, perpetual interest in what was happening at the other end of the map. It took the line that you should check the potential aggressor before he really emerged; in fact what you ought to attack are the conditions that make for aggression—what you ought to prevent is the excessive aggrandizement of any Power. It is too late to take action afterwards; it is a mistake to wait till the aggressor has actually shown his hand. The *Edinburgh Review* takes the line that the various Powers have the right to control one another—to prevent one of their number from becoming dangerous. I have come across the assertion that, if a state is becoming too powerful, it is legitimate to set out to weaken it even before it has made any aggressive move; though there were differences of opinion on this question. Francis Bacon held that if a Power had made itself formidable, your fear of what it might do was a sufficient justification for going to war. Grotius, however, had insisted that war was wrong unless the overpowerful state was itself about to attack. One could add that the whole system required what might be called an intelligent apprecia-

---

[1] *Annual Register* for 1760, pp. 2–3. Cf. *ibid.* for 1772, pp. 2–3.
[2] *The Decline and Fall of the Roman Empire*, 'General Observations on the Fall of the Roman Empire in the West', following ch. xxxviii.

K

tion of the international order as such. Everything was liable to be ruined if Englishmen hated the French too much and imagined that nobody but a Frenchman could ever be an aggressor. It was generally our fault that we went on fighting the old aggressor too long and thereby made it more easy for a new aggressor to emerge. It could be equally dangerous if the English as in 1814–15 loved the Prussians too much, and consented to excessive aggrandizement for them, on the assumption that they would always remain friends.

In fact, rigidity was always a serious danger and the system was under constant threat through the existence of deeply rooted prejudices. From the time of the Treaty of Utrecht, there was a tendency to regard the system as stable for the time being, and there existed a presumption in favour of keeping things as they were. There was even a version of the doctrine that tended to rigidity—a way of speaking about the balance of power as though it were the 'constitution' of Europe—a constitution partly written (in treaties, for example) but partly unwritten (like the balanced constitution of Great Britain). Gentz, who defended the whole system in the time of Napoleon, wrote:

'What is generally known as the balance of power is that constitution of neighbouring and more or less connected states, by means of which no one of them can damage another in its independence or essential rights without being restricted somewhere, and therefore endangering itself.'[1]

In reality, statesmen and writers would often tend to identify the balance of power with the existing map of European forces, disliking any change that would entail a redistribution of current alliance-arrangements. Alternatively, various states would set out to preserve what they regarded as their own system of the balance of power. States might continue alliances because they had become sentimental, or alliances might remain too fixed because of marriage-connections or commercial interest. The French, when in the eighteenth century they talked of maintaining the balance, often meant the preservation of the existing alliance-systems instead of rapid adjustments to a change in the distribution of power. In fact, by their attachment to Sweden, Poland and Turkey in this period, they may have been too lacking in flexibility, while Russia was coming to the front. On the other hand, if interests of state placed you in one alliance-system, but you had a standing marriage-connection or a regular commercial link with a member of the other group, this might help to

[1] *Fragments upon the Balance of Power in Europe*, ch. i, *ad init.*

form a bridge between the opposing alliance-groups, or to mitigate a war, or to facilitate an attempt to lure over a state that was in the other *bloc*.

Sometimes the principle of the balance of power is regarded as a precept, about which one can have a certain option—an injunction to behave in one manner rather than another. The eighteenth century regarded it rather as a law which operates wherever there is an international order and a states-system, a law which operates if governments are alive to their long-term interests. It is an injunction only in the sense that states are expected to pursue not merely local advantages but also their own long-term interest. Modern historical writing developed out of the literature on the balance of power. The historians of Göttingen adopted the concept of 'the European states-system', taking it over from the publicists and the practitioners of politics. They, too, regarded the system as a modern one, a Western creation, in spite of the fact that conditions somewhat analogous existed in ancient Greece, and in the monarchies that succeeded the empire of Alexander the Great. One of the Göttingen historians, Heeren, went on praising the system at a time when Napoleon, then at the height of his career, had entirely overturned it. Even at this inauspicious moment Heeren suggested that this international order, this European states-system, might gradually be expanded until it embraced the whole globe. Ranke took over from the Göttingen historians this whole idea of a European states-system, as well as the notion of the balance of power and the recognition of the operation of force in the resulting order of things. Englishmen in the twentieth century condemned Ranke as a Prussian for this aspect of his teaching, not realizing that the Hanoverian school from which he learned it, had developed it precisely as a result of its connection with England.

I should infer from all this that an international order is not a thing bestowed upon by nature, but is a matter of refined thought, careful contrivance and elaborate artifice. At best it is a precarious thing, and though it seems so abstract it requires the same kind of loyalty, the same constant attention, that people give to their country or to the other private causes which only the international order enables them to follow. I should infer, again, that the world was wrong in 1919 when it decided that hitherto everything had been in a state of nature, with only anarchy in the international field—all thought about foreign relations and international systems having to start at the beginning again. I personally would like to know what would have happened if the kind of international thought which we have been examining had received, not permanent establishment, but simply continued development during the last 150 years.

In reality it became crossed with ideological notions of foreign policy which greatly affected the world from the time of the French Revolution. In the nineteenth century it is interesting to see how revolutionaries and liberals could design to spread their system through an active foreign policy and through war; and there were many Frenchmen in 1793, 1830 and 1848 who would have been shocked to think that by the end of the nineteenth century a French republic would be allied with Czarist Russia. It seems that the world has constantly to be weaned out of the notion that wars ought to be war of religion and turned—if they exist at all—simply into wars for the creation of an international order.

I should infer finally that a given educational system is an odd one if it does not teach the young the profound ideas and principles which lie at the basis of the order in which they live.

CHAPTER 7

THE BALANCE OF POWER

MARTIN WIGHT

The theoretical analysis of international politics seems to move from a shallower to a deeper level, discovering at either level a 'law' or rule of political life. At the shallower level, it is the rule that neighbouring states are usually enemies, that common frontiers are usually disputed, and that your natural ally is the Power in the rear of your neighbour. Let us call this, for want of a better term, the conception of the pattern of power. It is developed with great elaboration in the *Arthashastra* of Kautilya, who did not however rise to the theory of the balance of power. The famous chapter in Commynes' *Memoirs*, which is usually credited with being the earliest account in modern European literature of the balance of power, is more truly a vivid description of the pattern of power, arguing that the universal hostility between neighbouring Powers must have been ordained by God to restrain 'la bestialité de plusieurs princes et . . . le mauvastié d'autres'.[1] Namier cogently restated 'the system of odd and even nembers' in international alignments, for the benefit of a generation that had chosen to forget it, and called it the 'sandwich system of international politics'.[2]

The idea of the *pattern* of power enables us to generalize about international politics in relation to their geographical framework. The idea of the *balance* of power involves a higher degree of abstraction. It means thinking of the Powers less as pieces on a chessboard than as weights in a pair of scales; we mentally pluck them out of their geographical setting and arrange them according to their alliances and affinities, with the underlying notion of matching their moral weight and material strength. The pattern of power leads to considerations of strategy; the balance of power leads to considerations of military potential, diplomatic initiative and economic strength.

Compared with the pattern of power, the notion of the balance of power is notoriously full of confusions, so that it is impossible to make any statement about the 'law' or principle of the balance of

---

[1] Book V, ch. xviii (ed. Calmette (Paris, Champion, 1925), vol. ii, p. 211).
[2] L. B. Namier, *Conflicts* (Macmillan, 1942), p. 14; cf. *Vanished Supremacies* (Hamish Hamilton, 1958), p. 170.

power that will command general acceptance. The sources of these confusions are at least three.

The first is the equivocalness and plasticity of the metaphor of 'balance' itself. In the notion of the balance of international power it may seem that the idea of equipoise is logically prior to the idea of preponderance. This is not borne out by the early history of the figurative meanings of 'balance' in the *N.E.D.* The meaning passed from the standard of justice or reason, through the wavering of fortune or chance, subjective uncertainty (hesitation), objective uncertainty (risk), to 'power to decide or determine: authoritative control', in a quotation from Gower as early as 1393. This was probably a hundred years earlier than the use of the metaphor in any European language to describe international politics, two hundred years earlier than the first recorded usage applied to international politics in English—and *that* happens to illustrate the sense of 'authoritative control'.[1] If it has always been the supreme task of international statesmanship to preserve the balance of power, the difficulty of the task is prefigured in the mutability and inconstancy of the metaphor itself. If we put it in an over-simplified way, we may say that the essential meaning of the verb 'to balance' is 'to compare weights'. But weights may be compared, either in order to find them equivalent; or in order to find and measure the difference; or (when they are human and social weights) in order to minister to the sense of authority of the balancer. All these meanings coexist in the phrase 'the balance of power'.

The second source of confusion is the overlap between the normative and the descriptive. Most sentences containing the phrase 'the balance of power' combine a normative with a descriptive sense. They are statements not only about what foreign policy ought to be pursued, but also about the tendency, law or principle that governs international alignments. For the balance of power means two things. It is, first, a system of foreign policy: a system which the agents in international politics uphold, neglect, or repudiate in favour of some other supposed system. It is, secondly, a historical law or theoretical principle of analysis which spectators of international politics (publicists, journalists, students) derive from or apply to their reflection on international politics. But agents and spectators are not distinct classes. All agents are partly spectators (of the other agents) and all policy presupposes some theory. And all spectators (above all in politically free societies) are frustrated agents.

The third source of confusion is that weighing in the balance implies an estimate, which requires judicial detachment. And the

[1] It is quoted below, p. 164.

international agent who estimates the balance of power is involved in what he estimates, and cannot be detached. His judgment of the balance is expressed as objective but is necessarily subjective. This obliquity of vision is inherent in social life, but it is most pronounced where the issue may be national survival or destruction.

This paper will try to show that 'the balance of power' has had the following distinct meanings in international politics:[1]

1. An even distribution of power.
2. The principle that power ought to be evenly distributed.
3. The existing distribution of power. Hence, any possible distribution of power.
4. The principle of equal aggrandizement of the Great Powers at the expense of the weak.
5. The principle that our side ought to have a margin of strength in order to avert the danger of power becoming unevenly distributed.
6. (When governed by the verb 'to hold':) A special role in maintaining an even distribution of power.
7. (Ditto:) A special advantage in the existing distribution of power.
8. Predominance.
9. An inherent tendency of international politics to produce an even distribution of power.

It is the fascination of the subject that these senses are difficult to disentangle, and almost any sentence about the balance of power, as this paper will perhaps illustrate involuntarily more than deliberately, is likely to imply two or more meanings at the same time.

The original application of the metaphor of the balance to international politics is in the sense of *an even distribution of power*, a state of affairs in which no Power is so preponderant that it can endanger the others. Let us call this sense 1. This is the primary meaning of 'the balance of power', to which there is always a tendency to return. If there are three or more weights that are thus considered as balanced (as with the five major Powers of Italy between 1454 and 1494, or the five Great Powers that formed the Concert of Europe in the nineteenth century) it may be called a multiple balance. If there are only two weights in consideration (as with the Habsburgs and France in the sixteenth and seventeenth

---

[1] We are not concerned with the idea of the balance of power in the internal politics of a state, which has had a distinct and parallel history from Aristotle and Polybius to Harrington, Montesquieu and the pluralists.

centuries, Britain and France in the eighteenth, the Triple Alliance and the Triple Entente before 1914, or America and Russia since 1945) it may be called a simple balance. The conception of the simple balance involves a higher degree of abstraction than that of the multiple balance. It means a selective concentration upon the greatest Powers. There has never yet, in the history of Western international society, actually been a simple balance. When there have been rival predominant Powers, they have always had lesser Powers around or between them, capable of being considered as contributing to a multiple balance. Even the confrontation of two world empires, as in the case of Rome and Persia, has been varied and enlivened by unreliable vassals and intractable buffers, an Armenia or an Osroene or a Palmyra; and the great contest between Heraclius and Chosroes was influenced, perhaps decisively, by the independent action of the Avars, Bulgars, Slavs, Gepids, and Chazars.

But the distinction between multiple and simple balance is immaterial to the conception of the balance of power as an even distribution. In both the multiple and the simple balance there is the idea of equipoise. When Machiavelli wrote that, before the French invasion of 1494, 'Italia era in un certo modo bilanciata', when Guicciardini wrote that Lorenzo de' Medici 'procurava con ogni studio che le cose d'Italia in modo bilanciate si mantenessino che piu in una che in un' altra parte non pendessino', they were trying to describe such an even distribution of power.[1] Thus Sir Thomas Overbury's description of the states-system a hundred years later, in 1609, when the Spanish attempt at predominance had been defeated:

'It is first to be considered that this part of Christendom is balanced betwixt the three Kings of Spain, France, and England; as the other part is betwixt the Russian, the Kings of Poland, Sweden and Denmark. For as for Germany, which if it were entirely subject to one Monarchy, would be terrible to all the rest; so being divided betwixt so many Princes and those of so equal power, it serves only to balance itself, and entertain easy war with the Turk; while the Persian withholds him in a greater.'[2]

By a similar use of the metaphor, Churchill described the European situation brought about by the Locarno Treaties: 'Thus there was a

---

[1] Machiavelli, *Il Principe*, ch. xx (ed. Burd, p. 329); Guicciardini, *La Storia d'Italia*, book I, ch. i.
[2] Sir Thomas Overbury, *Observations in his Travels*, in *Stuart Tracts 1603-1693*, ed. C. H. Firth (Constable, 1903), p. 227.

balance created in which Britain, whose major interest was the cessation of the quarrel between Germany and France, was to a large extent arbiter and umpire';[1] and Eden wrote, 'The fighting in Korea achieved a balance of power, recognized and respected as such'.[2] The same notion of even distribution appears in Lester Pearson's dictum that 'The balance of terror has replaced the balance of power'.[3] In this usage the word 'balance' retains its meaning of 'equilibrium', and it is perhaps most likely to appear as the object of such verbs as maintain and preserve, upset and overturn, or redress and restore.

Almost insensibly, the phrase passes from a descriptive to a normative use. It comes to mean (2) *the principle that power ought to be evenly distributed.* When during the American Revolutionary War George III was seeking the assistance of Catherine the Great, she replied: 'Her ideas perfectly correspond with his, as to the balance of power; and she never can see with indifference any essential aggrandizement or essential diminution, of any European state take place'.[4] The *Manchester Guardian* wrote in 1954: 'If there is to be coexistence there must be a balance of power, for if power is unbalanced the temptation to communism to resume its crusade will be irresistible'.[5] In each of these quotations sense 2 can be seen emerging out of sense 1. In 1713 the phrase was written into the Treaty of Utrecht to justify the perpetual separation of the crowns of France and Spain: 'for the end that all care and suspicions may be removed from the minds of men and that the Peace and Tranquillity of the Christian World may be ordered and stabilized in a just Balance of Power (which is the best and most solid foundation of mutual friendship and a lasting general concord)'.[6] Thenceforward, for two hundred years, the balance of power was generally spoken of as if it were the constituent principle of international society, and legal writers described it as the indispensable condition of international law.[7] It was even ironically apostrophized as the condition of private prosperity.

[1] *The Second World War* (Cassell, 1948), vol. i, p. 24.
[2] *Full Circle* (Cassell, 1960), p. 28.
[3] Speech at San Francisco, June 24, 1955 (*Commemoration of the Tenth Anniversary of the Signing of the United Nations Charter* (U.N.P. Sales No.: 1955. I.26), p. 215.) Cf. John Strachey, *On the Prevention of War* (Macmillan, 1962), p. 25.
[4] *Diaries and Correspondence of the First Earl of Malmesbury* (2nd ed., Bentley, 1845), vol. i, p. 344.
[5] Leading article, August 21, 1954.
[6] As translated in Sir Geoffrey Butler and Simon Maccoby, *The Development of International Law* (Longmans, 1928), p. 65.
[7] A distinction must be made between legal writers:
(i) Who, resting mainly on the declaration in the Treaty of Utrecht, regard

'The *balance of pow'r*? ah! till that is restor'd,
What solid delight can retirement afford?'

sang Isaac Hawkins Browne during the War of the Polish Succession.[1] 'The balance of power had ever been assumed as the known common law of Europe,' wrote Burke in the *Regicide Peace*, 'the question had only been (as it must happen) the more or less inclination of that balance.'[2] 'The balance of power in Europe,' said Lord John Russell sixty-five years later, 'means in effect the independence of its several states. The preponderance of any one Power threatens and destroys this independence.'[3] The Concert of Europe was in origin and essence a common agreement on the principle of the balance of power.

But it is the trouble about international politics that the distribution of power does not long remain constant and the Powers are usually in disagreement on its being an even distribution. Most arrangements of power favour some countries, which therefore seek to preserve the *status quo*, and justify it as being a true balance in the

the balance of power as being itself a fundamental legal principle. E.g. Sir Travers Twiss, *The Law of Nations considered as Independent Political Communities* (new edition, Clarendon Press, 1884), pp. 187–8; Robert Redslob, *Histoire des Grands Principes du Droit des Gens* (Paris, Rousseau, 1923), pp. 160–2, 251–3.

(ii) Who describe the balance of power as, not a legal principle, but the political condition of international law. E.g. L. Oppenheim, *International Law* (1st edition, Longmans, 1905), vol. i, pp. 73–4; A. Pearce Higgins, *Studies in International Law and Relations* (Cambridge University Press, 1928), pp. 138–42; Charles de Visscher, *Theory and Reality in Public International Law* (Princeton University Press, 1957), p. 157.

(iii) Who describe the maintenance of the balance of power as a legal right in international law deriving from the right of self-preservation. E.g. Vattel, *Le Droit des Gens*, book III, ch. iii, sections 47–8; G. F. von Martens, *A Compendium of the Law of Nations* (translated by William Cobbett, 1802), p. 127; Henry Wheaton, *History of the Law of Nations* (New York, Gould, Banks, 1845), pp. 20, 80–2; John Westlake, *Collected Papers on Public International Law* (Cambridge University Press, 1914), pp. 121–3; T. J. Lawrence, *The Principles of International Law* (Macmillan, 1925), pp. 128–31. W. E. Hall, *A Treatise on International Law* (Clarendon Press, 8th edition, 1924), austerely avoids the phrase balance of power, but substantially describes it as the point at which the right of self-preservation of several states may override the right to self-development of a menacing state (p. 51).

[1] 'The Fire Side: a Pastoral Soliloquy, on the Earl of Godolphin's taking the Seals', 1735 (*Oxford Book of Eighteenth Century Verse*, p. 300).

[2] *Letters on a Regicide Peace*, No. 3 (*Works*, ed. H. Rogers (Holdsworth, 1842), vol. ii, p. 333).

[3] H. Temperley and L. M. Penson, *Foundations of British Foreign Policy* (Cambridge University Press, 1938), p. 205.

THE BALANCE OF POWER

sense of an equilibrium; and are irksome to other countries whose policy is accordingly revisionist. Just as such phrases as 'the hereditary system' or 'property' ceased to have a sacrosanct ring in domestic politics when they were uttered by men of the self-made or unpropertied classes, so 'the balance of power' loses its connotation of being grounded on morality and law when it is uttered by representatives of Powers that believe themselves at a disadvantage. This linguistic process can be seen at work in a discussion between Cripps and Stalin in Moscow in July 1940. Cripps had been sent to Moscow as British ambassador with the task of persuading Stalin that Germany's conquest of Western Europe endangered Russia as well as Britain. 'Therefore both countries,' he argued, 'ought to agree on a common policy of self-protection against Germany and on the re-establishment of the European balance of power'. Stalin replied that he did not see any danger of Europe being engulfed by Germany. 'The so-called European balance of power,' he said, 'had hitherto oppressed not only Germany but also the Soviet Union. Therefore the Soviet Union would take all measures to prevent the re-establishment of the old balance of power in Europe.'[1] Similarly Hitler to Ciano in 1936: 'Any future modifications of the Mediterranean balance of power must be in Italy's favour.'[2] Here the phrase has lost any sense of an even distribution of power, and has come to mean simply (3) *the existing distribution of power*. The usage is not confined to revisionist Powers. When the Parliamentary Secretary to the Admiralty told the House of Commons in 1951 that 'the balance of sea power has tilted away from us very dramatically during the last ten years',[3] he was using the phrase neutrally and unemotionally. And by a natural extension it comes to mean *any possible distribution of power*, future as well as present or past. Thus Churchill wrote to Eden in 1942: 'No man can see how the balance of power will lie or where the winning armies will stand at the end of the war.'[4] This is possibly the most frequent usage—to describe the relationship of power prevailing at a given time. The word 'balance' has entirely lost its meaning of 'equilibrium'. There is less notion of stability, more of perpetual change about it than in sense 1; and it will frequently be found as the subject of a sentence (it will be said 'to have changed' or a new one will be said 'to be appearing') as though it lies largely beyond human control.

[1] *Nazi-Soviet Relations 1939-1941: Documents from the Archives of the German Foreign Office* (Washington D.C., Department of State, 1948), p. 167.
[2] *Ciano's Diplomatic Papers* (Odhams Press, 1948), p. 57.
[3] L. J. Callaghan, March 12, 1951 (485 H.C.Deb. 5s, col. 1093).
[4] Churchill, *The Second World War*, vol. iii, p. 616.

So far we have been considering 'the balance of power' roughly as a description of a state of affairs; it is now necessary to consider it as a policy; though it will be clear that the two conceptions are inseparable. The principle that power ought to be evenly distributed, raises the question, By whom? There seem to be three possible answers.

(*a*) It may be said that the even distribution of power will take place through the combined skill and effort of all the Powers concerned, or, in the case of a simple balance, of *both* the Powers or coalitions concerned. (*b*) It may be said that the even distribution of power will be the responsibility of a particular Power, which is said 'to hold the balance'. This answer presupposes a multiple balance. Where there is a truly simple balance, a holder of the balance is excluded. The holder of the balance is, ex-hypothesi, a third force; he may be *tertius gaudens*. (*c*) It may be said, again, that the even distribution of power will come about, over the widest field and in the long run, through a fundamental law or tendency of political forces to fall into equilibrium. Let us consider these answers in turn.

First, the argument that the maintenance of an even distribution of power can take place through the combined skill of all the Powers. If the broad test of an even distribution of power is the absence of a grand alliance against a Power aiming at universal monarchy, then there was such an even distribution from the defeat of Louis XIV to the French Revolution and from the defeat of Napoleon to the First World War. (Suitable qualifications must be made for the anti-British coalition in the American Revolutionary War, and the partial alliance against Russia in the Crimean. And by such a broad test, conflicts on the scale of the Polish Succession, Austrian Succession, and Seven Years Wars have to be rated as incidents in preserving an even distribution of power—a generous proviso.) The maintenance of a multiple balance of power during these periods must in some degree be attributed to the skill of the Powers concerned; but allowance must be made for external circumstances, especially the opportunity for expansion outside Europe. And it cannot be overlooked that these periods of multiple balance came to centre upon questions of partition—of Poland and Turkey at the end of the eighteenth century, of Turkey, Africa and China at the end of the nineteenth. The balance of power, in effect, came to mean (4) *the principle of equal aggrandizement of the Great Powers at the expense of the weak.*

'L'équilibre veut qu'il y ait balance entre les forces; la pesée implique un partage: il faut des contrepoids, ce sont les faibles et les vaincus qui les fournissent, et l'opération tourne inévitablement au profit des forts, des ambitieux et des habiles. L'avènement de la Prusse a été le résultat logique de ce système: elle a servi de contre-poids, jusqu'au jour ou elle s'est senti assez de ressort pour entraîner à son tour le plateau et faire trébucher la balance.'[1]

Nothing in European history has done more to discredit the idea of the balance of power than the belief that it led naturally to such a crime as the Partition of Poland.

'The inventors of this evil project, in the whole course of their enterprise invoked the principles of the balancing system as their guide and polar star, and actually followed them, so far as circumstances would permit, in their division of the spoil, and whilst they inflicted the most fatal wounds upon the spirit and very existence of this system, borrowed its external forms, and even its technical language. *Corruptio optimi pessima:* To behold this noble system, which the wisdom of the European community had devised for its security and welfare, thus perverted, was an odious spectacle.'[2]

The battle of the concessions in China in 1897–8 was similarly an exercise in adjusting the balance. For the British, the sole object of their acquisition of Wei-hai-wei was 'to maintain balance of power in Gulf of Pechili, menaced by Russian occupation of Port Arthur'.[3]

The multiple balance lasts as long as no conflict of interests has arisen to make a decisive schism between the Great Powers. Sooner or later this occurs, and the Powers divide into opposite camps. The multiple balance now resolves itself into a simple balance: it is no longer a merry-go-round but a seesaw. The multiple balance of the eighteenth century dissolved directly into a state of war, near-general war in 1778–9, general war in 1792–3. The nineteenth century Concert of Europe was more skilful in prolonging the peace; the transformation of the multiple into a simple balance began with the Franco-Russian alliance in 1892, or rather, with the lapse of the Reinsurance Treaty in 1890, and peace was maintained by a simple balance for another twenty years. The corresponding transformation from multiple to simple balance between the two World Wars occurred in 1936 with the formation of the Rome-Berlin Axis against the League Powers.

[1] Sorel, *L'Europe et la Révolution Française*, vol. i, p. 34.
[2] F. von Gentz, *Fragments upon the Balance of Power in Europe*, p. 77, as translated in Wheaton, *History of the Law of Nations*, pp. 279–80.
[3] *British Documents on the Origins of the War*, ed. Gooch and Temperley, vol. i, No. 47.

In the circumstances of a simple balance, when each of two Powers or coalitions is trying to maintain an even distribution of power between them by a competition in armaments or a diplomatic struggle for alliances, the idea of the balance of power as equality of aggrandizement tends to be eclipsed (though it may still have a place) by another idea of the balance of power (which may also appear in the circumstances of a multiple balance). This is (5) *the principle that my side ought to have a margin of strength, in order to avert the danger of power becoming unevenly distributed.* Here the word balance acquires the sense it has in the phrases 'balance of trade' or 'bank balance', i.e. not an equality of assets and debits but a surplus of one over the other. And here the contradiction between the subjective and objective estimates of the balance of power, between a political position as seen from the inside and as seen from the outside, becomes acute. When Dean Acheson first formulated the policy of 'negotiating from a position of strength', he apparently meant a levelling up of America's strength to an equality with Russia's, the restoration of an equipoise; but the phrase was equivocal from the start, and quickly acquired the sense of possessing a margin of strength.[1] It was sharply illustrated by headlines in *The Times* newspaper in 1963: 'Mr McNamara says West now has Superiority: US Forces nearing proper Balance for Peace.'[2]

The logic of this development of the idea of 'balance' is illustrated by a story which Norman Angell somewhere tells. Angell as a young man heard Churchill as a young Cabinet minister making a speech in Oxford in 1913. 'There is just one way in which you can make your country secure and have peace,' Churchill said, 'and that is to be so much stronger than any prospective enemy that he dare not attack you—and this is, I submit to you, gentlemen, a self-evident proposition.' Angell got up and asked him if the advice he had just given was the advice he would give to Germany.[3] But it is not simple patriotism or nationalism which has given this interpretation of the

---

[1] Coral Bell, *Negotiation from Strength* (Chatto and Windus, 1962), ch. i.

[2] *The Times*, November 19, 1963. The Washington correspondent wrote:

'In a policy speech today [18 Nov.] Mr Robert McNamara, the United States Secretary of Defence, said that the west enjoyed a military superiority over the Soviet block in conventional forces as well as strategic and tactical nuclear weapons. The significance of this position of strength was manifold. . . . He rejected the idea that the Soviet block could ever achieve superiority and thus initiate another arms race, although new technological developments might require important expenditures in future. He saw the American forces rapidly approaching the proper balance required to maintain peace.'

[3] The incident is recorded in C. E. M. Joad, *Why War?* (Penguin, 1939), pp. 71–2. Cf. Norman Angell, *Preface to Peace* (Hamish Hamilton, 1935), p. 122.

balance its greatest potency, but a system where 'my side' is a coalition identified with international virtue and legality. Collective security under the League of Nations, as we shall note below, was built upon the assumption that the law-abiding Powers would have a constant preponderance over any possible aggressor.

The fullest transformation of the idea of the balance of power seems to arise out of the notion of 'holding the balance'. The Power that 'holds the balance' is the Power that is in a position to contribute decisive strength to one side or the other.

The figure is seen at its simplest in Camden's famous description of Queen Elizabeth:

'There sat she as an heroical princess and umpire betwixt the Spaniards, the French, and the Estates; so as she might well have used that saying of her father, *Cui adhaereo, praeest*, that is, 'the party to which I adhere getteth the upper hand'. And true it was which one hath written, that France and Spain are as it were the scales in the balance of Europe, and England the tongue or the holder of the balance.'[1]

There is a little confusion in the metaphor, since the tongue of a balance is an index to show which way the scales incline, not a stabilizer. The idea appears in an equally pure form in a letter from Palmerston to William IV in 1832. He is explaining the quarrels between France on the one side and Austria, Prussia and Russia on the other, about the treaty establishing Belgian independence.

'Upon the occasion of all these pretensions the British Government brought the three Powers to bear upon France, and France was upon all compelled to yield; latterly the three Powers have in their turn been unreasonable and deficient in good faith, and have endeavoured, under false pretences, to defeat the treaty they had ratified and to mar the arrangement they had guaranteed. The British Government then brought France to bear upon the three Powers, and it is to be hoped with ultimate success. Rivals in military strength, as France and the three Powers are, Your Majesty may be said practically to hold the scales of the balance of Europe. France will not venture to attack the three Powers, if she is also to be opposed by England; and the three Powers will pause long before they attack France, if they think that France could in that case reckon upon the support of England. Thus, then, it appears . . . that Your Majesty has peculiarly the power of preserving the general peace and that by

[1] William Camden, *History of Elizabeth* (translated 3rd edition, 1675), p. 223.

throwing the moral influence of Great Britain into one scale or the other, according as the opposite side may manifest a spirit of encroachment or injustice, Your Majesty may . . . become on many occasions the arbiter of events in Europe.'[1]

This is the traditional conception, expressed in the simple terms suited to its recipient. Here, to hold the balance of power means, (6) *possessing a special role in maintaining an even distribution of power.*

It became part of the traditional British doctrine on the matter that a holder of the balance was essential to the very idea of the balance of power. Swift explicated the metaphor with characteristic clarity:

'It will be an eternal Rule in Politicks, among every free People, that there is a Ballance of Power to be carefully held by every State within it self, as well as among several States with each other.

'The true Meaning of a Ballance of Power, either without, or within a State, is best conceived by considering what the Nature of a Ballance is. It supposes three things. First, the part which is held, together with the Hand that holds it; and then the two Scales, with whatever is weighed therein. Now consider several States in a Neighbourhood: In order to preserve Peace between these States, it is necessary they should be formed into a Ballance, whereof one, or more are to be Directors, who are to divide the rest into equal Scales, and upon Occasions remove from one into the other, or else fall with their own Weight into the lightest: So in a State within it self, the Ballance must be held by a third Hand, who is to deal the remaining Power with the utmost Exactness into each Scale. Now it is not necessary, that the Power should be equally divided between these three; for the Ballance may be held by the Weakest, who by his Address and Conduct, removing from either Scale, and adding of his own, may keep the Scales duly poised.[2]

One of Swift's editors dogmatically contradicted his author on this point: 'Swift forgot that a balance ceases to be true, as soon as its adjustment is entrusted to any one. It must either be maintained by its own equilibrium or it becomes a pretence sustained only by the application of arbitrary force.'[3] This comment illustrates the growing

[1] C. K. Webster, *The Foreign Policy of Palmerston* (Bell, 1951), vol. ii, pp. 801–2.
[2] *A Discourse of the Contests and Dissentions in Athens and Rome* (1701), ch. i (*A Tale of a Tub and other Early Works*, ed. Herbert Davis (Blackwell, 1957) p. 197).
[3] Henry Craik, *Selections from Swift* (Clarendon Press, 1892), vol. i, p. 367.

repudiation of the policy of the balance of power by a strand of British opinion in the nineteenth century, but it also indicates the ambiguities in the idea of holding the balance. They become apparent if we ask two questions: *Who* holds the balance in any given situation? and if the function of holding the balance be defined as an ability to contribute decisive strength to one side or the other, what is implied in the notion of *decisive strength*?

Who holds the balance? There are good grounds for the traditional British belief that it has been peculiarly Britain's role to hold the balance of Europe. From 1727 down to 1868 (with one or two lapses) the annual Mutiny Act described the function of the British army as 'the preservation of the balance of power in Europe'. To hold the balance has been a policy suited to an insular Power enjoying a certain detachment from Continental rivalries. But there have been other Powers with a degree of geographical detachment, particularly Russia.[1] At the end of the War of the Austrian Succession the Tsaritsa Elizabeth controlled the balance of Europe. In the American Revolutionary War Catherine the Great held the balance between Britain and the anti-British coalition of France, Spain and Holland. In the War of the Bavarian Succession she was in a similar position, courted by both Austria and Prussia, and assuming the role of the protectress of the German constitution, hitherto played by France. Likewise, between March and September 1939 Stalin held the balance between the Western Powers and the Axis. In other words, a Power holds the balance only so long as it does not commit itself; and when it has committed itself, there is a new situation in which the balance will probably be held by another Power.

Indeed, holding the balance of power has its nth Power problem. It is not only the Great Powers that can aspire to the role. Sometimes a small Power, through the accident of strategic position or the energy of its ruler, can contribute useful if not decisive strength to one side or the other, as Savoy in the seventeenth and eighteenth centuries used to hold the balance on the Alps, or as Yugoslavia today holds a balance in South-eastern Europe between the Communist and Western blocs. The belief that they can hold the balance of power may soothe the pride of Great Powers in decline. Immediately after the War de Gaulle stated his aim of grouping together the states which touch the Rhine, Alps and Pyrenees, and making of this organization the arbiter between the Anglo-Saxon and Soviet camps. 'France, in equipping herself with a nuclear weapon,' he said in 1959,

---

[1] 'It is a fundamental law that the outer regions in the west and east function, directly or indirectly, as counterweights to a concentration at the centre.' L. Dehio, *The Precarious Balance* (Chatto and Windus, 1963), p. 102.

L

'will render a service to world equilibrium'.[1] (The equilibrium between the Western and Communist blocs, or the equilibrium within NATO?) Many Japanese and some Germans have had the same idea for their own country. Acton argued that it was the Papacy itself which invented the system of the balance of power at the time of the Reformation to replace the Papal ascendancy of the Middle Ages. 'The Popes undertook to maintain their spiritual freedom through their territorial independence by the opposite plan to that of the *respublicana Christiana* under pope and emperor, by *preventing* predominance of any one power, not by courting it. So they created the system of balance of power as the security of their temporal power, as of old the imperial supremacy had been the implement and safeguard of their spiritual predominance.'[2] Others have attributed the beginnings of this policy to Venice. The Italian states aimed to hold the balance between the Kings of Spain and France as early as did Henry VIII. In 1553 Mary, Regent of the Netherlands, wrote to the imperial ambassador in England about the dangers which the Franco-Turkish alliance was bringing upon Italy, and added that if the Italian states knew their own interests they would confederate against the French King. 'Mais vous scavez les craintes qu'ilz ont de la grandeur de l'ung ou l'autre de ces deux princes [Charles V and Henry II] et soing de balancer leur pouvoir.'[3]

Sometimes a balance has been held by barbarians outside the pale of international society: the Iroquois held the balance in the first half of the eighteenth century between the English and French in North America. Whenever a Power is courted by both sides, it holds in some degree the balance of power. Turkish policy in the Second World War held a delicate balance both between the two belligerent blocs and between the Western Powers and Russia. Many a Small Power likes to think that it holds a balance, if only between its allies. The balance of power (in sense 2) is incompatible with the doctrines professed by the Afro-Asian states, and Nehru argued that the neutralist states cannot be a third force to maintain the balance of power, because they lack military strength to throw into the scales—they can only be a third area, united on moral not military grounds, through which efforts at conciliation could be channelled. But this implies a devaluation of the moral element in politics which seems inconsistent with much of Afro-Asian doctrine. Indian

[1] Statement on November 10, 1959 (*Guardian*, November 11, 1959).
[2] F. N. Gasquet, *Lord Acton and his Circle* (Allen, 1906), p. 250. Cf. Ranke, *History of the Popes*, book I, ch. iii (Bohn Library, Bell, 1913, vol. i, p. 67).
[3] Letter of October 8, 1553 (*Papiers d'Etat du Cardinal de Granvelle* (Paris, Imprimerie Royale, 1843), vol. iv, p. 121).

mediation over the repatriating of prisoners taken in the Korean War, the role of Krishna Menon at the Geneva Conference in 1954, Indian chairmanship of the three international commissions for supervizing the Indo-Chinese armistice, seemed to show to many Afro-Asians and others that India could act as an arbiter. The *Manchester Guardian* early in 1953 described the Indian attitude in these words: 'Their view about their duties in Asia is like that of European statesmen of the eighteenth century, who, in a situation which was constantly changing, planned the combinations of the Powers by which a certain stability might be achieved.'[1] There comes a point at which it is difficult to draw any clear distinction between 'maintaining' the balance of power (a function connected with sense 2) and 'holding' it. For any Power may find, in some circumstances, that it possesses a special role in preserving an even distribution of power. And we encounter here the confusion between the objective and the subjective estimates. There are many international situations in which an involved Power, and a Power relatively detached, will each interpret its policy by a responsibility for holding the balance. The notion of holding the balance shades easily into the hope of contributing some strength, whether decisive or not, which is almost equivalent to possessing some degree of freedom of action.

This brings us to the second question. What are the implications and consequences of holding the balance? If he who holds the scales is weaker than either of the Powers or coalitions which make the scales, his function will only be that of conciliator; but if he is as strong as either of them, or stronger, he will tend to become an arbiter. The answer lurks in Churchill's description of Locarno, and in the last sentence of the passage from Palmerston, both quoted above: 'Your Majesty may become the arbiter of events in Europe.' And a Power in this role may not always play it in a way that other Powers regard as just. It may be concerned less to maintain an even distribution of power than to improve its own position, 'The great danger of inviting, and accustoming Russia, on every emergency, to be the Mediatrix of Europe,' wrote the *Observer* in 1803, 'is that she will at length consider herself the Mistress of it also'.[1] The activity of holding the balance easily slides from possessing a special role (which implies a sense of duty) to possessing a special advantage; as easily as the notion of the balance of power slides from *an even* distribution to *any* distribution. There is an equivocality about most of the English claims to hold the balance of power from the sixteenth to the nineteenth centuries. It is illustrated by the earliest recorded

[1] Leading article, February 18, 1953.
[2] *Observer*, July 17, 1803, quoted in the issue of July 19, 1953.

use of the phrase in English, in Fenton's dedication to Queen Elizabeth of his translation of Guicciardini: 'And lastly [God] hath erected your seate upon a high hill or sanctuarie, and put into your hands the ballance of power and justice, to peaze and counterpeaze [appease and counterpoise] at your will the actions and counsels of all the Christian Kingdomes of your time.'[1] 'Balance' here means 'control'. Compare Waller's *Panegyric to My Lord Protector* in 1655:

> 'Heaven, (that has placed this island to give law,
> To balance Europe, and her states to awe)
> In this conjunction does on Britain smile:
> The greatest leader, and the greatest isle!'

When an English politician in 1704 rejoiced that the battle of Blenheim 'has given the balance of Europe into the Queen's hands', he meant that it had made England the strongest Power on the continent, with a freedom of action greater than that of other Powers.[2] Canning's doctrine that Britain should hold the balance between the conflicting ideologies on the Continent was similar. As he wrote to his friend Bagot, the British ambassador at St Petersburg, soon after the enunciation of the Monroe Doctrine, 'The effect of the ultra-liberalism of our Yankee co-operators, on the ultra-despotism of our Aix la Chapelle allies, gives me just the balance that I wanted.'[3] But this was Canning's private comment on what he afterwards publicly described as calling 'the New World into existence to redress the balance of the Old', and it contains perhaps a flavour of sense 5, that my side ought to have a margin of strength. Continental Powers have always noted that while Britain traditionally claimed to hold the balance of Europe with her right hand, with her left hand she was establishing an oceanic hegemony which refused for two centuries to admit any principle of equilibrium. Thus, from possessing a special role in maintaining an even distribution of power, holding the balance imperceptibly slides into (7) *possessing a special advantage in the existing distribution of power*. When Coral Bell writes:

'A consistent and in some ways a justified criticism of the policies of the western Powers in the period of the Cold War has been that

---

[1] Geffray Fenton, *The Historie of Guicciardin* . . . *reduced into English* (1579), epistle dedicatorie to the Queen, p. iv.
[2] G. M. Trevelyan, *Blenheim* (Longmans, 1930), p. 419.
[3] Letter of January 22, 1824 (*George Canning and his Friends*, ed. J. Bagot (Murray, 1909), vol. ii, pp. 217–18).

they have tended to deliver the balance of power into the hands of Germany and Japan, both potential revisionist states'.[1]

it is the second rather than the first of these meanings of the phrase that is conveyed.

It will be seen that the idea of the balance of power as a description of a state of affairs tends to slip away from the meaning of an even distribution to that of any possible distribution of power; and that the idea of the balance of power as a policy tends to slip away from the meaning of a duty or responsibility for preserving an even distribution, to that of enjoying a margin of strength or some special advantage. By these routes the balance of power comes to mean possessing a decisive advantage, or (8) *possessing predominance*. In this sense Chester Bowles wrote in 1956 that 'the two-thirds of the world who live in the undeveloped continents . . . will ultimately constitute the world balance of power'.[2] In this sense Bonaparte wrote to the Directory in 1797: 'Nous tenons la balance de l'Europe; nous la ferons pencher comme nous voudrons.'[3] And more dramatically, the Kaiser, visiting England for Queen Victoria's funeral in 1901, told Lord Lansdowne that the traditional English policy of upholding the balance of power was exploded: 'Die balance of power in Europa sei ich.'[4] Here at last the word balance has come to mean the opposite of its primary diplomatic sense: equilibrium has become preponderance, balance has become overbalance. Or, if you prefer, the word has returned to its still earlier pre-diplomatic sense of authoritative control. And the verbs that govern the phrase pass from possession to identification: from holding, through inclining, to 'constituting' or 'being'.

There remains to be considered the third answer to the question, By whom is power to be evenly distributed? 'The balance of power' sometimes implies an assertion that the groupings of Powers fall into ever-changing but ever reliable conditions of equilibrium. Thus it means (9) *an inherent tendency of international politics to produce an even distribution of power*. This assets a 'law' of international politics

---

[1] Coral Bell, *Survey of International Affairs 1954* (Oxford University Press, 1957), p. 10.
[2] 'Why I will vote Democratic', *Christianity and Crisis*, October 15, 1956, p. 137.
[3] Sorel, *L'Europe et la Révolution Française*, vol. v, p. 185.
[4] *Die Grosse Politik*, vol. xvii, p. 28. 'It was not the British fleet but the twenty-two German Army Corps that were the Balance of Power', H. von Eckardstein, *Ten Years at the Court of St James's* (Butterworth, 1921), p. 194. 'Lord Salisbury is antiquated. He is obsessed by the idea that there is a balance of power in Europe. There is no balance of power in Europe except *me*—me and my twenty-five corps', H. H. Asquith, *Genesis of the War* (Cassell, 1923), pp. 19–20.

that underlies and reinforces the 'principle' of the balance of power in sense 2; so that even if Powers neglect or repudiate the principle, the law will be seen at work overruling them. Rousseau saw it in this light when he wrote:

'Ne pensons pas que cet équilibre si vanté ait été établi par personne, et que personne ait rien fait à dessein de la conserver: on trouve qu'il existe; et ceux qui ne sentent pas en eux-mêmes assez de poids pour le rompre, couvrent leurs vues particulières du prétexte de la soutenir. Mais qu'on y songe ou non, cet équilibre subsiste, et n'a besoin que de lui-même pour se conserver, sans que personne s'en mêle; et quand il se romproit un moment d'un côté, il se rétabliroit bientôt d'un autre: de sorte que si les princes qu'on accusoit d'aspirer à la monarchie universelle y ont réellement aspiré, ils montroient en cela plus d'ambition que de génie.'[1]

Between 1848 and 1914, says A. J. P. Taylor, the balance of power 'seemed to be the political equivalent of the laws of economics, both self-operating. If every man followed his own interest, all would be prosperous; and if every state followed its own interest, all would be peaceful and secure.'[2] 'The Balance of Power', says Toynbee, 'is a system of political dynamics that comes into play whenever a society articulates itself into a number of mutually independent local states.' It 'operates in a general way to keep the average calibre of states low in terms of every criterion for the measurement of political power . . . a state which threatens to increase its calibre above the prevailing average becomes subject, almost automatically, to pressure from all the other states that are members of the same political constellation'.[3] It might even be said that in contemporary political writings, the balance of power as this kind of sociological law has tended to replace the balance of power as moral and legal principle.

But even in this usage there is a tendency to slide away from the notion of even distribution of power—to express rather the endless shiftings and regroupings of power, the scales perpetually oscillating without coming to rest. When Rostovtzeff writes 'The complicated political situation which constituted the balance of power among the

[1] Rousseau, *Projet de Paix Perpetuelle* (with translation by E. M. Nuttall, Cobden-Sanderson, 1927), pp. 26–8.
[2] *The Struggle for Mastery in Europe 1848-1918* (Clarendon Press, 1954), p. xx.
[3] A. J. Toynbee, *A Study of History* (Oxford University Press, 1934), vol. iii, pp. 301–2.

Hellenistic States gave rise to almost uninterrupted warfare',[1] the long perspective almost loses sight of the recurring equilibria of power, and the phrase becomes almost synonymous with the states-system itself.

The law of the balance of power has a certain fascination and credibility in relation to Western international history since the beginning of the sixteenth century. 'The balance of power', said Stubbs in 1880, 'however it be defined, i.e. whatever the powers were between which it was necessary to maintain such equilibrium, that the weaker should not be crushed by the union of the stronger, is the principle which gives unity to the political plot of modern European history.'[2] (Here the usage seems nearer sense 9 than sense 2.) But it is necessary to take account of contrary indications. It has often been remarked that, while international society has widened from Western Europe to cover the whole world, there has been a steady reduction in the number of Great Powers, from the eight of the years before 1914 to the Big Two of today. Though the field of the balance of power expanded, the number of decisive weights has decreased. The precedent of earlier states-systems, such as that of ancient China before the establishment of the Ts'in empire, and of the Hellenistic world before the Roman Empire, have also been noted. Barraclough has argued, following Dehio, that the law of the balance of power has been good for Europe, but that 'outside Europe, the principle of preponderant Powers is securely established'.[3] This seems an over-simplification. On the one hand, within Europe (if it be considered by itself) the balance of power has worked itself out by 1945, with the partition of the continent between the two remaining Great Powers, both of them extra-European. On the other hand, outside Europe the operation of the balance of power is evident enough. In North America there was a kind of balance of power between Spanish, English, French and Indians for two hundred years before the infant United States became predominant. In India there was a balance of power between English, French and various succession states of the Mogul Empire for a hundred years before Britain became pre-

[1] M. Rostovtzeff, *Social and Economic History of the Hellenistic World* (Clarendon Press, 1941), vol. i, p. 36; cf. p. 43. Cf. D. M. Bueno de Mesquita, *Giangaleazzo Visconti* (Cambridge University Press, 1941), p. 60: 'The rivalries of these states formed the main content of Italian politics; the smaller cities and lesser rulers precariously survived by means of a rapid adjustment to the momentary balance of the five powers.'

[2] W. Stubbs, *Seventeen Lectures on the Study of Medieval and Modern History* (Clarendon Press, 1887), p. 258.

[3] G. Barraclough, *History in a Changing World* (Blackwell, 1955), p. 176. Cf. L. Dehio, *The Precarious Balance*, p. 123.

dominant. In China there was a balance of power between all the Western Great Powers, except Austria-Hungary and Italy but including Japan, for a hundred years before it was overthrown by Japan. In the Middle East there was a balance of power—the Eastern Question was one of the most famous essays in the balance of power—for more than a hundred years before Britain acquired in 1919 the lion's share of the Ottoman Empire. And in Africa, a balance was achieved between French and British power which continued until the emancipation of the African states in the past couple of years. In all these regions, as well as in the world as a whole, the balance of power is discernible. But *equally* discernible is 'the principle of preponderant Powers', so that it may be wondered whether the two are not complementary. It has been argued in this paper that the very idea and language of the balance of power has a mobility that tends, so to speak, to defeat its own original purpose, so that the phrase comes to mean predominance instead of equilibrium. And if political 'laws' are in question, it may be wondered whether there may not be another law of international politics besides the balance of power, slower in operation and ultimately overriding it: a law of the concentration or monopoly of power.

The idea of the balance of power has been repudiated from opposite sides. It is always rejected by Powers aspiring to predominance; and in the past two hundred years it has been rejected by a large body of radical opinion, both liberal and socialist. But both kinds of critic have in the end found themselves entangled in what they disbelieved.

Instead of the independence of nations based on and secured by a system of equilibrium, Powers aiming at predominance have asserted some ideal of solidarity and unification, from the Tridentine Catholicism of Philip II's Spain down to Hitler's New Order in Europe, and the United Soviet Republics of the World which seems to be the long-term aim, in so far as there is one, of the rulers of the USSR.[1] 'What Britain called the balance of power,' said Hitler with some truth, 'was nothing but the disintegration and disorganization of the Continent.'[2]

'As for the balance of power,' said Burke of the Jacobins, 'it was so far from being admitted by France . . . that in the whole body of their authorized or encouraged reports and discussions on the theory

[1] Elliott R. Goodman, *The Soviet Design for a World State* (Columbia University Press, 1960).

[2] Speech in the Berliner Sportpalast, January 30, 1941 (*The Times*, January 31, 1941).

of the diplomatick system, they constantly rejected the very idea of the balance of power, and treated it as the true cause of all the wars and calamities that had afflicted Europe . . . Exploding, therefore, all sorts of balances, they avow their design to erect themselves into a new description of empire, which is not grounded on any balance, but forms a sort of impious hierarchy, of which France is to be the head and guardian.'[1]

Nor was it simply idealism that made the United States in her earliest years repudiate the balance of power along with entangling alliances. From the moment of her independence, she was the predominant Power in the New World, as Hamilton clearly saw. 'We may hope, ere long,' he wrote in 1787, 'to become the arbiter of Europe in America, and to be able to incline the balance of European competitions in this part of the world as our interest may dictate. . . . Our situation invites and our interests prompt us to aim at an ascendant in the system of American affairs.'[2]

Nevertheless, when facing defeat by a grand alliance, a predominant Power may hasten to seek the protection of the principle it has formerly neglected. George III, writing to Catherine the Great for her assistance in the American Revolutionary War, said that a mere naval demonstration by her 'pourra restituer et assurer le repos de l'Europe entière, en dissipant la ligue qui s'est formée contre moi, et en maintenant ce système d'équilibre que cette ligue cherche à détruire'.[3] After the battle of Stalingrad, German propaganda began appealing to the principle of the balance of power against the overmighty strength of Russia, just as Napoleon at St Helena sometimes argued that his own policy had been directed by the same principle against the same danger. Holland Rose could write thus of Britain's defeat in the American War:

'Thus, the trend of European politics in the East, in Germany, and in the Netherlands told heavily against England, and increased the natural reluctance of any Power to seek the friendship of a beaten nation. It is at such times that the artificiality of the idea of the Balance of Power is seen. No State took the slightest interest in restoring the islanders to their rightful position in the world.'[4]

Here is a naïve expression of the belief that one's own nation, when

[1] *Letters on a Regicide Peace*, No. 3 (*Works*, vol. ii, pp. 333–4).
[2] *The Federalist*, No. xi (Everyman edition, pp. 50, 53).
[3] *Diaries and Correspondence of the First Earl of Malmesbury*, vol. i, p. 228.
[4] J. Holland Rose, *William Pitt and National Revival* (Bell, 1911), pp. 300–1.

deprived of its hegemony, has a right to appeal to the principle of the balance of power, coupled with the belief that the balance of power is pretty ineffective anyway.

On the other hand, there were those who thought that, though the balance of power might be desirable, the price to be paid might be too high.

> 'Now *Europe's* balanc'd, neither Side prevails,
> For nothing's left in either of the Scales,'

wrote Pope towards the end of the Spanish Succession War,[1] with more wit than truth—showing that the politicians' appeal to the principle of the balance of power was beginning to yield diminishing returns in public conviction. Men who were told that taxation and wars were necessary to maintain the balance of power, naturally blamed the balance of power when they were tired of taxation and wars. In 1758 a book was published at Altona with the title *Die Chimaere des Gleichgewichts von Europa*, arguing against the balance of power as an excuse for endless mutual interference:

'If the equilibrium were ever realized nothing could be more terrible than the enslavement of every state with regard to its neighbours—it would be necessary to recognize in every state the right to intervene in the domestic affairs of the others—it would be better indeed to have a universal monarchy, for to be subject to several states at the same time would be much harder than to be dependent on the one.'[2]

The argument has been revived by critics of the United Nations. Kant's treatment of the balance of power perhaps shows the intellectual rejection of the idea consolidating itself. In the *Idee zu einer allgemeinen Geschichte* (1784) he seems to see 'ein Gesetz des Gleichgewichts', for the regulation of the wholesome antagonism of contiguous states as if springing up out of their freedom, as a halfway house to the international federation which he advocates.[3] In the *Verhaeltnis der Theorie zur Praxis im Voelkerrecht* (1793) he wrote:

'The maintenance of universal peace by means of the so-called

---

[1] In 1711. Alexander Pope, *Minor Poems*, ed. Norman Ault and John Butt (Twickenham Edition, vol. vi, Methuen, 1954), p. 82.
[2] Quoted in Butler and Maccoby, *Development of International Law*, p. 68.
[3] Seventh principle (Kant, *Werke* (Academy edition), vol. viii, p. 26; Hastie, *Kant's Principles of Politics*, pp. 19–20).

Balance of Power in Europe is—like Swift's house, which a master-builder constructed in such perfect accord with all the laws of equilibrium, that when a sparrow alighted upon it, it immediately collapsed—a mere figment of the imagination.'[1]

The doctrines of the American and French Revolutions seemed to offer an alternative principle for international society, fraternal, uncompetitive, above all simple. For all who were touched by these doctrines the balance of power was condemned as an obsolete principle of the Ancien Regime, the diplomatic counterpart of hereditary absolute monarchy. The example of the United States, serenely aloof from the ordinary rules of foreign politics, had a powerful influence on English radicals in the nineteenth century. The policy of the balance of power was criticized by Cobden and Bright, mainly on practical grounds, as a source of constant wars and unnecessary entanglements, but with more lasting cogency on intellectual grounds, as a mischievous delusion that means so many different things that it means nothing at all. 'So far as we can understand the subject', said Cobden, 'the theory of a balance of power is a mere chimera—a creation of the politician's brain—a phantasm without definite form or tangible existence—a mere conjunction of syllables, forming words which convey sound without meaning.' He combined ridicule with the most powerful reasoned attack in English political writing on the whole conception:

'The balance of power, then might, in the first place, be very well dismissed as *chimera*, because no state of things, such as the "disposition", "constitution", or "union", of European powers, referred to as the basis of their system, by Vattel, Gentz, and Brougham, ever did exist;—and, secondly, the theory could, on other grounds, be discarded as *fallacious*, since it gives no definition —whether by breadth of territory, number of inhabitants, or extent of wealth—according to which, in balancing the respective powers, each state shall be estimated;—whilst, lastly, it would be altogether incomplete and inoperative, from neglecting or refusing to provide against, the silent and peaceful aggrandizements which spring from movements and labour. Upon these triple grounds, the question of the balance of power might be dismissed from further consideration.'[2]

This sketches almost all the points of subsequent debate, from Cobden's day to our own.

[1] *Werke*, vol. viii, p. 312.
[2] *The Political Writings of Richard Cobden* (Ridgway, 1868), vol. i, pp. 263, 269

The English tradition of idealist internationalism and the American tradition of rejecting the balance of power converged in the First World War, to produce the League of Nations. In Wilson's view, 'the great game, now forever discredited, of the balance of power' was abolished.[1] 'There must be, not a balance of power, but a community of power; not organized rivalries, but an organized common peace.'[2] And it became accepted doctrine that the balance of power was no longer the constituent principle of international society. Probably the most influential English textbook of international law is Oppenheim's. In its pre-War editions of 1905 and 1911 it described the balance of power as a political principle indispensable to the existence of international law. In its post-War editions, and especially after Lauterpacht took over the editorship of it, this was replaced by a reference to the new international organizations. During the 1920s, that unique interlude in diplomatic history when no Great Power was left on the European continent except an exhausted and pacific France, and the two Anglo-Saxon Great Powers had in their degrees retreated into self-sufficiency, the balance of power was banished from writings about contemporary international relations. Historians played their part. In a notable Chatham House address in 1923, Pollard sought with learning and acuteness to bury the idea[3]; and it became customary to refer to it as an obsolete principle, 'that favourite objective of eighteenth-century statesmanship'.[4]

But in the 1930s it became increasingly difficult to suppress the obsolete principle of interpretation. By a coincidence there were published in 1932 two books with titles that incorporated the phrase. *The Balance of the Continents* described a balance transformed through the sublimation of the element of power: 'the continents are impelled to establish the equilibrium by economic interests and juridical ideals endangered by financial or political recklessness: it is the balance of co-operation, spiritualized social elements seeking a universal rhythm'.[5] This may be taken as a late flower of the new orthodoxy: almost, in the circumstances, its *reductio ad absurdum*.

---

[1] Address to Congress, February 11, 1918 (*The Messages and Papers of Woodrow Wilson* (New York, Review of Reviews Corporation, 1924), vol. i, p. 478).
[2] Address to the Senate, January 22, 1917 (*ibid.*, p. 351).
[3] A. F. Pollard, 'The Balance of Power', *Journal of the British Institute of International Affairs*, March 1923. Cf. his *Wolsey* (Longmans, 1929), pp. 119–20, and his letter to *The Times*, July 24, 1939, with the letter in reply from Sir John Orr, August 29, 1939.
[4] E.g. A. Aspinall, reviewing Guedalla's *Palmerston* in *History*, July 1929, N.S., vol. xiv, p. 166.
[5] M. H. Cornejo, *The Balance of the Continents* (Oxford University Press, 1932), p. 206.

The second book showed the older doctrine reasserting itself. *The New Balance of Power in Europe* was a straight political study of European developments: 'Two political groups are racing to attain military supremacy. One of these groups seeks to maintain the political structure of Europe, the other strives to change it.'[1]

Wilson had been able to repudiate the conception of the balance of power in 1918–19 with such immense authority, only because the United States under his leadership had been drawn into the system of the balance. The original idea of the League of Nations was to transform the temporary preponderance of power thus brought about into a permanent preponderance of law-abiding states against any breaker of the new Covenant. To the defeated Germans this resembled the balance of power in sense 8: predominance—a Pax Anglo-Saxonica. To the victors it resembled implicitly (for the phrase was seldom used) a transformation of the balance of power in sense 5; that the upholders of the collective system should have a margin of strength, as Smuts said, 'which will give stability to that decentralization (brought about by the principle of national self-determination) and thereby guarantee the weak against the strong'.[2] 'It is obvious that the one indispensable condition of such a system of collective security is that the States who can be relied upon to be loyal to it shall be superior in strength to those who may assail it.'[3] Thus, at the centre of all the surrounding controversy about the relations between Great Powers and small, the supposed injustice of the peace settlement, and the inadequate provisions for peaceful change, the League's supporters came to understand the League not as replacing but as perfecting the Concert of the Powers, and the principle of collective security not as a substitute for the balance of power but as improving, regulating, institutionalizing it. It was 'only a more scientific development of the doctrine of the balance of

---

[1] Valentine de Balla, *The New Balance of Power in Europe* (Johns Hopkins Press, 1932), preface.

[2] *The League of Nations—Practical Suggestions*, December 16, 1918. Extracts from this pamphlet are printed in *The History of the Peace Conference*, ed. H. W. V. Temperley, vol. iii (Frowde, 1920), pp. 52–4. On the balance of power and the founding of the League see further, *History of the Peace Conference*, vol. vi (Frowde, 1924), pp. 575–7, and A. J. Toynbee, *The World after the Peace Conference* (Oxford University Press, 1925), pp. 47–51.

[3] A. Salter, *Security* (Macmillan, 1939), p. 108. Cf. his *Recovery* (Bell, 1932), p. 278: 'The definite addition of America's influence' to 'the forces in the world supporting the "collective" system of Covenant and [Kellogg] Pact' 'would turn the balance decisively in their favour'. Cf. J. L. Brierly, writing in 1942: 'What is essential is a preponderance of force in the hands of those who are determined to maintain the peace' (*The Basis of Obligation in International Law* (Clarendon Press, 1958), p. 272).

power as laid down by Pitt, Castlereagh and Palmerston'.[1] The decisive breakdown of the League was in the end over a disputed interpretation of the balance of power—whether it was more important to check actual but local Italian aggrandizement in Africa, or to preserve the Stresa Front against potential but general German aggrandizement in Europe.

The First World War had transformed the United States into the holder of the balance of power; the Second World War completed her involvement by making her into one of the weights of a simple balance. But at the same time the Charter of the United Nations proposed an institution further removed from the balance of power than the League had been. The voting procedure of the Security Council was the negation of the principle of balance: giving every Great Power the right to jam the movement of the scales at will, it offered the alternatives of community of power or anarchy. Its undesigned blessing was that it was incapable of working, and the idea of the community of power had a shorter life after 1945 than it had had after 1919. It can be found in Bevin's speeches until the Communist seizure of Czechoslovakia. After that the balance of power becomes once more a respectable and indeed indispensable part of the diplomatic vocabulary, and an object of almost metaphysical contemplation by the strategic analysts.

Is then the balance of power the guarantee of the independence of nations? or is it the occasion of war? The only answer is that it is both. So long as the absence of international government means that Powers are primarily preoccupied with their survival, so long will they seek to maintain some kind of balance between them. It is easy to point to instances in which the final move in the rectification of the balance has been war. It is less easy, either to remember, or to establish, how often the balance of power has averted war. For the balance of power is not the 'cause' of war; the cause of war, however one chooses to identify it, lies in the political conditions which the balance of power in some degree regulates and reduces to order. The alternative to the balance of power is not the community of power: unless this means federation, it is a chimera. International politics have never revealed, nor do they today, a habitual recognition among states of a community of interest overriding their separate interest, comparable to that which normally binds individuals within the state. And where conflicts of interest between organized groups are insurmountable, the only principle of order is to try to maintain, at the price of perpetual vigilance, an even distribution of power. The alternatives are either universal anarchy, or universal

[1] C. K. Webster, *The Art and Practice of Diplomacy* (Chatto and Windus, 1961).

dominion. The balance of power is generally regarded as preferable to the first, and most people have not yet been persuaded that the second is so preferable to the balance of power that they will easily submit to it.

CHAPTER 8

COLLECTIVE SECURITY AND MILITARY ALLIANCES

G. F. HUDSON

A fundamental change in the nature of war between earlier and recent times has been the increased possibility of decisive operations at the very outset of war, or even before declaration of it, with the consequence that plans and preparations made before the outbreak have come to be ever more important as compared with measures taken when the war is already in progress. This development has not only affected each nation's own peace-time defence preparations; it has had a vital bearing on the formation of military alliances, for unless the allies have concerted in advance their strategic plans for the emergency foreseen in the alliance, they have little chance of effectively co-ordinating their military efforts in time to meet the initial major effort of the enemy when war comes, and their alliance is consequently of only limited value, even though its *casus foederis* may be acknowledged without delay. This is fairly obvious where formally concluded military alliances between two or more nations are concerned. What has been less generally recognized, however, has been that such considerations are also relevant to the concept of collective security as it has been evolved by the promoters of the League of Nations and the United Nations, and of multilateral guarantee treaties such as the Locarno Treaty of 1925.

The basic idea of collective security is that a country will be protected against aggression, not by an alliance which is specifically directed against a particular country or group of countries, but by a treaty system binding its signatories to come to the assistance of any nation which is a victim of aggression. By assistance is here meant military aid such as would be expected from a partner in a military alliance, and not merely the moral support or economic measures which some theorists of international organization formerly believed to be sufficient to restrain even a Great Power from the use of force. The principle of collective security is that state A is pledged to go to the aid of B if B is attacked by C, and thus far the effect is the same as if A and B had an ordinary military alliance. But A is also pledged to go to the aid of C if C is attacked by A, and A cannot regard itself as the ally of B more than of C, because theoretically it is an open question whether, if an act of war should occur, B or C would be the aggressor. In the same way B has indeterminate obligations towards A and C, and C towards A and B, and so on with a vast number of variants as the system is extended to more and more states. The point of practical military importance about such a system is that, although the obligations assumed and the protection expected are supposed to be as in an ordinary military alliance, the preliminary planning appropriate to an alliance cannot be undertaken because it is impossible to know what the alignment of states will be if there is an armed conflict.

The problem may be illustrated by a comparison of British-French military relations before 1914 and during the period of the Locarno Treaty. Before 1914 there was not even a formal defensive alliance between Britain and France, but so sure were the political and military leaders in both countries that their national interests would compel them to be on the same side against Germany in a European war that the General Staffs were allowed to enter into detailed discussion of military co-operation to be put into effect in the first stage of such a war. It was decided by what route the British Expeditionary Force was to go to France, what port and railway facilities were to be reserved for it, and where it was to go in relation to the planned deployment of the French Army. Without these pre-war arrangements the British participation in the war in France in August and September of 1914 would not have been possible. In the period of the Locarno Treaty, however, Britain, although now bound by a treaty commitment to aid France against a German attack, was also bound to aid Germany in case of a French invasion. Nothing was done to prepare for a possible fulfilment of these obligations by staff conversations with either France or Germany, for it was psychologically impossible to make plans with the one for fighting the other after having made plans with the other for fighting the war the other way round. Any operational agreement with either France or Germany would have had to be made after the outbrdak of hostilities according to the decision on intervention on the particular issue arising. Down to March 1936 there were no Anglo-French staff conversations; only after the German repudiation of the Locarno Treaty at the time of the reoccupation of the Rhineland were there again such inter-staff arrangements, with the result that a British expeditionary force was again in 1939, as in 1914, quickly put into the field in France—though this time, because of the different direction of German strategy, the need was less urgent. The absence of any Anglo-French inter-staff planning in 1936 was not indeed the decisive factor in the French failure to take action in the Rhineland, for the French army was at that time still strong enough to have

M

dealt with the Germans by itself, but the military aloofness certainly made it easier for the Baldwin Cabinet to follow its isolationalist impulses and disclaim any responsibility for implementing the British guarantee of the demilitarized zone.

The Locarno Treaty had been framed in accordance with the principles embodied in the Covenant of the League of Nations and was linked to it by a provision for appeal to the League Council. The League system displayed on a grand scale the characteristic features of the Locarno formula; in theory all members of the League were equally likely or unlikely to commit aggression, and there could be no knowing against whom the collective force of the League might have to be directed any more than a policeman knows in advance whom he may be called on at any time to arrest. It may be held that the League was not really a military security system at all, since the Covenant—a document full of ambiguous compromises—nowhere specifically bound members to wage war against an aggressor. On the other hand, Article 16 certainly implied naval blockade as well as embargoes, and even the application of embargoes depended on ability to resist coercive action designed to avert them. But there were no schemes for joint defence or for sharing the sacrifices which might be involved. Since nobody could have any idea who would be in conflict with whom, it was impossible to plan anything in advance. One of the headaches for military planners in Britain after 1918 was the uncertainty as to what tasks the armed forces might be called to carry out under the League Covenant, and what assistance the country might expect to receive in an emergency from the new international organization.

The essence of a genuine alliance system is that both the commitments and the aid to be expected are precisely defined. In a fully developed alliance the contingents to be provided and the initial strategy to be adopted against a common enemy are specified. Thus the government and the service staffs know the limit of their liabilities and also on what they can count in a war crisis, provided, of course, that the ally fulfils his obligations. Confidence that the ally will fulfil his obligations is in turn increased by the extent of peace-time co-operation and joint planning. Habits of mutual consultation, the pooling of resources, of intelligence and of technical skills, and the interlocking of command organizations, all bind together the partners in an alliance so that in an emergency they will tend automatically to help one another even in advance of definite decisions to do so. In the dozen years since the establishment of NATO, the peace-time military amalgamation of its members has already gone much further than could have been imagined among allied sovereign states in the nineteenth century. A similar amalgamation exists among the states adhering to the Warsaw Pact, but there it is based on a community of political faith professed by ruling parties which have long been accustomed to accept directives from a single centre, whereas NATO is an association of democratic states brought together by a sense of common danger but without uniformity of doctrine or social pattern.

Britain today, as never before in time of peace, has become dependent on allies for her security, and has yielded her cherished freedom of action to the collective decisions of a combination of powers. The bitter experience of two world wars and awareness of economic and strategic weakness in a dangerous world has led Britain to abandon the idea of keeping clear of international entanglements and judging every issue on its merits when the time comes. The partial surrender of freedom in policy has been made, however, not to the world organization posited by idealists as the alternative to a system of sovereign states, but to a power bloc which in the contemporary international situation is arrayed against another power bloc of comparable strength, with a relatively weak, though numerous, aggregate of states outside both of them.

Membership of an organization such as NATO involves a special kind of dilemma for a nation which depends on it for security. Should the responses of the allies to an attack on any one of them be as rapid and nearly automatic as possible, or should there be provision for joint deliberation and judgment before commitment of forces? Or in a popular phrase, 'How many fingers on the trigger?' The answer to this question must depend primarily on whether one thinks of one's own country being attacked or of being called on to go to the aid of someone else's. If Britain were threatened with aggression, perhaps with nuclear bombardment, we should want to be sure that aid from allies, and particularly from America, would be immediate and unrestricted, without the native hue of resolution being sicklied o'er by discussions between a dozen states to decide whether they should take action or not. On the other hand, if one of our allies were to incur the danger of attack by what we considered provocative behaviour, we should want some kind of machinery of consulation and collective decision to ensure that we were not dragged into war by the selfish unilateral policy of another state. The principle of 'My ally, right or wrong' is one which cuts both ways; it can be reassuring as a guarantee for oneself but alarming as a liability to help others.

Twice since NATO was founded have situations arisen in which it seemed that the coalition might be committed to war by unilateral acts of its members. During the Korean war Britain was afraid that American retaliation against China might start a general conflagration, and exerted maximum pressure in Washington to prevent this from happening; if the war had spread, however, Britain could hardly have kept out of it or allowed America to be defeated by abstaining from the conflict. In 1956, when Britain and France attacked Egypt without consulting America, America condemned their action and yet gave warning that Russian intervention would bring her in on their side. If the basic consideration in an alliance is that one cannot afford to see one's ally crushed, whatever his behaviour, then disapproval of his actions will not prevent participation in war in his support; on the other hand, a coalition war in such circumstances clearly involves an extreme moral disarray such as may jeopardize the whole war effort. It is of the greatest importance to endeavour by full and continuous consultation between allies to prevent such situations from arising.

But even if the members of a power bloc restrain one another from adventures, the bloc remains judge in its own cause since there is no authority to which it is subject. Both the Great Power blocs of the contemporary world are contained within the United Nations, but the latter has no supreme power over them such as was envisaged by its makers, as also by those who framed the Covenant of 1919. The idea of a world security organization issuing impartial injunctions, and third-party verdicts enforceable against an aggressor by the overwhelming power of nations 'not parties to the dispute', remains in the realm of dreams. But the United Nations has recently performed with some success a more modest, but very valuable, role. The 'Dagforces' formed of contingents from 'uncommitted' nations are not capable of coercing the rival Power blocs, but they can curb and limit conflicts which might otherwise grow into major wars through being aggravated by bloc rivalry. Since the Great Powers are so bitterly at odds among themselves they have had to depute to Indians, Swedes and Irishmen the policing of the world outside the borders of their alliances.

CHAPTER 9

THE NEW DIPLOMACY AND HISTORICAL DIPLOMACY

H. BUTTERFIELD

I

Since the First World War it has often been argued that old rules of policy and traditional techniques of international action are superseded because the methods and maxims of 'cabinet diplomacy' are not relevant in the world of modern democracies. The point is still liable to appear in discussions of these matters, when an attempt is made to see a present-day problem in the light of history. Nobody can doubt that adaptability to change is of the first importance in a world as dynamic as that of the twentieth century; but discrimination may be needed, if there are lessons of long-term experience which, once they are lost, it might be a costly matter to recover. It was once the assumption that there are important things which are not to be learned within the space of a single lifetime. According to this view, if each generation (or each new class of society that moves into the ascendancy) has to learn all its lessons over again through bitter experience, the wisdom is likely always to come too late. The matters that are in question are liable to be of a fundamental character, like the lesson that had to be learned in the 1930s: namely, that in a world of armed states a nation that is relatively disarmed must not expect to prevail in negotiation, as though reason held the sovereignty in human affairs. It is possible therefore that, while there is danger because at a certain level the mind is not sufficiently flexible to meet the needs of a dynamic age, there may exist at the same time (and at a profounder level) too little realization of what might be called the long-term lessons of experience. The point has some relevance for the whole structure of our thinking if we are contemplating international affairs not merely in their connection with present-day issues but as a whole aspect of the history and experience of mankind. It concerns, also, the question of political education— particularly the education of a democracy.

After the First World War it was easy to imagine that the diplomats were responsible for the catastrophe—responsible for the wars they had been unable to prevent. There occurred, therefore, a strong reaction against the 'old diplomacy', and particularly against what was called 'secret diplomacy'. In any case, it was asserted (sometimes even in the highest quarters) that, in the future, policy would have to be tailored to the needs of modern democracy—conducted under 'simpler' rules than in the eighteenth and nineteenth centuries. In 1919 there existed amongst the Western powers a utopianism which had no parallel after the end of the Second World War.

On the other hand, there were people in the nineteenth century who, as they contemplated the advent of democracy, already feared that the coming age would be prone to wilfulness in foreign policy. They thought that the masses would give way to passions, moral indignations and short-cut forms of reasoning, lacking the patience for the understanding of 'the other party' (the foreigner), lacking the foresight for the pursuit of long-term objects, and failing to realize the things that might be achieved by diplomatic methods—failing even to see that diplomacy, instead of being a mere game of intrigue and subtlety, might actually be a creative art.

We may wonder whether the proclamation of a 'new diplomacy' and 'simpler' types of policy in 1919 was not itself an example of the danger which some of our predecessors were dreading—in fact, a facile attempt to pander to the self-esteem of the masses. The call for a 'simpler' diplomacy envisaged a world in which there were 'good' states harassed only because they had to deal with the possible emergence of 'bad' ones and it involved just the inflexible kind of self-righteousness, and the unhistorical attitude towards the past, which might be expected to characterize an age of young democracies. It might have been better, after 1919, therefore, not to humour the inexperienced democracies so much, but to press upon them the urgent need for education in the whole problem of international affairs, now that they were taking upon themselves such great responsibilities in these matters. Parliaments themselves (at least in their better days) had shown a kind of self-discipline in this field, and in many parts of Europe had allowed the royal prerogative a special authority in foreign policy. Perhaps, instead of proclaiming so complete a break in 1919, it would have been better to take the line that here was the moment for asserting (and insisting upon) the continuity of history, or the importance of gaining every possible benefit from man's long-term experience. In any case, it is possible that statesmanship and rules of policy are not amenable to the kind of arbitrary re-definition that was envisaged in the years after 1919—not capable of being rendered 'simpler' by an act of will, or by the mere fact that democracies needed to have them simplified.

In favour of this critical attitude towards the developments which took place after 1919, it might be argued that, if there are rules of diplomacy and laws of foreign policy, these must be valid whether the business is conducted by men or women, whites or blacks, monarchies or democracies, cabinets or parliaments. If it is unwise to exploit a victory over-much, or to forget that the enemy of today may be needed as an ally tomorrow—if it is wrong, through reliance upon the virtue of a certain power, to allow that power to get into a position in which it can misbehave with impunity—these things do not become more admissible when practised by democracies rather than by monarchies. It may be true that some of the routines of diplomacy—some of the techniques and detailed practices—may depend on conditions (on the state of communications, for example, or the character of the *régimes* involved); but this can hardly be the case with rules of policy and the way in which consequences proceed out of causes in international relations. Out of the experience of centuries, there ought to have arisen, if not something like a science of diplomacy, at least a ripe kind of wisdom in regard to the conduct of foreign policy—rules or maxims possessing a permanent validity, at any rate so long as policy is being operated within a system of nation-states. After 1919 the principle of 'the balance of power' was treated as a kind of prescription—a policy which it was open to one to adopt or to reject. In fact it is rather a formulation of the way in which national interests do actually operate, and already operated before the principle came to its conscious formulation. If the principle of the balance of power was useful or valid in the eighteenth century, it was likely to be useful or valid in the twentieth century, for its *rationale* never had anything to do with the character of particular *régimes*. In reality the principle first came to consciousness not even in the world of nation-states at all, but amongst the city-states of the Renaissance.

We may ask therefore: Is there not something which can be condensed from the experience of many centuries, and is there not a point in extracting or collecting this, and turning it into a teachable form? Or are we to say that a new kind of *régime* must face the additional difficulty of inventing a new type of diplomacy? The Napoleonic Empire represented a new type of *régime*, but it is remarkable to see how much Napoleon learned of the fundamental rules of policy from a conscious use of history—a use only feasible perhaps for a man of peculiar insight. Also, the lines of his foreign policy projected themselves in quite an astonishing way from the grooves that had been formed by traditional French diplomacy. Something of the same would appear to have been true in the development of the policies of Soviet Russia. In a world where so many Powers, great and small, are continually pulling and thrusting, are there no rules about the play of forces that remain fundamentally the same, whatever further complications may have been superimposed by the advent of a new *régime*? This prompts the further query: whether the twentieth century has done justice to the permanent and fundamental elements in the structure of what we call a foreign policy—whether it would not have developed faster and further if, instead of emphasizing the break with the past in 1919, it had set out to retain the accumulated wisdom and experience, and build its superstructure on the top of that. The new democracies have had to learn at great cost the consequences of the breach of certain maxims the importance of which our predecessors had already deduced from bitter experiences. Even old democracies failed to acquire the necessary knowledge of the nature of diplomacy itself, remaining unaware, for example, of the need for armaments under the conditions of the inter-war period—the need for armaments not for the purpose of war-making but for the purpose of e.g. securing the necessary 'pull' in negotiations.

In this connection, it may not be entirely irrelevant to take note of the very considerable decline in the study of diplomatic history which has been taking place in recent decades in this country. It is partly an incident in the general decline of what we customarily call political history. Partly also it is due to the fact that our 'general history' (i.e. our European history), instead of being a dry account of the external relations of states has been turning into a survey of the development of our whole civilization. The decline is most remarkable of all amongst research students, however, and here it is particularly regrettable; for diplomatic history, owing to the nature of its documentation and to the kind of precision-work it requires, happens to be an excellent initial training for an historian. A conscious reaction against diplomatic history in general began to occur in the latter half of the nineteen-thirties, and this was partly due to the influence of Marxist history and the tendency to reduce policy to certain economic determinants. A particular campaign was waged against the kind of history that was written out of diplomatic documents, on the ground that the actions and policies of states were based on considerations not recorded in such documents. Diplomatic documents had been the first to occupy the historian after the rise of a more scientific history and the gradual opening of the archives in the nineteenth century. They acquired such status that, pending the release of further types of documentation, diplomatic reports were used as the authorities for the *internal* histories of countries in a way that would not be admissible at the present time. Diplomatic history was an old subject, therefore, and by the middle of the nineteen-thirties research-students were pressing upon the date-limits of our archives. Whereas in 1919 these students were grouped in the period around the Congress of Vienna, by 1934 they were congested around the period 1875–77, and many of them were finding it difficult to discover untrodden ground. Economic history, on the other hand, was a comparatively new subject, and Marxism had important effects even on non-Marxist historians in the latter half of the nineteen-thirties. A further reason for the decline of diplomatic history was the fact that its writers were sometimes too dry and austere, producing a history that was too much a mere digest of the documents, without sufficient reflection on policy or its attendant circumstances—without sufficient thought about the nature of diplomacy as such. In my young days, students of European (as distinguished from British) history often received their introduction to the study of a foreign country through an initial piece of research in diplomatic history. They could find at least one important section of the necessary documents in our own Foreign Office archives, and they could gradually acquire experience of a foreign country, whereas the internal history of that country would have been more appropriate to its own native students. In recent years there is a serious decline of European History in our universities, and there have been periods when it has been difficult for us to fill chairs (either here or in Commonwealth countries that have approached us) where a 'European' historian is required. Sometimes, when a chair in European history has been vacant the most obvious candidates for it in this country have been refugees who have settled here). Nothing contributes so much to rescuing a University History School from insularity as a strong department or a strong representative of European history. Certain disadvantages seem to spring from the fact that military history and naval history are almost entirely neglected in practically all our Universities. Hardly more than one or two Universities in Great Britain have a department of International Relations. There is a danger that the country at large may lack the nucleus of people which it certainly had until 1914—people, outside the circle of government, who are equipped to understand something of the real nature of a foreign policy. For this reason the present question brings to one's mind the further problem: Whether the character of twentieth-century diplomacy has really rendered the historical study of the subject less relevant than it was forty years ago?

II

In one sense the reaction which took place in 1919 against the 'old diplomacy' may have had a certain amount of justification. There was considerable subtlety in much of the diplomacy of the eighteenth century, as though cabinets could weave their spider-webs, almost pursuing their policies as one pursues 'art for art's sake'. In reality, however, it is probably true that the arguments which have usually been made from this fact require to be completely reversed. We ought not to infer that the twentieth century presents us with a special case, to which the long-term experience of the past cannot apply. It is the eighteenth century which is the special case, being handicapped for the conduct of diplomacy in a way that neither the Renaissance city-states nor the twentieth-century nation-states were handicapped.

In the monarchies of the eighteenth century the modern idea of the state was as yet unachieved. The interests of the king, as in a certain sense the owner of the property, was sometimes to be distinguished from the interests of the country itself, so that 'dynastic' policy sometimes ran counter to 'public' policy. In the first half of the century in particular, two systems of policy might be open to a given government, and on many occasions these two systems were simultaneously pursued. In the case of the Hanoverian Kings of England, in the Spain of Elizabeth Farnese, in the France of Louis XV and, later, even in Russia, the monarch could actually be at feud with his own foreign minister, or could conduct a second diplomatic system, almost as a kind of palace-intrigue. The atmosphere of melodrama, and the flavour of conspiracy which attend the conclusion of the famous Anglo-French alliance of 1717 (and surround the Diplomatic Revolution of 1756) are the result of an anomalous system in which secret agents, political adventurers and adroit manipulators flourished. Here is the primary reason for the excessive subtlety of much of the diplomatic manoeuvring of the eighteenth century. Many of the features which diplomacy came to acquire as a result of this situation must be regarded as incidental to the situation itself, and as unconnected with that inheritance of long-term experience with which the present paper has so far been concerned. But in view of this fact, it is remarkable that the eighteenth century did at the time appropriate so much of the world's past experience, and consciously reflected upon this experience, producing comments and inferences that possibly have permanent value.

On the other hand, it is not clear that even the anomalies of the eighteenth-century situation do not have their subtle parallels in our own day. To an outsider, at least, it seems possible that such changes as have taken place in the conduct of foreign affairs in our time have not been in the direction that the men of 1919 so blithely expected. In so far as the coming of democracy has added a new factor that has to be taken into account—an extra ball to keep in the air—it may have rendered the task of a diplomat more complicated than before. A Foreign Office that has to steer amid the vagaries of public opinion may have analogies with the public minister of the eighteenth century who had to make himself palatable to a court. In so far as 'open diplomacy' came to mean 'diplomacy by conference' it must have entailed certain changes in technique and procedure—perhaps the introduction of new practical devices. But certainly it must have had disadvantages as well as advantages, and one wonders whether the success of conferences must not ultimately depend on new forms of what used to be called 'secret diplomacy'. The development of communications must have influenced the conduct of foreign policy almost as radically as the coming of democracy. In some respects the machinery must have worked very differently, e.g. in the Napoleonic age, when a diplomat abroad sometimes had to wait for months before receiving an answer to a request for instructions. Perhaps the speeding-up of communications and the advent of democracy have combined, therefore, to make the ambassador less significant in both the manufacture and the execution of policy. Together, they have both produced the need and provided the facilities for frequent direct meetings between Foreign Ministers or Heads of States. On the other hand, the effect of ambassadors in the days when they had an important independent influence was a qualifying or complicating one, tending to cushion or mediate or mitigate the consequences of a policy or the conflict between national interests, because residence tended to produce a sympathetic understanding of the foreigner or the foreign country. Without this complicating factor, the play of forces is more direct—the operation of national interests becomes all the more clear and clean. Policy is not more free of whatever rules or laws may permanently govern it—it is subject to them in a more unqualified manner than before.

Since 1919 it is possible that there has been a further change or development in technique. A certain move may be made in foreign policy not so much for the sake of its immediate diplomatic effect, but rather with an eye to the impression that it will make on public opinion either at home or abroad. In a converse manner, one suspects that certain lines of propaganda, adopted at home, really envisage some negotiation with a foreign power—that is to say, even an article in a newspaper or a question in the House of Commons may itself be a move in the diplomatic game. One can hardly believe that the effect of this is to make the work of the diplomat less complicated than it was in the days of our fathers. I am not clear that it is more easy for the members of a democracy to understand movements in diplomacy today than it would have been (if they had had the information) under the conditions of the year 1913. Indeed, fundamentally, modern democracies may be more at the mercy of their own governments or foreign offices (where these latter are strong-minded enough to desire and to take the lead) than the Liberals in the time of Sir Edward Grey. One of the serious effects of the coming of democracy may be the way in which foreign policy may become a party matter; and this, whether right or wrong, must sometimes weaken very seriously the diplomacy of the country concerned.

But neither this nor the other well-known effects of democracy on foreign policy can be regarded as really new. The changes that have taken place are only a prolongation of tendencies that were visible long before the outbreak of the war of 1914. The attachment to the 'conference' method (and to direct meetings between Foreign Ministers) is to be seen already in the years after 1815. Movements in public opinion were factors of which statesmen in the eighteenth as well as the nineteenth century were often compelled to take account. The public opinion in question would correspond with what was the politically effective part of the nation; but Walpole was overborne by e.g. the commercial interests in England in 1739, and was forced to enter upon a war that he wished to avoid. Even Cardinal Fleury was similarly overborne (and forced to go to war with Austria) in 1740 by a party of younger people at the court of Versailles.

It has been argued that the principle of the balance of power is difficult to reconcile with the facts of the twentieth century, when the 'rights' of democratic peoples have come to receive such thorough recognition. In the eighteenth century, however, a parallel system of 'rights' did exist and received similar recognition; and the operation of this was bound to be very much the same, even though the nature of the 'right' was different, i.e. was dynastic in character. Diplomacy had to be conducted within the limiting terms that were set for it by this system of recognized 'rights'; though if there was any juggling it was with genealogical tables rather than with historical or ethnographical claims, such as have been so familiar in more recent times. In both cases the balance of power (for example) had to be engineered with due regard to the accepted theory of rights. Where these were contravened, it was held, in the eighteenth century as well as in the twentieth (e.g. in the case of a Partition of Poland in both centuries) that a great crime had been committed against the whole order.

One radical suggestion has been made about the present state of Western diplomacy and it is perhaps interesting because its very radicalism springs from the use which it makes of an historical analogy. In the centuries before 1914, views of European diplomacy were greatly affected by the fact that international relations were supposed to be conducted within a 'state-system', and, though the system was virtually a European one, Heeren, a hundred and fifty years ago, was contemplating its possible extension to all the countries of the world. The states within the system (however bitter their rivalries) belonged to a recognizable cultural group, and were like members of the same 'club'—ready to compete for position within the 'club', but anxious not to destroy the 'club' itself. On the other hand, there had always been a realization of the existence of countries and powers that lay entirely outside the recognized state-system. The Greek city-states had treated the inhabitants of such regions as mere barbarians, while the Christians of the Middle Ages had also been compelled to fight the total outsider—the power of Islam in particular. It is sometimes held that the conflict between the democratic West and the communist East creates the necessity for this more drastic kind of diplomacy—that here is a kind of super-rivalry or super-warfare, comparable to the struggle of Civilization against Barbarism, Christianity against Paganism. A similar situation may have existed during the conflict with Hitler, who may have won some of his initial victories because the other powers were expecting that he would play the game according to the rules of the 'club'.

It is doubtful whether this whole attitude implies anything more than a counsel of desperation—an insistence, for example, that communism shall not be included in the international order to which we belong. It is always a temptation to believe that the enemy of the moment ought to be cast out of the whole system, and during the First World War we became accustomed to regarding Germany as the single Great Power unworthy to be accepted as part of the civilized order. It is possibly the case that such an extremist measure tends to make its own prophecies come true or turn its own myth into reality—turn the Germany of Wilhelm II into Nazi Germany, for example. And the analogies in history are liable to be over-stressed for the purpose of making desperation-policies more plausible; for in point of fact, the Christians did extend their conception of law to embrace the case of warfare against infidels and barbarians. The Turks may have stood outside the order of Christendom, and till nearly the close of the seventeenth century it was possible to form Holy Leagues against them. From the time of the Renaissance, however, they formed part of the regular system of European alliances, though their handling required certain peculiar techniques. In the eighteenth and nineteenth centuries their preservation came to be regarded as essential for the European balance of power. In the sixteenth and seventeenth centuries the Protestants and Catholics would have liked to annihilate one another; but diplomacy naturally operated in favour of a new and creative achievement—an international order that comprehended both. Russia today is a member of the United Nations; that is to say, she, too, is within the system even while she is working in favour of a counter-system. So long as actual war is avoided, the diplomacy of the twentieth century can hardly escape its traditional role—the preservation of an international order, or the further development of such form of order as already exists. If in our diplomacy we are still working for peace (and not merely strengthening our own position for what is regarded as the inevitable eventuality of war), we are *ipso facto* working for the development of an over-all 'international order' and for the achievement of a kind of stability. In this sense, twentieth-century diplomacy can hardly help having continuity with the past.

The most remarkable feature of the kind of diplomacy that has developed since the end of the Second World War is one which represents the converse of the suggestion that the issue lies between the representatives of Civilization and the representatives of Barbarism. Recent years have seen an important development of the role of what might be called the 'moral factor' in international relations; and it is strange that in this period, when armaments have become formidable beyond all precedent, actual weapons have lost some of their relevance and power, and an imponderable factor has acquired unusual importance. It is this which is altering (or which ought to alter) the character of twentieth-century diplomacy more than anything else.

The dread of actual war has not put an end to the desire for changes in the *status quo* but has meant that governments feel compelled to seek victories other than the victories of brute force. The existence of so many undeveloped and uncommitted countries (or of regions under various forms of imperialistic control) has meant that a tremendous conflict for 'influence' has been taking place in time of peace. The Marxists (developing the methods of the French Revolution) had long ago brought propaganda and diplomacy to a closer fusion (and at a higher degree of temperature) than ever before. That fusion has now become a momentous matter for both East and West, and has enhanced the importance of the moral factor in international relations everywhere.

The change would not be so remarkable if it took place at the

UN, where one might have expected it. But in reality, the remarkable thing about the UN may be the way in which so much of what might be called the 'old diplomacy' underlies its proceedings or decides the grouping of votes. It is rather through the traditional diplomatic channels and in the ordinary relations between governments that the introduction of a new factor seems to be producing something like a qualitative change. In this new kind of world the Egyptians can secure a victory that has no correlation with the power that they actually possess, and they can proceed to make changes in the *status quo* which the West may fail to check, or can only check if they enlist the aid of the moral factor themselves. It was apparent for some time that Khrushchev was determined to secure victories of this moral (or quasi-moral) kind; and (just as Acton seemed to do) he realized that the moral factor tends in reality to make for changes in the *status quo*. In fact it has become more powerful than 'legalism'—than those rights (or that *status quo*) which could claim to be established in international law. But Khrushchev seemed to see also that, by means of this moral factor, he had a possibility of producing important changes in the distribution of power in the world. The episode of the U-2 spy-plane in 1960 makes one wonder whether the dramatic use of this kind of sensation may not be capable of having effects comparable to those of a victory in battle. In the case of the Suez episode the moral factor seemed stronger than the claims of friendship, alliance and even immediate self-interest, over-riding all purposes shorter than the ultimate and long-term purpose, i.e. the aim of acquiring the confidence of the uncommitted areas of the globe. Sheer accumulated power has not lost its relevance, and violent declamation is one of the remarkable features of the game as it is now played. But an imponderable factor has acquired an importance that is possibly unprecedented; and, so long as the colossal giants confront one another with fabulous weapons which, humanly speaking, they cannot use and do not intend to use (and which they will certainly not find it practicable to use for any peripheral or doubtful purpose) this imponderable factor may operate with over-riding effect. There could possibly be a great shifting of power, while the Great Powers most adversely affected by this might not be allowed an opportunity for firing a gun. It is precisely because the guns cannot be brought into play that violent anger, thunderous denunciation and apparent wilfulness may have a significant place in a calculated strategy. In other words, the situation may entail (or require) a change in the character of diplomacy—though even this change would not constitute an absolute revolution.

This leads me to wonder in what way operations at the UN may have required a new kind of diplomacy, or resulted in the development of new techniques.

CHAPTER 10

WAR AS AN INSTRUMENT OF POLICY

MICHAEL HOWARD

At least twice in Karl Maria von Clausewitz's posthumous work *Vom Kriege* this famous, much misunderstood phrase is to be found. The first occasion is in section 24 of book I, chapter 1: 'War is not only a political act but also a real political instrument, a continuation of political commerce, a carrying out of the same by other means.' ('... *der Kriege nicht blos ein politischer Akt, sondern ein wahres politisches Instrument ist, eine Fortsetzung des politisches Verkehrs, ein Durchführen desselben mit andern Mitteln*'.) This thought is developed through several sections and the phrase, like a musical motif, recurs with different twists and combinations. It is then dropped as Clausewitz goes on to examine in detail the various forms, requirements, and problems of war. But in the final book of the work, book VIII, in which war is once again considered as a whole, there is an entire section (ch. 6 (B)) entitled 'War as an Instrument of Policy' ('*Der Krieg ist ein Instrument der Politik*'), in which the statement recurs with renewed emphasis: 'We maintain ... that War is nothing but a continuation of political intercourse, with a mixture of other means' ('*Wir behaupten ... Der Krieg ist nichts als eine Fortsetzung des politischen Verkehrs mit Einmischung anderer Mittel*'). We can truly say that this is the main theme of the entire work, the lesson which above all others Clausewitz wished to impart. The popular view which links his name with the phrase is not at fault. This was no casual *obiter dictum*, but the essence of his thought.

None the less there is, in the popular view, a grave misinterpretation, both of the significance which Clausewitz attached to the phrase and, largely as a result, of Clausewitz's entire teaching about war. The concept of 'war as an instrument of policy', taken from its context, sounds ruthless, cold-blooded, militaristic and abhorrent. War, it seems to suggest, should to the statesman be just another means for the attaining of the national end, to be judged by a purely teleological standard. In the minds of British and American thinkers during the First World War, the alleged teaching of Clausewitz combined with the alleged practices of Bismarck and the only too well authenticated atrocities of German troops in Belgium to embellish the image of Prussian 'militarism'. It was a powerful factor in the consequent peacemaking, and in the state of mind

N

which fed the nations of Europe and the United States, in the Kellogg Pact, solemnly to abjure 'recourse to war for the solution of international controversies, and renounce it as an instrument of national policy in their relations with one another'.

It is doubtful whether Clausewitz would have seen anything contrary to his own teaching in the Kellogg Pact, although he might have found it grimly reminiscent of the Kantian proposals for perpetual peace which were current in Germany on the eve of the Napoleonic invasions. The point which he was trying to make, and which indeed he did make repeatedly and explicitly, was not that the policy of a state is incomplete unless war is one of its instruments. It was that war is not an independent thing-in-itself, which can be considered in isolation from the circumstances which give rise to it and the object for which it is conducted. The context of the passage already quoted from book VIII, ch. 6 (B), is as follows:

'We know, certainly, that War is only called forth through the political intercourse of Government and Nations; but in general it is supposed that such intercourse is broken off by War, and that a totally different state of things ensues, subject to no laws but its own.

We maintain, on the contrary, that War is nothing but a continuation of political intercourse, with a mixture of other means. We say mixed with other means in order thereby to maintain at the same time that this political intercourse does not cease by the War itself, is not changed into something quite different, but that, in its essence, it continues to exist, whatever may be the form of the means which it uses, and that the chief lines on which the events of the War progress, and to which they are attached, are only the general feature of policy which run all through the War until peace takes place.'

These unexceptionable reflections were not put forward by Clausewitz simply as maxims for the guidance of statesmen and commanders on the lines of those prepared by Sun Tzu or Frederick the Great. They are links in a chain of hard dialectical reasoning which can be summarized as follows: War 'in its absolute form was' an act of unlimited violence. 'This absolute form' (*absoluten Gestalt*') or 'perfection' (*Volkommenheit*') of war was not simply a Platonic idea: it was what, in logic, one would assume war necessarily to be.

'As the use of physical power to the utmost extent by no means excludes the co-operation of the intelligence, it follows that he who uses force unsparingly, without reference to the bloodshed involved, must obtain a superiority if his adversary uses less vigour in its application. The former then dictates the law to the latter, and both proceed to extremities to which the only limitations are those imposed by the amount of counteracting force on each side' (book I, ch. 1, section 3).

Thus by 'reciprocal action' one would have expected to see war pushed rapidly to the ultimate extremes of violence. But in fact it never was. The reality and the absolute never coincided. This was not because of the effectiveness of any laws or restraints upon war. These, arising from the social climate of the belligerent states, might control or modify hostilities, but 'these things do not belong to war itself; they are only given conditions; and to introduce into the philosophy of War itself a principle of moderation would be an absurdity' (ibid). The effective restraints on war lay in the nature of the belligerents, their motives and their actions. War was not an isolated act. It was fought between states whose organization was incomplete and imperfect, 'and thus these deficiencies, having an influence on both sides, became a modifying principle' (book I, ch. 1, section 7).

Secondly, war—in the early part of the nineteenth century—was a long-drawn-out affair of successive actions whose course and interactions could not be foreseen. 'Therefore, in that way both parties, by the influence of the mutual reaction, remain below the line of extreme effort, and therefore all forces are not at once brought forward '(book I, ch. 1, section 8). A sentence shortly before this reads:

'If War ended in a single solution, or a number of simultaneous ones, then naturally all the preparation for the same would have a tendency to the extreme, for an omission could not in any way be repaired' (ibid.).

Such a single solution seemed possible to Schlieffen, and yet more possible to the strategists of the missile era. Technological development was to narrow the gap between 'Absolute' and 'Real' war: in 1914 the belligerents did proceed very rapidly to extremes. But Clausewitz's last moderating factor was to remain valid, that:

'even the final decision of a whole War is not to be regarded as absolute. The conquered State often sees it only as a passing evil, which may be repaired in after times by means of political combinations. How much this must modify the degree of tension, and the vigour of the efforts made, is evident in itself' (book I, ch. 1, section 9).

N*

Thus in the world of fact the laws of logic yield to those of probability, and the actions of belligerents will be dictated, not by the intrinsic nature of war, but by the political objective aimed at.

'The smaller the sacrifices we demand from our opponent, the smaller, it may be expected, will be the means of resistance which he will employ; but the smaller his preparation, the smaller will ours require to be. Further, the smaller our political object, the less value shall we set upon it, and the more easily shall we be induced to give it up altogether. . . . Thus it is explained how, without any contradiction in itself, there may be Wars of all degrees of importance and energy, from the War of extermination down to the mere use of an army of observation' (book I, ch. 1, section 11).

Clausewitz thus resolves his apparent contradiction, and on the resulting synthesis he goes on to base his subsequent studies. At the end of the work, as we have seen, he returns to re-assert his original premise; but when he comes back to restate it, he does so with a subtle change of emphasis. In book I he is analytical, resolving an abstract contradiction: in book VIII he is didactic, providing a guide to action—and recognizing the possibility, apparently excluded by the terms of the argument in book I, that the circumstances might arise in which war *did* become absolute, independent, and unaffected by political objects. We have seen him admitting this to be a common delusion—'in general it is supposed that such (political) intercourse is broken off by War, and that a totally different state of things ensues, subject to no laws but its own' (book I, ch. 1, section 23). Now he argues, not just that wars are necessarily instruments of policy, but that they *should* be so.

'That the political point of view should end completely when War begins is only conceivable in contests which are Wars of life and death, from pure hatred. . . . The subordination of the political point of view to the military would be contrary to common sense, for policy has declared the War; it is the intelligent faculty, War only the instrument, and not the reverse. The subordination of the military point of view to the political is, therefore, the only thing which is possible. . . . To leave a great military enterprise, or the plan for one, to *a purely military judgment and decision* is a distinction which cannot be allowed, and is even prejudicial; indeed it is an irrational proceeding to consult professional soldiers on the plan of a War, that they may give *a purely military opinion* upon what the Cabinet ought to do . . . notwithstanding the multifarious branches and scientific character of military art in the present day, still the leading outlines of a War are always determined by the Cabinet, that is, if we would use technical language, by a political not a military organ' (book VIII, ch. 6 (B)).

Clausewitz, in short, is still saying that war *must* be an instrument of national policy but the imperative is now one less of tautological necessity than of moral obligation. An a-political war is something not so much impossible as stupid and wrong.

This apparent inconsistency in argument resulted from a shrewd appreciation of the historical facts. The limitations which the nature of the belligerents impose on the realization of the 'absolute form' of war varied from era to era according to the political structure and economic potential of the states concerned. In the eighteenth century 'the Army with its fortresses and some prepared positions, constituted a State in a State, within which the element of War slowly consumed itself' (book VIII, ch. 3 (B)). With the coming of the French Revolution, national energies and resources were made available as never before for the prosecution of war, and in Napoleon there appeared a man able to organize and make use of them. War, therefore, 'has assumed quite a new nature, or rather it has approached much nearer to its real nature, to its absolute perfection' (*ibid.*). The bonds which had prevented the unrestrained use of violence had been weakened, largely by the injection of new popular and nationalist passions into conflicts which had hitherto been waged by mercenaries over matters of State policy; and once weakened, they could not easily be restored. Clausewitz's prognosis was cautious, but to the point:

'Now, whether this will be the case always in future, whether all Wars hereafter in Europe will be carried on with the whole power of the States, and consequently, will only take place on account of great interests closely affecting the people, or whether a separation of the interests of the Government from those of the people will again gradually arise, would be a difficult point to settle; least of all shall we take it upon ourselves to settle it. But everyone will agree with us, that bounds, which to a certain extent existed only in an unconsciousness of what was possible, when once thrown down, are not easily built up again; and that at least, whenever great interests are in dispute, mutual hostility will discharge itself in the same manner as it has done in our times' (*ibid.*).

Clausewitz's foresight was based on a purely political analysis.

Technical developments were to give it an absolute confirmation. The railways which were to bring the people to the battlefield in numbers undreamed of by Napoleon; the air power which was to extend the slaughter of the battlefield to the homes of the peoples; finally the nuclear explosive power which was to eliminate the element of attrition from war and resolve it into that 'single solution, or a number of simultaneous ones', which Clausewitz had *a priori* ruled to be impossible; all were progressively to eliminate the qualifications and mitigations in which Clausewitz had wrapped up his 'absolute conception'. The political aim did thus cease to be the automatic 'built-in' restraint described in book I of *Vom Kriege*. It became rather a moral categorical imperative, obedience to which became ever more difficult, while the penalties for transgression have become unendurably severe.

During the twentieth century, indeed, military considerations have not merely become independent of the political aim: often they have dictated it. The classic instance, of course, is to be found in the plans of the German General Staff in 1914, drawn up without reference to civilian ministers and accepted by them without question, whereby the military mechanism for aiding Austria-Hungary in a Balkan conflict against Russia involved an unprovoked attack, not only on France, but on Belgium, a country whose neutrality Germany had pledged itself to respect and the infringement of which was a challenge no British government could be expected to ignore. The unleashing of unrestricted submarine warfare—and more remotely yet no less fatally—the subvention of Bolshevism in Russia are further examples of military considerations moulding a policy which in the long run was to prove fatal to the interests of the nation as a whole.

Germany's enemies were not slow to follow. To end a war in which millions have died or suffered by a compromise peace, rectifying frontiers and exchanging compensations in eighteenth-century fashion, requires—as the Americans found after the Korean conflict—a degree of national self-control of which few States have hitherto found themselves capable. Absolute weapons, whether mass armies or nuclear explosives, require absolute war aims and absolute enemies. To maintain that the victims of Verdun and the Somme had died to maintain the balance of power between Austria-Hungary and Russia in the Balkans would have appeared an obscene blasphemy. Vaster, if more shadowy objectives alone could justify the prolonged sacrifice that modern techniques of war demanded of belligerents; and in the process the disintegration both of Russia and of Austria-Hungary passed unnoticed. A quarter of a century later, the destruction of German cities by Allied air-forces—a *pis aller* after precision bombing of military objectives had been found impossible with existing equipment—made it impossible to maintain any longer the claim—perhaps in any case an untenable one—that the Allies were fighting Nazi tyranny, and not the German people. And today the increasing armament of national forces, even those allegedly devised for fighting 'limited wars', with nuclear weapons gives rise to a legitimate fear lest once again—and yet more disastrously—the means will dictate the end, and not *vice versa*.

It was natural enough, once the nations of the world could look back calmly on the events of the First World War, that they should have wondered whether war, as it had developed in their generation, could ever be an instrument of national policy again. Clausewitz had written that 'policy makes out of the all-overpowering element of War a mere instrument, changes the tremendous battlesword, which should be lifted with both hands and the whole power of the body to strike once for all, into a light handy weapon, which is even sometimes nothing more than a rapier to exchange thrusts and feints and parries'. But had not the battlesword now become too heavy even for policy to wield and transform? That seemed to be the lesson of the First World War; and to abjure the use of the sword altogether seemed the only rational course to pursue.

But the statesmen who believe this to be possible overlooked another passage in *Vom Kriege*—one buried in a chapter on technicalities and easily ignored.

'War actually takes place (he wrote) more for the defensive than for the conqueror, for invasion only calls forth resistance, and it is not until there is resistance that there is War. A conqueror is always a lover of peace (as Buonaparte always asserted of himself); he would like to make his entry into our State unopposed; in order to prevent this, we must choose War, and therefore also to make preparations, that is in other words, it is just the weak, or that side which must defend itself, which should always be armed in order not to be taken by surprise' (book VI, ch. 5).

The state which defends itself against invasion is using war as an instrument of policy no less than the invader. The Austrians and the Czechs in 1938 did not use this instrument; the Poles and the Finns in 1939 did, and so in 1941 did the Russians and the Americans. The nations which signed the North Atlantic Treaty resolved to use it, in 1949, to preserve an apparently precarious independence. Heavy and murderous the instrument might be, but there was no other in sight;

and neither is there one today. A politic and apparently necessary war was fought in Korea, and in the course of it, we may note in conclusion, there occurred a classic and decisive conflict between the political and military elements, in the persons of President Truman and General MacArthur. MacArthur, after his suspension, declared to the Senate:

'The general definition which for many decades has been accepted was that war was the ultimate process of politics; that when all other political means failed, you then go to force; and when you do that, the balance of control, the balance of concept, the main interest involved, the minute you reach the killing stage, is the control of the military. A theater commander, in any campaign, is not merely limited to the handling of his troops; he commands that whole area politically, economically, and militarily. You have got to trust at that stage of the game when politics fails, and the military takes over, you must trust the military, or otherwise you will have the system that the Soviet once employed of the political commissar, who would run the military as well as the politics of the country.

.... I do unquestionably state that when men become locked in battle, that there should be no artifice under the name of politics, which should handicap your own men, decrease their chances for winning, and increase their losses.'[1]

MacArthur in short rejected Clausewitz entirely. It is an understandable point of view. Many great soldiers have shared it, the elder Moltke among them. The idea that the soldier is, in von Roon's words, a lancet in the hands of the diplomatic surgeon, is not always an easy one to accept. But today more than ever before it must be accepted; not simply because of the increased destructiveness of warfare, but also because, in many areas, the distinction between war and peace has become so blurred. Korea was possibly the last 'war' which would be recognizable as such to Clausewitz and his contemporaries—a conflict with clear-cut fronts conducted by organized and uniformed military forces depending on regular lines of supply. The Truman-MacArthur controversy—like that between Bismarck and Moltke, or Lloyd George and Haig—was one to which Clausewitzian analysis still applied. How far it will remain valid for those conflicts of subversion, insurrection, and civil revolt of which wars in future are likely to consist must remain an open question.

[1] *Military Situation in the Far East*, Hearings before the Committee on Armed Services and the Committee on Foreign Relations, U.S. Senate, 82nd Congress, 1st Session (Washington D.C., U.S.G.P.O., 1951), p. 45 (May 3, 1951).

CHAPTER 11

THREATS OF FORCE IN INTERNATIONAL RELATIONS[1]

G. F. HUDSON

The place of threats in diplomacy between armed sovereign states should be considered in connection with the belief (whether well or ill founded) that the nuclear stalemate has now made war unthinkable between Great Powers. As long as war was the *ultima ratio regum*, which could and did occur from time to time, the threat of resort to war if certain demands were not met or if vital interests were infringed was always present in peace time in relations between states. In this sense it can be said that in traditional international politics the use of force has not been confined to actual war, but has won its greatest successes when governments have been intimidated into compliance with the will of a stronger (or more determined) Power without any clash of arms taking place. War can even be regarded as a failure in the application of force, just as the killing of a cashier by a bank robber usually implies that the robber has failed to intimidate by pointing a gun and has had to carry out his threat in action.

Three degrees of pressure may be distinguished in traditional peace time diplomacy, leaving out of account pressures of an essentially moral or economic type. In the first and lowest degree an awareness on both sides of the relative power of each side in terms of war potential is present as a background to negotiation without ever having to be mentioned by the diplomats. Thus if A is substantially stronger than B in man-power, war industries and strategic position, this has its effect in any dispute, for the authorities of B concerned with foreign policy know in the back of their minds that, if the dispute were to develop into a crisis, and if B could find no ally or other power likely to intervene on its behalf, A might go to war and would almost certainly win. They might, however, think that the government of A was not sufficiently serious in its claims to carry the dispute to crisis, or was paralysed by domestic dissension or other causes, and the A government, in order to impress B with its resolution, might then proceed to a second degree of pressure, in which it would be plainly hinted in diplomatic language that war might be the

[1] This paper was written in April 1961. We have printed it without alteration, so that the reader may test it against subsequent events.—Ed.

result of B's recalcitrance. The third degree in the scale is that of the time-limit ultimatum, and perhaps the most memorable successful use of it in recent times was when President Hacha of Czechoslovakia was summoned to Berlin and confronted at midnight with the threat that Prague would be bombed at dawn unless he accepted an occupation of his country by German troops.

It is clear that all these three degrees of pressure, even the lowest, involve a belief that force may be used, and that even if it is not to be employed lightly, it is there as a last resort for a state which is prepared to risk a contest at arms and cannot get its way otherwise. But if war is regarded as impossible because the destructive effects of certain weapons have made it virtually suicidal even for the strongest Power, how can any threat of war be convincing? The very idea of a Great Power then disappears, for (again leaving out of account means of economic compulsion it may have) A is by hypothesis stronger than B in its war potential, but if there cannot be any war, it no longer matters how much stronger it is. A may have ten times the man-power, and resources of B, but it cannot threaten B with resort to force, so that unless a ground of agreement satisfactory to both sides 'as from a willing seller to a willing buyer' can be found, A will simply be defied by B.

In conditions, therefore, of unacceptable risks in war even for the strongest Power, aggressive policies which depend not on agreements for mutual advantage, but on blackmail and intimidation, are logically ruled out. Concretely, this should mean that Russia can no longer threaten any nation, even a very weak one, because nobody will be frightened by threats of a war which nobody believes any longer that Moscow would risk. Even before there was any nuclear stalemate with full development of the weapons involved Churchill once said that 'Russia does not want war, but wants the fruits of war'[1] i.e. objectives of policy that normally no state could attain without winning a war. This was a conception of Russian policy as one of bullying, but with a large element of bluff. On the whole, the Western Powers and exposed neutral countries which can rely to varying degrees on their protection have stood up to Soviet menaces far better than might have been expected in the days of appeasement just after the end of the last war. It has for a long time been almost a routine for the Soviet Union to make most alarming threats of the dire consequences which will be incurred by a country which allies itself with, or accepts military aid from, the United States, and for these threats to be ignored. But such defiance has not up to now

[1] Speech at Fulton, Missouri, March 5, 1946 (*The Sinews of Peace*, Post-War Speeches by Winston S. Churchill, Cassell, 1948, p. 103).

produced any modifications of the minatory tone of Soviet official language in these cases.

Berlin provides an example, both before and since the phase of nuclear stalemate, of Soviet threats and Western response to them. In the Berlin blockade of 1948 the Russians clearly did not expect that it would be possible to supply the city by air and were ready to challenge the West to force a way through on the ground in the face of superior Russian military strength—a decision in which the Western powers (by agreement among themselves) would have had to take the initiative. But when the airlift proved sufficient to supply West Berlin, Stalin refrained from trying to shoot down the transport planes—a move in which *he* would have had to take the initiative. At that time nobody considered that war was impossible, and there was sufficient disagreement about the relative efficiency of various weapons to make it very doubtful which side would emerge victorious from a contest of arms; America still had a monopoly of the atomic bomb, but no H-bomb and no big stockpile, while Russia had a great superiority in ground forces. Neither side, however, had the will to press the issue to the point of war, and the success of the airlift made it possible to maintain the *status quo* without fighting. When ten years later Khrushchev renewed the demand for control over West Berlin with the threat of a new blockade, there was for a time great alarm in Western official circles because of the 'missile gap'—the temporary lead gained by the Soviet Union in rocketry, and it was probably Khrushchev's confidence in the intimidating effect of this technical advance which made him commit his prestige so much to the demand for Berlin. Up to the autumn of 1959 the threat of a new blockade combined with the impression made by Khrushchev's state visit on a large section of the American public and on President Eisenhower in particular was gradually pushing American policy in the direction of capitulation, but after Khrushchev's departure from America, it began to harden again, and the most important factor in this reversal of the trend was the growing conviction in Washington that, whatever was done or not done about Berlin, there would be no war. This conviction was largely due to evidence that Khrushchev was himself fully convinced of the dangers of a full-scale nuclear war to the Soviet Union and was not prepared to risk it. This being so, there was no need to give way over Berlin, for Khrushchev had never made any offer of a *quid pro quo* for a Western surrender of Berlin; the only reward was to be 'relaxation of tension'. But who cares about a tension which the Russians themselves are continually creating if it cannot lead to war?

When Khrushchev discovered that the West was no longer being

intimidated, he had no alternative but to wreck the summit conference in May 1960, for the only purpose of the conference from his
point of view was to provide him with a spectacular diplomatic
victory over Berlin, and he had to find some way of getting out of the
conference by making a scene as champion of his country against
intolerable insults instead of having to return empty-handed from a
negotiation—as he certainly would have done if the conference had
continued, since he had nothing to offer and could no longer blackmail.

The problem of Khrushchev's foreign policy between 1958 and
1962 was how to combine his advocacy of 'peaceful co-existence'—
meaning avoidance of the risk of atomic war—with a diplomacy of
demands which only a threat of war could make acceptable to the
West, i.e. as issues on which they were not sufficiently resolute or
united to fight. Khrushchev had to proclaim the dangers of atomic
war for the Soviet Union as well as for the West because he was
steadily pushed towards more aggressive courses by pressures of the
Chinese and undoubtedly of an element inside Russia, saying to him
in effect: 'If we are now so powerful, why don't you go and have a
showdown with the imperialists?' To resist these pressures
Khrushchev was compelled to emphasize the principle of co-existence
and engage in a bitter public controversy about it with the Chinese
Communists. But this means he lost his power of successful bullying,
because he had virtually declared himself to be a dog who barked,
but would not bite.

The logic of this situation should be a move of the Soviet régime
towards policies involving not merely a propaganda show of conciliation, but old-fashioned negotiation on the principle that in genuinely
peaceful diplomacy one can only get what one wants by offering
something substantial in return. Such an idea was unfortunately alien
to Khrushchev's diplomacy, because in a period of spectacular
industrial and technological successes for the Soviet he was more of a
demagogue than Stalin, and thus more susceptible to the expectations
(not the opinions) of the party (or parties) which he leads. Because
historically, as every Marxist-Leninist knows, the victory of Communism is inevitable, and its cause should always be advancing, the
leader should always be winning diplomatic victories without having
to pay a price for them, e.g. he should get the West to abandon West
Berlin without making any concessions which would endanger the
Communist régime in West Germany. The fear of being repudiated
by his own followers makes Khrushchev too intransigent to reach
satisfactory agreements through peaceful negotiations, while on the
other hand he has no prospect of getting his way by threats as long as
it is not believed that he may carry them out.

There is nevertheless in this state of affairs a danger for the West because Khrushchev's dilemma may lead him to brinkmanship if he feels his personal power in danger and thinks he detects in the West an irresolution which would give him political victories through crises without war. He may be fully aware of the dangers of an atomic war for the Soviet Union and yet be confident that he can make certain moves of a warlike character without provoking any resort to war by the West. Every Cold War episode is something of a test; it indicates how far the Western powers are prepared to go in defence of their interests, how united (or disunited) they are among themselves, and how their public opinion reacts to crises. For the corollary to the nuclear stalemate is the maintenance of the *status quo* —that neither side will invade the territorial spheres of the other for fear of provoking hostilities which might lead to full-scale nuclear war. Intimidation must, therefore, still exist in the sense that nations must 'threaten' to defend themselves—and their allies— whatever their fear of atomic war, and must make this will convincing to the prospective attacker. It is no use having a nuclear 'deterrent' if there is any doubt whether it would be used for a *casus foederis* or even in direct self-defence. If it were once to become clear that one side in a technical nuclear stalemate was more afraid of nuclear war than the other, the side that was more afraid would have to climb down politically and keep on climbing down to the point of complete capitulation. The 'balance of terror' must therefore be a balance of will as well as of technical 'capability'. It is in fact for this very reason a highly precarious balance, as much a matter of politics, attitudes and states of mind as of military organization and armaments. If a state A makes unacceptable demands on state B and B believes that A will not go to war if they are rejected, B will reject them, but if A believes that B will give way if pressed hard enough, it may take steps which will bring on war through miscalculation. This is the peculiar peril of our time and we have no immediate prospect of emerging from it.

CHAPTER 12

PROBLEMS OF A DISARMED WORLD

MICHAEL HOWARD

Through all the discussions, planning, and negotiations about disarmament which have taken place since the Second World War, and to which the development of thermonuclear weapons has given an understandable urgency, there has run a common assumption which is seldom dispassionately examined. It is that a disarmed world is likely to be a more peaceful place than an armed world; that 'peace' and 'disarmament' are different words to describe a single state of affairs; that the major problems which face us are the technical and political ones of how to disarm, rather than the political ones, of how to run an organized and orderly society in a world in which major armaments no longer exist. It is not unusual to ask whether a disarmed world is possible; but it *is* unusual to ask whether, if it were possible, it would be desirable—that is, whether men as individuals and the societies in which they live would be more secure, or happier, or more self-confident than they are today. Would a disarmed world in fact be a *peaceful* world?

In examining the problem, we have to make the very considerable assumption that general and complete disarmament is possible. We must accept that all difficulties with respect to phasing, verification, inspection, and control have been solved. Nations will have discarded all weapons except those needed for the maintenance of internal order. All military and paramilitary formations, except militias and domestic police forces, will have been dissolved. The manufacture of armaments will have been discontinued, and the national resources so liberated converted to peaceful uses. An International Disarmament Organization will have been established and be working without undue friction. Its orders would be unquestioningly accepted and its officials enjoying free access to all parts of every nation's territory, all sectors of industry, all archives of government. We have also to assume—for this is implied in the current disarmament proposals both of East and West—that the political organization of the world is still recognizably the same as it is today, with sovereign national states pursuing distinct ambitions and interests, and antagonistic ideologies co-existing in an international community, but regulating their affairs by mutual negotiations under some form of international authority with powers sufficient to prevent recourse to armed force.

If the Soviet proposals[1] were implemented and disarmament was achieved in four years, there could be little if any alteration in the present pattern of world politics. The same statesmen, the same bureaucracies, the same great ideological and much the same great economic pressures which mould international affairs today would still prevail. Even the eight or nine years foreseen as necessary to implement the Western proposals would hardly be enough to witness any substantial transformation in the nature of international intercourse. The military element would be to a large extent removed —though not entirely, for reasons which we will consider further below: but it is unlikely that, for example, East and West Germans, Chinese and Formosans, or Arabs and Israelis would regard one another with any greater amity; or that the United States would look with any greater benevolence on Dr Castro; or that the Communist world would cease to expect the final disintegration of its capitalist adversaries, and lend that disintegration, if occasion arose, a helping hand.

In order to determine whether such a world would be 'peaceful' in any recognizable sense, we must be quite clear in our minds in what sense we use the word 'peace'. It is so emotive a term, one which lends itself so easily to political propaganda and abuse, that if it is to be used as a tool in intelligent discussion—especially intelligent international discussion—it must be precisely defined. It certainly implies absence of war; yet even more it means social and political *order*, absence of anarchy, and escape from that miserable civil chaos of which Thomas Hobbes wrote: 'In such condition, there is no place for industry, because the fruit thereof is uncertain, and consequently no culture of the earth; no navigation, nor use of the commodities that may be imported by sea; no commodious building; no instruments of moving, and removing such things as require much force; no knowledge of the face of the earth; no account of time, no arts, no letters; no society; and which is worst of all, continual fear, and danger of violent death; and the life of man solitary, poor, nasty brutish and short.'[2] Peace, in short, is the maintenance of an orderly and just society: orderly in that man is defended against the violence or extortion of his neighbour, and just in that he is defended against the arbitrary violence or extortion of his rulers. There can be lasting peace neither in anarchies nor in despotisms. Indeed peace is more likely to be found within a well-ordered society at war with its neighbours than in a community which, although formally at peace, has relapsed into barbarism and civil war. Should any reader doubt

[1] Written in 1962.—Ed.
[2] *Leviathan*, ch. xiii (Everyman ed., pp. 64–5).

this, let him ask himself whether he would prefer to have lived in London in 1941, or in Oran twenty years later.

The first characteristic of peace, then, is social and political order; and if such order is to be effective and continuing, it must be freely accepted by all politically-conscious members of the community where it prevails. An order which is felt to be imposed by an alien group—alien in terms of race, class, or social caste—may be accepted as a lesser evil, when the alternative is subjugation by a yet more odious group or perhaps total social disintegration; but it is unlikely to remain stable for long. Economic developments, the contagion of ideas, the general flux of history, perpetually create situations in which the political patterns and mechanisms which were thought by an earlier generation to be adequate to the maintenance of a peaceful life appear in their new context, to a significant and articulate élite, as obstacles to a truly just political and social organization and in consequence obstacles to, rather than instruments of, peace.

This impermanence applies not only to the internal structure of states: it involves equally their very existence in the world community. Empires disintegrate under the pressure of dissident nationalist minorities; new nation-states are formed, divide, coagulate, or become empires in their turn as they extend their influence over technically retarded or politically immature communities. Those international thinkers and lawyers who wish to create or stabilize an international order on the pattern of a domestic order, with sovereign states playing the parts of individuals within it, entering into mutual contacts and accepting a common jurisdiction, inevitably find the analogy applicable only within very narrow limits. States are not, like men, finite. They bear less resemblance to men than they do to cells, splitting, reassembling, and forming new entities. This process of division and coagulation, under the pressure of emergent nationalism or social revolution, has been one of the principal causes of international conflict over the past 150 years; and there are no signs that it is anywhere near its end. When the leaders of the Communist world declared, at their meeting in Moscow in November 1960, that 'national liberation wars' were bound to continue, they were doing no more than stating an evident fact about international society. They were at fault only in implying that at some stage in the future a world order would emerge so just, so wise, and so balanced, that such struggles would cease. It is not out of place to observe that only one such war of 'national liberation' has been waged in Europe since 1945. It took place in Hungary in 1956. The Communist world is no more likely to be immune from them than is the West.

The history of Europe since the close of the Middle Ages, with the possible exception of the period 1870–1914, gives little ground for supposing that the tensions produced by rival armaments-systems have been the sole, or even the principal cause of international conflicts; and the history of North America, whose greatest war arose between two communities which at its outset were virtually unarmed, gives even less. The factors making for war over the centuries have been complex and it is dangerous to oversimplify: but there are two very basic ones, which are as strong today as they ever were.

The first consists in the absorption—economic, political and cultural—of weak, passive or politically impotent communities by their better organized or more dynamic neighbours—a process today condemned as 'imperialism' but one without which no great state in the contemporary world would exist at all: neither the state which originated in the expansion of the Grand Duchy of Muscovy, nor that which, planted on the western coasts of the North Atlantic, absorbed or eliminated the primitive tribal communities which had previously subsisted on the North American continent. This process of expansion and absorption ceases only when two equally positive and expanding cultures meet. The result of this meeting may be conflict, as it was when the French and the Spanish met in Italy at the end of the fifteenth century, or the French and the British met in North America at the end of the seventeenth, or the Slav and the Austrian met in the Balkans at the end of the nineteenth; or it may result in an uneasy balance such as that struck by the British and the Russians in Central Asia in the nineteenth century. We are faced by a similar confrontation between two dynamic cultures in the contemporary world; and the tensions and rivalries which result are not to be eliminated by a purely military disarmament.

This type of rivalry, between major Powers, can be kept under control so long as each Power conducts its affairs in a rational manner. The gains from overt military conflict today would be so negligible compared with the damage which would be suffered, that only the adventurist or the desperate are likely to provoke it; although it cannot be denied that within our lifetime we have seen such men seize power in at least two of the major states of the world. The Great Powers, by exercising rational self-control, might keep the peace, and avoid overt conflict, in a disarmed world, as they have in an armed. Moreover, even if they did not, direct clashes of interest are usually susceptible of arbitration and compromise under the aegis of an international authority.

It is questionable, however, whether the same can as confidently be said about conflicts provoked by dissident, revolutionary elements within states, whose activities may call the jurisdiction and even the existence of those states in question. This, the second category of forces making for international instability, is perhaps even more dangerous than the first. The activities of these elements, élites inspired by nationalist or social ideas incompatible with the political framework within which they are compelled to operate, have been the principal source of internal and international conflict over the past hundred years. Active revolutionary minorities inspired by national ideas destroyed the Europe created by the Congress of Vienna; they destroyed the Habsburg Empire and in so doing precipitated the First World War. They destroyed the British and the French Empires; and there is no sign that these and similar movements have either lost their force or would be likely to do so in a disarmed world.

Indeed, dynamic nationalism is likely to increase rather than diminish in the foreseeable future, irrespective of whether disarmament is achieved or not. The increase of education will bring about an increase in political self-consciousness on the part of hitherto dormant minorities, even within recently independent states, and to this inherently fissiparous process there is no logical end. The suppression of such minority desires for independence requires both political ruthlessness and military power. The Great Powers indeed, rather than repress these tendencies, have increasingly preferred to encourage them, hoping to acquire the newly-independent states as their *protégés*, or at least keep them from entering the political systems of their rivals. The fact that the new states have technical and administrative needs far beyond the capacity of the original revolutionary élites which created them to provide, forcing them to turn to larger and wealthier Powers for loans, advice and technical expertise, creates the continuing danger that new nationalism may, in spite of itself, provide fuel for the older pattern of imperialism which we have already examined. Nor is there any reason to suppose that the new states which are emerging today will be more distinct and permanent in their form that were the empires out of whose ruins they were born. They may be so small and non-viable that they must depend on strong protectors to save them from unwelcome absorption by powerful and historically uncongenial neighbours. They may be as liable to disintegration as is the Congo, or as was the Yugoslavia which emerged from the First World War. It would be a bold man who prophesied that the frontiers on maps of Asia and Africa in 1962 will remain unchanged at the end of the century, or that the changes will come peacefully by mutual consent—disarmament or no disarmament.

It is not easy to see why either of these great forces making for conflict and change—the clash of cultures, and the internal revolution

—should cease to operate in a disarmed world. Disarmament would, it is true, eliminate the strategic factor in international mistrust. A Russia with no cause to fear irruption from the West might take a less direct interest in Central Europe, and vice versa. A relaxation of world tension might make possible the dismantling of alliance-structures which each side at present considers necessary for its security against the threat presented by the other. The Great Powers might be thus less liable to pressure from their most vulnerable allies. But the effect even of this must not be overestimated. Military forces reflect political tensions as much as they create them. Even in a disarmed world, Great Britain would be alarmed if the oil-bearing states of the Middle East entered into a close association with the Soviet Union and adopted her political system. The United States would feel even more strongly about Central and South America; and it is not probable that the Soviet Union would acquiesce without some protest if the states of Eastern Europe joined a Common Market administered from Brussels—or if Outer Mongolia transferred its allegiance to Peking. It may be that the purely strategic element in international affairs, even in an armed world, is so little decisive that its total abolition would have surprisingly little effect on the pattern of international relations.

Indeed the possibility must be examined that the effect of the abolition of major military force would be to embitter certain aspects of international relations, even if it improved others. The brooding fear of war today acts as a brake on national and ideological ambitions. It holds back the Great Powers from forwarding their interests and exploiting the weakness of their rivals to the fullest extent of which they are capable. The Western world might be doing far more than it is to encourage counter-revolution and dissident nationalist movements in Eastern Europe and the Baltic States. The Communist Powers might exploit far more ruthlessly the anti-Western nationalism of the Asian and African states, besides encouraging activities subversive of the existing governments in the West. It is no secret that in both camps strong pressure is constantly being exercised in this direction; pressures held in check by the understanding among the responsible statesmen that the deliberate exacerbation of world tensions, is, in a thermonuclear age, too dangerous an activity to be freely indulged. If those fears were to be removed by general and complete disarmament, the checks might also be removed on the deliberate exploitation by major Powers of the weaknesses of minor ones and of each other—exploitation of a kind which no international authority or 'peace-keeping force' would be able to check. To wonder whether, under such circumstances, the world would remain disarmed for very long, is to go beyond the bounds imposed at the beginning of this paper. But one can reasonably ask whether such a world would be, in any meaningful sense, any more stable, peaceful and secure than that in which we live today.

It is, of course, often argued that even if disarmament failed and mutual rivalries, mistrust and recrimination led to rearmament, we would be no worse off than we are now; that we have therefore nothing to lose by disarmament, and everything to gain. But this is not self-evident. The present situation is dangerous, but it is not unfamiliar. The statesmen and diplomats of the world have been living with these dangers for a long time and have acquired certain techniques of dealing with them. The declaratory policies of both sides may appear irreconcilable, occasional *gaffes* and miscalculations may make us shudder with horror, but a perceptible tact has grown up on both sides of the Iron Curtain as to what questions are negotiable and what questions are not, which declarations are to be taken seriously and which are designed for domestic consumption, how far pressure can be applied and at what point it begins to be dangerous. In a disarmed world, the art of international dialogue would have to be re-learned, in an unfamiliar environment where rivalries and ambitions, might, as we have seen, be intensified rather than abandoned. Hostility might be exacerbated to the point when rearmament became inevitable, in an atmosphere far more bedevilled with mutual exasperation and hatred than exists today. This hypothesis may appear far-fetched, yet a simple return to the *status quo ante* is certainly not to be looked for; and an unsuccessful attempt at disarmament, for the failure of which each side would certainly loudly and plangently blame the other, would have contributed little to mutual tolerance and understanding.

All these dangers would, of course, be reduced by an effective supra-national Authority, with the will and the power to intervene swiftly, and with an overwhelming preponderance of force, to settle international conflicts. Existing plans for a disarmed world all recognize the need for national states to retain police forces and militias; and the legitimate requirements for these might be considerable. Large states could keep on foot forces tens of thousands strong—not an excessive number for their internal needs, but a powerful military weapon if concentrated. States with turbulent frontier-areas might reasonably demand military aircraft as the most economical way of keeping the peace. Iraq is a case in point; and if Iraq possessed such aircraft, could they reasonably be denied to Israel? In the presence of such powerful neighbouring 'police forces', no states could be expected to abandon the right and power of self-defence without the assurance that their interests and independence would be protected by the supra-national Authority as sedulously and swiftly as they would protect them themselves. The effectiveness of such assurance would depend not only on the size, efficiency and swift action of the force at the disposal of the Authority, but on the will unhesitatingly to use it. The Authority would need to be immune from political pressure by majority or minority interest groups. Its officials would need in fact to possess a degree of power for immediate and drastic action far exceeding anything entrusted to those of the United Nations—a power indeed such as few sovereign states today have shown themselves prepared to grant. The risk that an Authority armed with such powers might fall into the hands of their political adversaries is no doubt responsible for the understandably cautious attitude adopted in the Soviet disarmament proposals towards the whole question of an international force; yet no statesman could consider risking the very survival of the society for whose welfare and independence he was responsible, by entrusting it to the mercies of a body whose capacity to protect it might, at the crucial moment, be paralysed by indecision, timidity, or political intrigue. Until this elementary dilemma is solved, a disarmed world is likely to present as many occasions for mutual distrust as an armed one; and many more temptations to limited aggression by unscrupulous Powers.

This preoccupation with minor conflicts and local revolutionary situations may appear trivial at a time when the main threat to world survival seems to spring from the damage which the Great Powers can inflict on each other and on the world in the course of a major struggle. If the Great Powers can agree to disarm, it may be argued, the quarrels of minor Powers will be insignificant brawls of little consequence to the peace of the world. Such a hope does not stand up to serious analysis. The relations of Great Powers with one another is conditioned to a very large extent by their attitude towards, and interest in, their smaller neighbours: and this interest is not a purely strategic one. Even in a disarmed world—which would be a world, as we have seen, where there would still be a considerable amount of military force available—Russia would be unlikely to stand aloof from a quarrel between Poland and Germany; or the United States, from one between China and Taiwan; or Great Britain from one between Iraq and Kuwait. Even if they did not intervene directly, they would do their best to aid their *protégés* by bringing their influence to bear in the international Authority; which, subjected to such pressures, would find it no easier to judge impartially and act swiftly than have its predecessors. Only in those cases where the interests of no Great Power or its *protégés* were involved could rapid

o

action be taken, or alternatively, the conflict be left to burn itself out. Such instances are likely to be few; and such joint action, or abstention, is as possible in an armed world as in a disarmed one.

It does not seem unreasonable therefore to suggest that General and Complete Disarmament, if it were rapidly achieved, would do little to eliminate world tensions and disorders; and it might even increase them unless it were accompanied by the creation of something indistinguishable from a supra-national state. We must not underestimate the degree of peace and order which obtains in the world today—a greater degree, perhaps, than at any moment in man's recorded history. The actual peace enjoyed in their private lives by the readers of this paper—their domestic security, their confidence in their government, their harmonious relations with society—it is not likely to be substantially increased by general disarmament. It is possible that it would be diminished—particularly if they are citizens of small or unstable states. What *would* be reduced would be the risk of mutual annihilation inherent in the politico-military structure on which that peace now depends. The fundamental dangers of our situation, in spite of its placid surface, may be so great that no price is too high to pay in order to escape from it—even international anarchy, chronic disorder, the whole Hobbesian state of nature which the state, with all its panoply of police and armed forces, exists to avert. Better this, perhaps, than the annihilation of mankind: such would be a perfectly rational choice for us to make. Whether such a world could for long stay disarmed, whether an International Disarmament Organization could really function within it, is open to question. In any case the possibility must be faced, that it may not be possible to have both disarmament, and that degree of peaceful order which, with all its many imperfections, so much of the world enjoys today.

INDEX

Abyssinian War (1935–36), 71, 104, 174
Acheson, Dean, 158
Acton, Lord, 162, 191
Actium, battle of (31 BC), 127
Adams, Henry, 33
Africa, partition of, 156, 168
Afro-Asian states, 162–3, 211
Aggression, 104–11; Grotius's conception of, 54–5, 69–70; political not moral causes, 139, 146. *See* War, just
Alliances: and disarmament, 211; grand, 108–9, 156, 169; military, 176–80; 'my ally, right or wrong', 178; obligation of, 62–3; disparagement of, 63. *See* Collective security
America, North, 162, 167, 209
American Civil War (1861–65), 23, 209
American Revolution, 171; Revolutionary War (1775–83), 153, 156, 161, 169
Ancillon, Johann Peter Friedrich, 47
Angell, Sir Norman, 158
Annual Register, 144–5
Anthropology and international relations, 44, 48
Anti-colonialism, 114
Antigone, 77
Aquinas, St Thomas, 89; on natural law, 74, 88; on perfect communities, 95n.
Aristides, 124–5
Aristotle, 18; and constitutional tradition, 89; and internal balance, 151n.; ontological, 87; on perfect communities, 95n.; political life natural to man, 77
Armaments competition, 27, 209
Aspinall, Arthur, 172
Asquith, Herbert Henry, 165n.
Attlee, C. R., Earl, 129
Atomic bomb (1945), 85–6
Austrian Succession War (1740–48), 27, 156, 188

Bacon, Francis: and balance of power, 137–9, 141; and preventive war, 145
Bagot, Sir Charles, 164
Balance of power: as advantage, 164–5; as aggrandisement, 156–7; antiquity, whether found in, 132–3, 145, 166–7; and collective security, 47, 173–4; and community of power, 172, 174; confusions of meaning, 148–51; as constitution of international society, 146, 153–4; and constitutionalism, 141, 151n.; descriptive, 151–3, 155, 165; deterrent function, 110–11, 145; European states-system and, 132, 147; as even distribution, 103–4, 152–4; and freedom of states, 142–3, 154, 174; Grotius ignores, 39, 72, 106; growth of idea of, 23, 139–40; holding of, 159–65; inequality of states and, 46–7, 142; and international law, 72, 153n.; and international order, 39, 106–8, 140–1; and international society, 96, 103; intervention for, 63, 116–19; Italy, Renaissance, in, 43, 133–7, 151, 152, 167n., 183; 'law' of, 147, 165–8, 183; legitimacy and, 72, 104, 188; as margin of power, 158–9; masterpiece of international politics, 21, 32; meanings of, 150–1; into monopoly of power? 168; multiple, 151, 156–7; normative, 153–5; outside Europe, 167–8, 189–90; and partition, 156–7; and pattern of power, 148–9; policy of, 156, 157, 165, 183; as predominance, 165, 173–4; principle of, 153–4, 166, 183; regional, 143–4, 152; rejection of, 168–73, 198; and self-limitation, 140–1, 144; simple, 151–2, 156–7; and *status quo*, 146, 154–5; *vs.* universal empire, 142, 145, 174–5; Utrecht Settlement and, 104, 153; Ver-